AF575077

INSPIRED TRAVELLER'S GUIDE

ARTISTIC PLACES

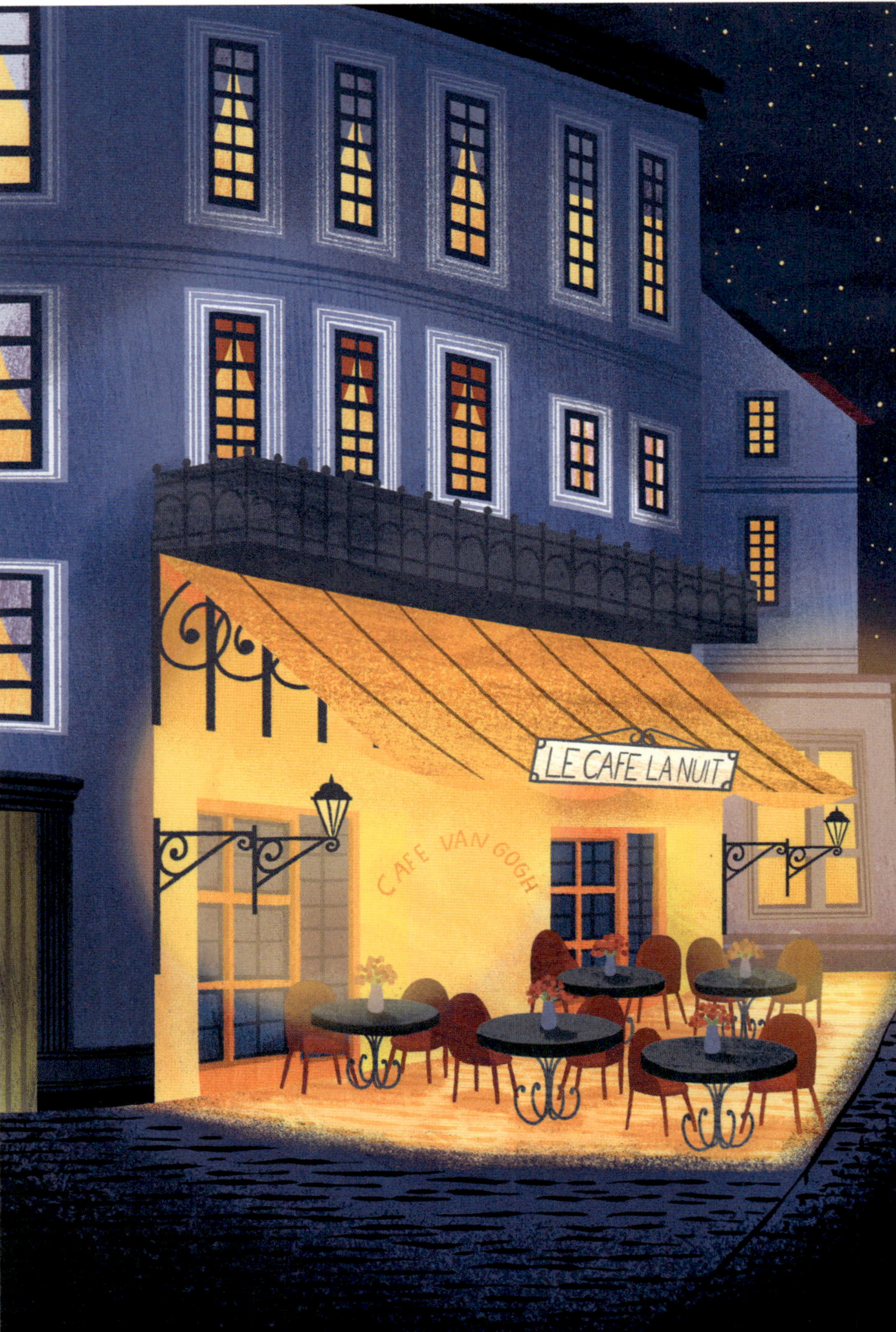
LE CAFE LA NUIT
CAFE VAN GOGH

INSPIRED TRAVELLER'S GUIDE

ARTISTIC PLACES

SUSIE HODGE

ILLUSTRATIONS BY
AMY GRIMES

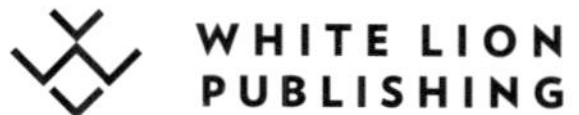

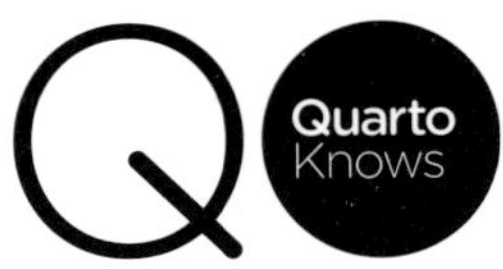

First published in 2021 by White Lion Publishing,
an imprint of The Quarto Group.
The Old Brewery, 6 Blundell Street,
London, N7 9BH,
United Kingdom
T (0)20 7700 6700
www.QuartoKnows.com

A catalogue record for this book is available from the British Library.

ISBN 978 0 7112 5453 4
Ebook ISBN 978 0 7112 5454 1

10 9 8 7 6 5 4 3 2 1

Design by Paileen Currie and Maisy Ruffels

Printed in China

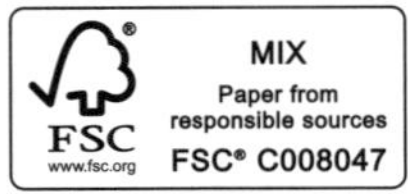

CONTENTS

INTRODUCTION

EVEN IF we've never been there, some places in the world can be uncannily familiar. They might be misty mountain ranges or craggy ravines, dense forests or sunlit waterways, imposing architecture with ornamented façades, flower-filled fields, secluded interiors, mystical mountains or tranquil ponds. They may be exhilarating places that take our breath away or calm locations that fill us with comfort, like a warm scarf on a cold day. Because these places have been interpreted by talented artists, entire worlds are created for us in pencil, paint, ink or pastel, or marble or bronze, or even in wool, silk and other textiles; sometimes colourful, sometimes sombre, often uplifting or contemplative, threatening or restful. And we have seen them often, in galleries or in reproductions – localities that have become iconic, presented to us by an artist's skilful hand.

Places such as Dedham in Suffolk, England, where John Constable grew up and later depicted the landscapes of his childhood, a world that he feared was changing in the wake of the Industrial Revolution; or the desert landscapes, bones, shells and skies of New Mexico that inspired and occupied Georgia O'Keeffe for 56 years – over half her life; or the small town of Eldon in Iowa where Grant Wood made a feature of the peaceful-looking domestic architecture – all have become well-known to us, whether we have actually been there or not. Rouen Cathedral and the Gare Saint-Lazare, for instance, are now easily recognised because of Monet's paintings, while on seeing the actual wheat fields and church of Auvers-sur-Oise in France for the first time, you can be forgiven for feeling as if you've been here before when really, it's all down to Vincent van Gogh and his brushes. As Leonardo da Vinci once said, 'The artist sees what others only catch a glimpse of.'

Some of the most proficient artists have conveyed the entirety of a place; others capture an overall feeling or an atmosphere. The art that connects with a particular place doesn't necessarily present a panoramic view; locations are often implied through connotations, or perhaps colours or shapes. The place may be exemplified by one seminal work, or through many different renditions and interpretations by a number of artists. There may be one relatively small, flat image, or something created with minimal marks and distorted shapes and colours. It may be a work of sculpture, a print, or the place itself may have become familiar because either many artists have chosen to portray it or the one depiction of it sums up a feeling or a particular time. Often, as art captures a place, that place becomes imbued with a richness, a mystery and even a sense of celebrity. Whatever it is, this art can conjure up the intrinsic ambience of a place; the light, colours, vegetation or architecture, for instance, even sometimes evoking sounds and smells. For example, Claude Monet, J.M.W. Turner, John Singer Sargent and Canaletto have all captured Venice uniquely, while Hokusai's prints of Mount Fuji from several locations and in different seasons and weather conditions have become quintessential images that epitomise Japan for those far beyond its shores. Gauguin's prints and paintings of Tahiti may have been created largely from his imagination, but for many now, the colours, figures and landscapes have become unmistakable depictions of French Polynesia. Barbara Hepworth's biomorphic sculptures embody the sea, sand, cobbled streets and coastline of St Ives, and David Hockney's swimming pools, which are individually anonymous, clearly convey California through the light, colours and atmosphere.

Many artists simply paint their own domestic surroundings, what they see, just inside or outside their own front doors, whereas others have travelled, often afar and sometimes quite remarkably considering the difficulties of their times, to remote and even dangerous locations in order to capture dramatic or exotic landscapes. Turner's 1802 *The Schöllenen Gorge from the Devil's Bridge, Pass of St Gotthard,* and Caspar David Friedrich's 1818 *Chalk Cliffs on Rügen* are just some examples of precarious mountain views created by two intrepid artists in the early 19th century, while Eugène Delacroix's 1838 *Fanatics of Tangier* and Paul Klee's

1914 *View of Kairouan* both capture the essence, light and heat of North Africa in completely different ways.

This book explores 25 places that are associated with a range of international artists, who lived and worked at different times. It takes you on an enlightening journey, investigating some of the artists' thought processes, some of the situations they found themselves in, and comparing the places they portrayed and what you can see of them and their surroundings now. Of course, considering how many evocatively artistic places there are in the world, 25 is not a lot, and it has been extremely difficult to choose, but each place has been selected carefully for its strong artistic links. All the locations are fascinating in their own ways, from the cool fjords of Norway to the sizzling heat of Coyoacán in Mexico, or from downtown New York to Dessau in Germany between the two world wars. Visit the desert plains of Georgia O'Keeffe's New Mexico, follow the footsteps of the Renaissance masters in Florence, explore the crags of Caspar David Friedrich's Elbe Sandstone Mountains or the canals and Gothic palaces of Canaletto's Venice.

Like a rich tapestry, the book weaves through the stories of the artists and the places connected to them through their art. You can dip in and out, selecting one or more of the places featured, or read it in entirety from cover to cover. Or use it as a guide for your own journeys of discovery, to find out more about the locations and paintings, and where you can retrace some of those artists' footsteps today.

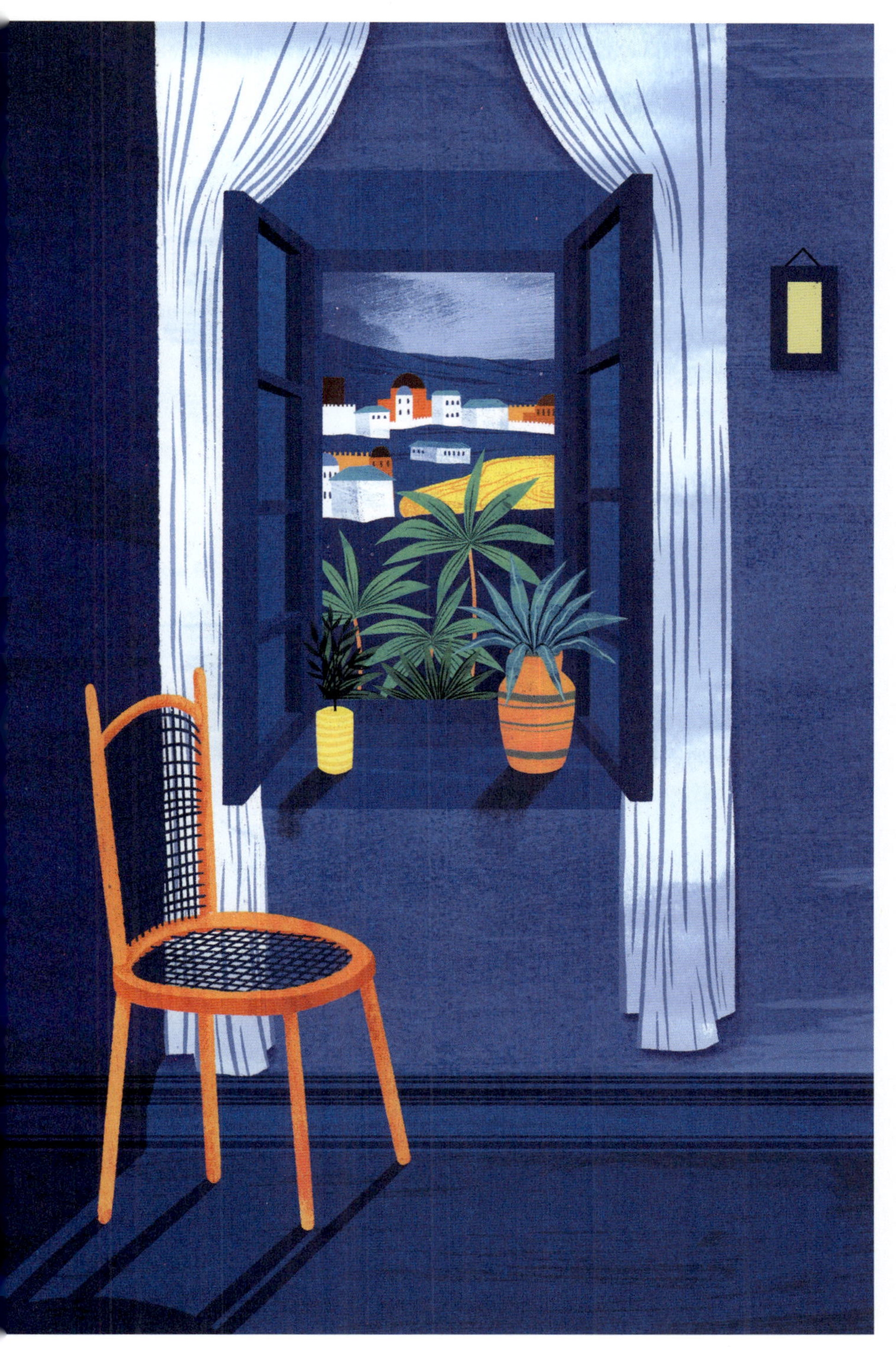

Where?	London
Which?	*Nocturne: Blue and Gold – Old Battersea Bridge* (1872–75) by J.A.M. Whistler
What?	Atmospheric scenes on the River Thames

LONDON

THE FOG that defined it for centuries has long gone, but parts of London, especially around the River Thames, remain as atmospheric as ever. London continues to be brimming with people – busy, active, enjoying all it has to offer as one of the world's most important cities for business, finance and culture. At approximately 2,000 years old, London is steeped in history, pageantry and culture, and much of this is still in evidence in many parts of this sprawling metropolis, where you'll find Roman remains, Gothic churches, Tudor halls, Georgian palaces and Victorian bridges. Red brick and slate are adjacent to sheet glass, steel and concrete, while cosy pubs, stately houses, opulent theatres, narrow alleyways, luxurious hotels, broad thoroughfares, peaceful parks and lively squares are all in close proximity to each other.

Over the centuries, this city of eclectic layers has been explored and depicted by hundreds of artists and writers who have appreciated its breadth and diversity, its famous landmarks and its lesser-known gems. It's worth walking off the beaten track to discover some of these gems that crop up almost everywhere. London is the biggest city in Western Europe, and the square mile of the City, its financial hub, has long been joined by the many villages that surrounded it, such as Battersea, Camden, Westminster, Chelsea, Kensington and Marylebone. Although now one huge conurbation, each area has its own personality, characteristics and charm. In 1870, the American artist James Abbott McNeill Whistler (1834–1903), who had been born in Massachusetts, was living in London. He had first stayed there in the late 1840s for a year with

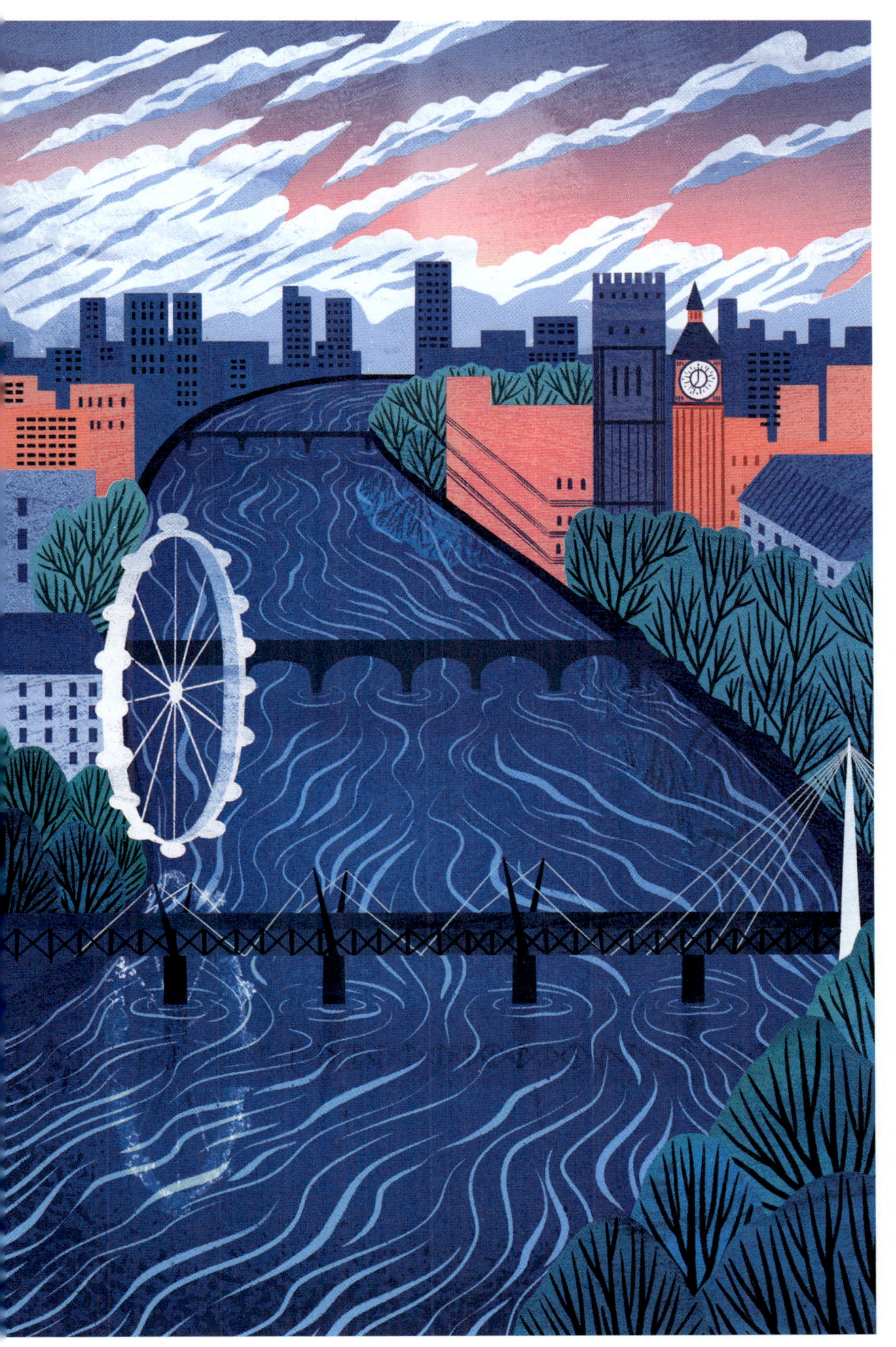

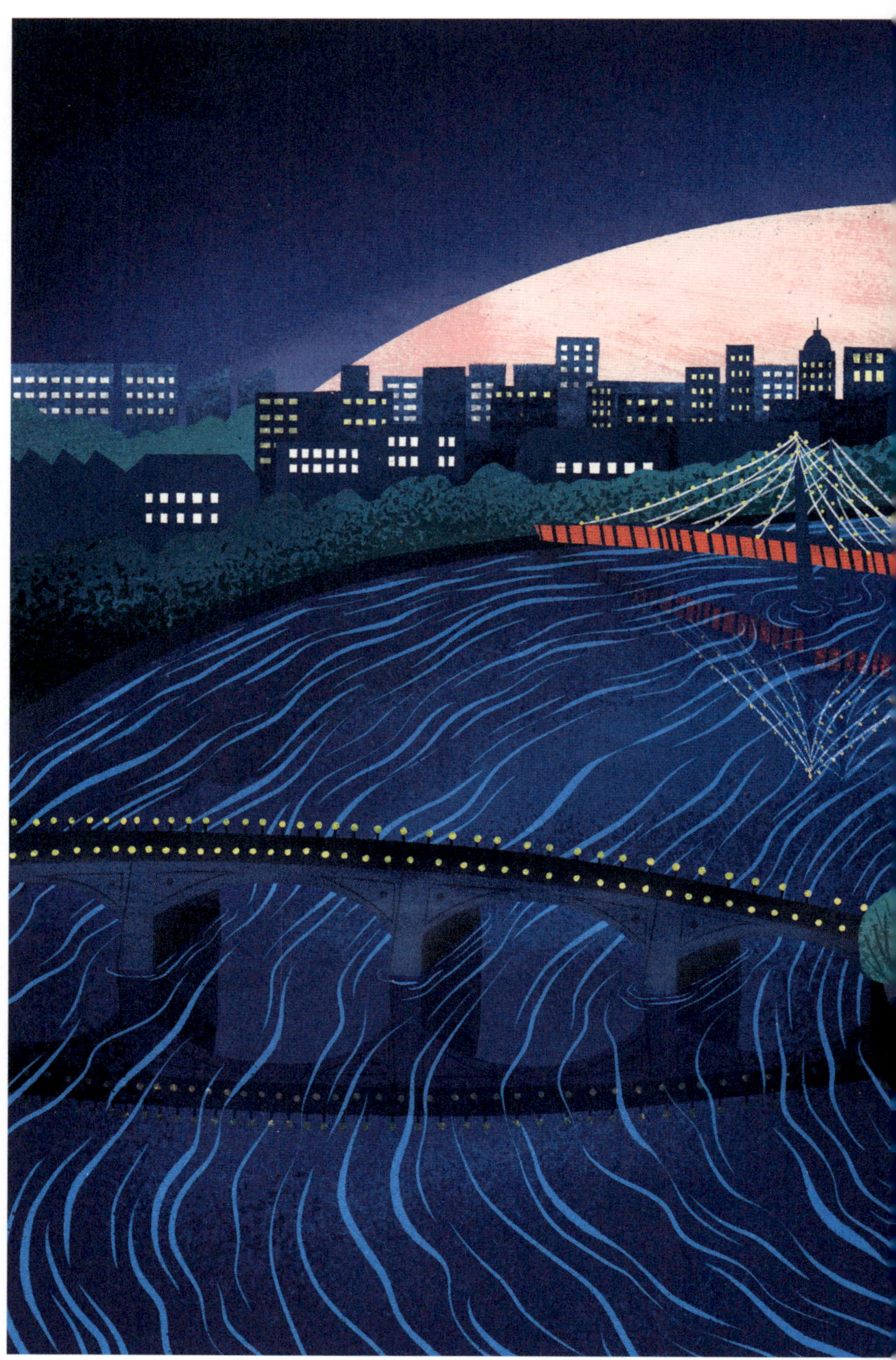

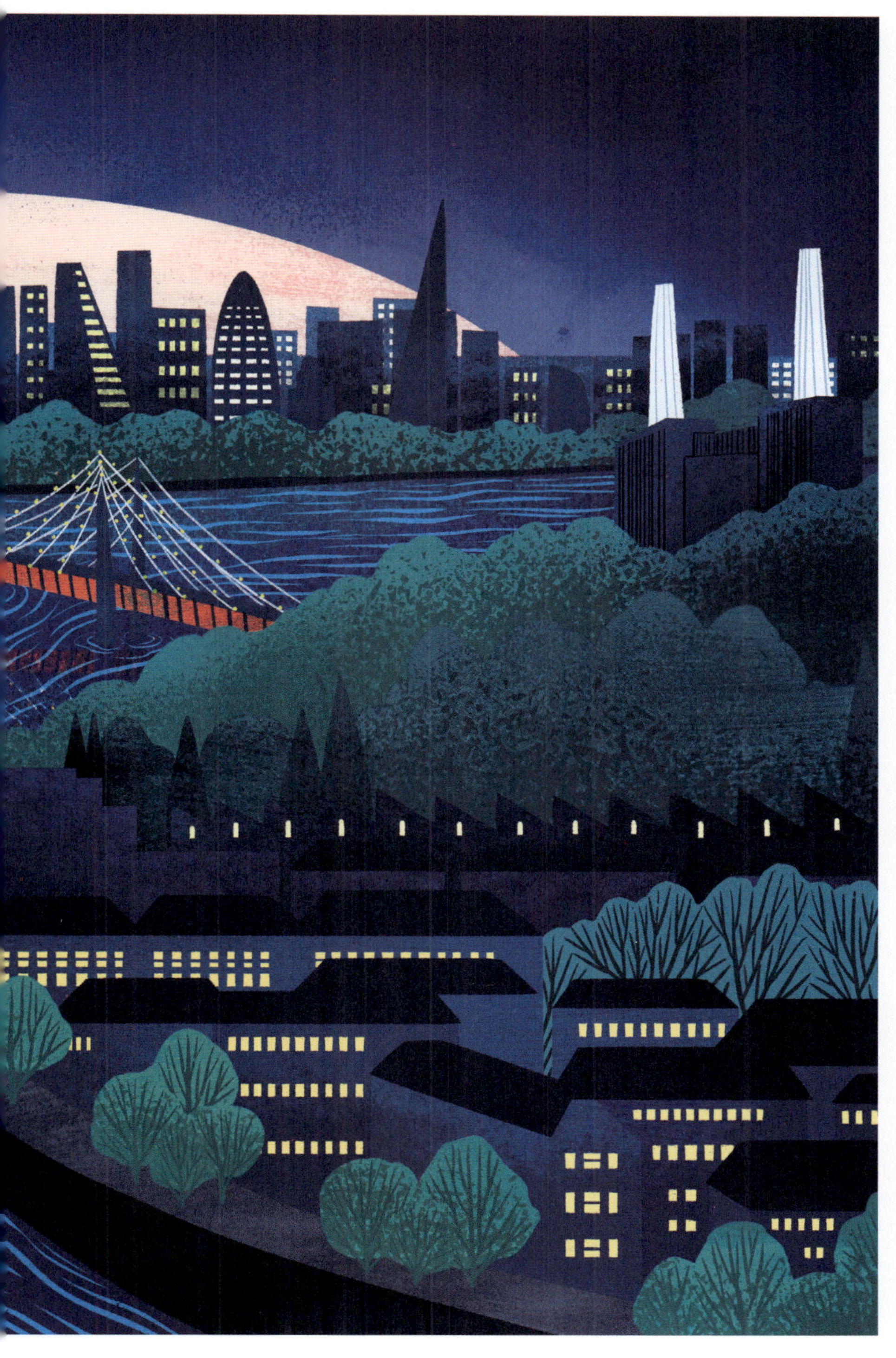

his half-sister and her husband. In May 1859, he returned permanently, rejecting the hospitality of his half-sister in Sloane Street, Knightsbridge, and instead taking lodgings in Wapping, where he was one of the first artists to appreciate the working-class environment of the East End, seeing beauty in the urban landscape and its inhabitants. There he lived near to the dockers, watermen and lightermen who occupied ramshackle dwellings by the riverside. He frequented the pubs where they ate and drank, sketching and capturing the environment in etchings, making a feature of the wooden wharfs, jetties, sheds, warehouses, docks and yards, often including portraits of the characterful men who lived and worked there; characters that his contemporary Charles Dickens also captured, in words. With the demolition and rebuilding that soon took place, much of the architecture and character of Wapping began changing, and Whistler's prints became admired as records of an already vanishing London. Today, Wapping's former docks have been redeveloped with residential apartments filling the converted warehouses, and popular pubs, bars and restaurants appearing all along the river. The bustling St Katharine and Tobacco Docks are also regenerated, now thriving with homes, businesses, bars, restaurants and shops.

By 1867, Whistler had moved further west to Chelsea, and his linear etchings became replaced by evocations of the misty atmosphere that resulted from increasing pollution and smog. He lived for years in Chelsea, beside the River Thames that became an enduring source of inspiration to him. Years later, when far from London, he reminisced: 'I begin rather to wish myself back in my own lovely London fogs! They are lovely those fogs – and I am their painter!' Based on his memory and pencil sketches made from a boat taken along the River Thames, he painted scenes of Chelsea, Battersea and the river, seeking to convey the sense of tranquillity he saw there. He called these atmospheric paintings 'Nocturnes', and *Nocturne: Blue and Gold – Old Battersea Bridge* of 1872–75 was the fifth in a series, featuring Battersea Bridge as a shadowy arc high in the composition, with Chelsea Church and the lights of the newly built Albert Bridge in the distance. Another of his nocturnes became the centre of the most famous lawsuit in art history when in November 1878, he sued the writer and critic John Ruskin for libel. Not understanding the concept of Whistler's paintings, Ruskin wrote about his 1875 *Nocturne in Black and Gold: The Falling Rocket*:

'I have seen, and heard, much of Cockney impudence before now; but never expected to hear a coxcomb ask two hundred guineas for flinging a pot of paint in the public's face.'

In court, Whistler was asked about the atmospheric, hazy painting that represented sparkling fireworks cascading over a London park at night. He explained that a nocturne 'is an arrangement of line, form and colour first. As to what it represents, that depends on who looks at it. To some persons it may represent all that I intended; to others it may represent nothing.' When the judge asked him if he asked for 200 guineas for the labour of two days for the work, Whistler replied: 'No; I ask it for the knowledge of a lifetime.' He won the case, but received inadequate damages and was forced into bankruptcy.

Nowadays, houseboats of all shapes and sizes are moored along the Chelsea side of the River Thames. Nearby are some of the most desirable residential areas in London. Rows of Georgian houses face the river and preserve the village atmosphere that made Chelsea so popular during the 18th and 19th centuries. Chelsea Embankment was built in 1871, and before that, much of Battersea's riverside was undrained marshland. Battersea Park was created and opened in 1858.

Early in 1896, two years after Whistler's wife Beatrix had been diagnosed with cancer, they took a suite at the brand new Savoy Hotel on the north bank of the River Thames. Sitting by Beatrix's bedside, Whistler worked on a series of lithographs, mainly depicting the view of the river from the hotel window. Three years later, on his advice, his friend Claude Monet also stayed at the Savoy, and over the next few years painted more than 70 views of Charing Cross and Waterloo Bridges and the Houses of Parliament in changing light and weather conditions. Since opening in 1889, the Savoy Hotel has hosted numerous artists, including Whistler, Monet, Pablo Picasso, Oskar Kokoschka and Andy Warhol. The stunning views of the River Thames that mesmerised them can still be seen from many of its sumptuous bars, restaurants and bedrooms, but you don't have to stay there to experience the charm of London. That can be found almost anywhere in this richly diverse city, and the beautiful flowing river remains an oasis of calm in an ever-bustling metropolis.

Where?	East Bergholt, Suffolk
Which?	*Flatford Mill (Scene on a Navigable River)* (1816) by John Constable
What?	English countryside with bucolic views

SUFFOLK

TOWARDS THE end of his life, widowed and depressed, the artist John Constable (1776–1837) travelled by train to his summer home in Dedham Vale on the Essex–Suffolk border. Worn down with worries over finances and the pressures of raising seven children on his own, his heart lifted as he caught sight of the countryside that was so familiar to him. A place where he had grown up, he had painted it countless times and he still loved it; the thickets and hedgerows, the open fields and the broad, bright skies. Impulsively, he turned to his fellow passengers and declared, 'It really is rather beautiful here, isn't it?' Glancing up, an elderly gentleman replied, 'But of course it is! This, Sir, is Constable country.'

While Constable was surprised and delighted at his fame (though admired by the French, he had been largely dismissed by his fellow countrymen and women), few have been surprised since, and the landscape of the Essex–Suffolk border remains linked to him. The area was also the inspiration for one of England's other finest rural and horse painters, Sir Alfred James Munnings, who similarly grew up nearby, the son of a mill-owner. In 1919, Munnings bought Castle House in Dedham, and lived and worked there for the rest of his life. Before that, during the 18th century, one of the founders of the influential British Landscape School, Sir Thomas Gainsborough, lived in Sudbury, less than 24 kilometres (15 miles) from Dedham.

When you arrive in Dedham, it's like stepping straight into a Constable painting. With its rural landscapes and leisurely pace of life, the place epitomises the spirit and nostalgic traditions of the

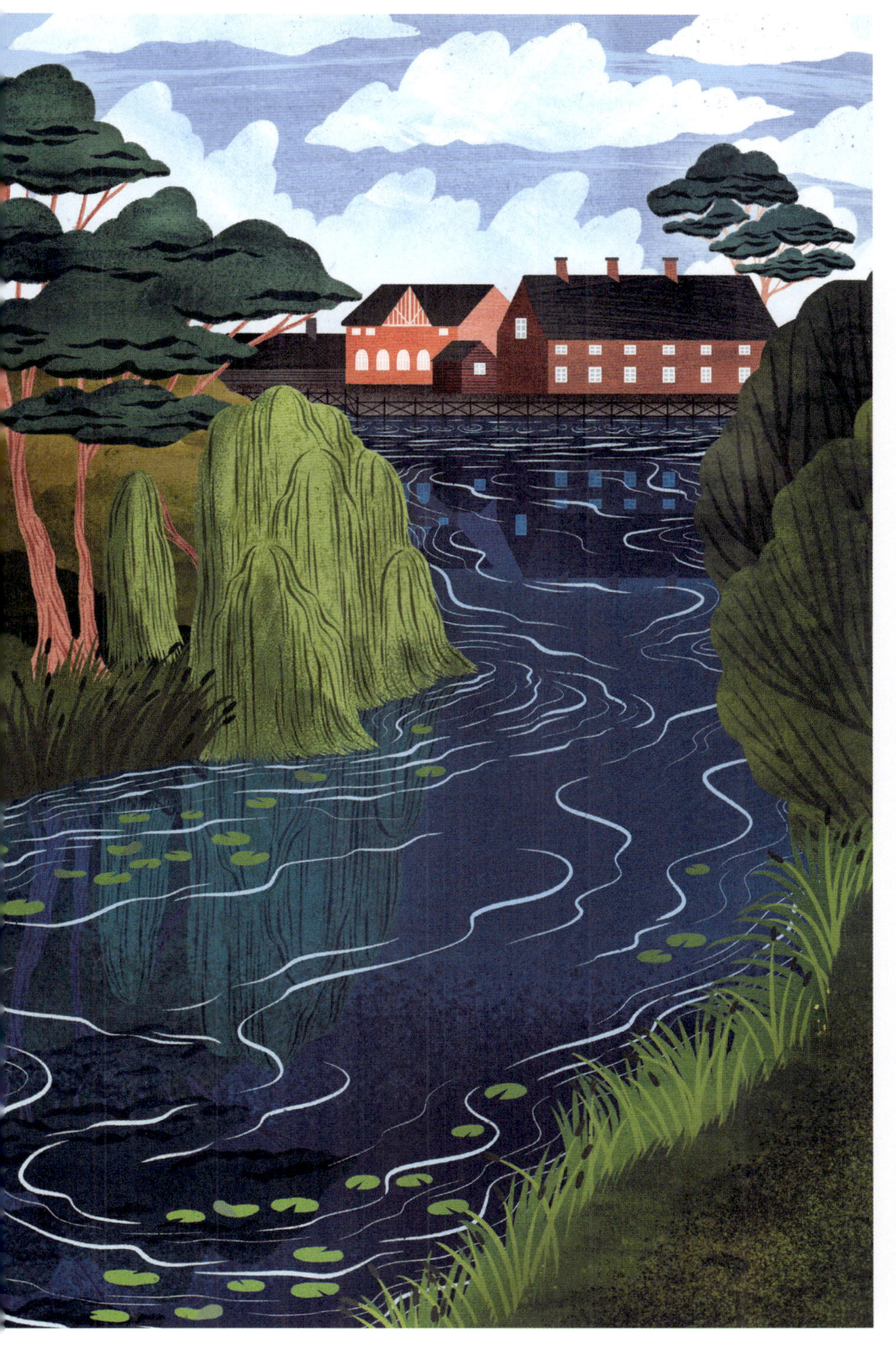

English countryside. This is where Constable was inspired to paint some of his most famous works, including *The Hay Wain* (1821), *The Cornfield* (1826) and *Flatford Mill (Scene on a Navigable River)* of 1816. Although he also painted elsewhere, Constable's favourite location remained the Essex–Suffolk border, around the River Stour.

Flatford Mill (Scene on a Navigable River) depicts a working rural locale during the early 19th century, when the Industrial Revolution was changing the face of the countryside. Constable captured a scene that he thought would not last much longer. He prepared the painting with sketches on site and back in his studio, but little did he know that his huge, leafy trees, chattering river, dramatic, cloud-filled sky and East Bergholt itself in the distance would still be virtually the same over two centuries later. Every year, visitors flock there, to walk, picnic, cycle or paint, and to explore such things as the white cottage where Constable's neighbour, the tenant farmer Willy Lott lived; Flatford Mill itself, which was owned by the Constable family, and Bridge Cottage, which now houses a permanent Constable exhibition. Constable walked these same fields as he grew up in the late 18th century. His father's successful business was about a mile from the village at Flatford, and it included a watermill on the River Stour near Dedham for grinding corn and a dry dock for building the barges to transport grain. Constable had no idea that his myriad views of the area would become truly iconic for so many, nor that these same scenes would remain recognisable so long after he painted them. His love for the place is apparent in his work.

Charming and quintessentially English, the landscape that so inspired him is still fondly known as Constable Country. You can wander through rolling farmland, meadows and ancient woodlands, next to babbling brooks or under leafy trees. Take a stroll in the sun to nearby Flatford Lock, as umpteen boat trippers meander by on the River Stour. Pass through narrow cobbled lanes or along grassy paths, then amble over the bridge to the old granary building and Flatford Mill, both red-brick structures with gables and overhanging eaves that exude an air of rustic simplicity, capturing a time when craft skills were at the centre of rural life. Much here may at first seem familiar – instantly recognisable from the many Constable prints seen worldwide on merchandise – but some of the beauty is unexpected and as abundant as when Constable first captured it.

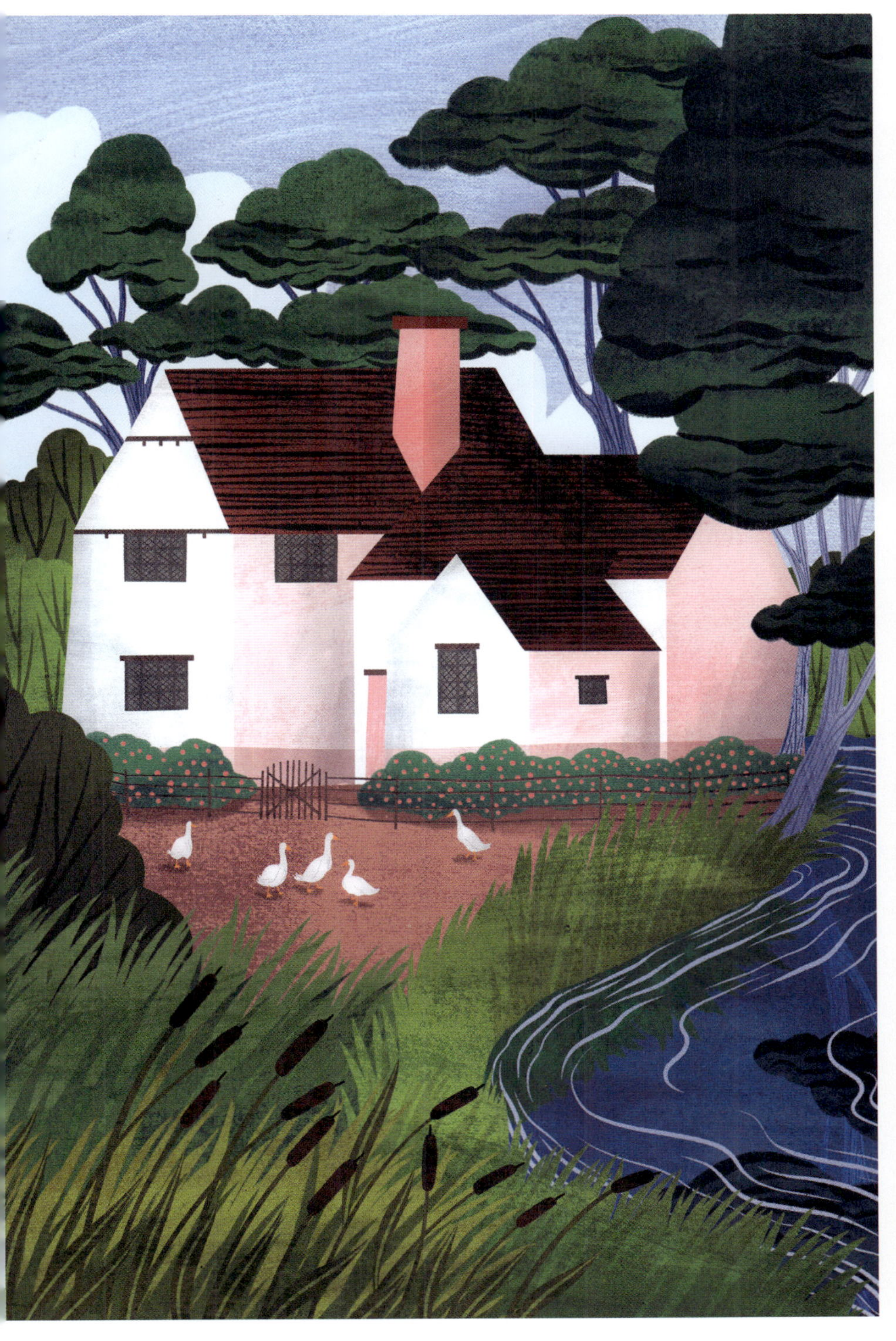

Where?	St Ives, Cornwall
Which?	*Pelagos* (1946) by Barbara Hepworth
What?	Renowned hub for artists inspired by light, sea, wind and hills

ST IVES

EVEN ON a cloudy day, the light is clear. It slants down to the earth, highlighting and intensifying all it touches. Ferns, mosses, liverworts, lichens and fungi spread across the rich soil and rockier areas, bristling in the gentle breeze or sometimes stronger winds, catching the same dazzling light that shines on the sea, the fishing harbour, the narrow streets of the old part of town, and the soft sandy beaches, and even silhouettes the distant, undulating hills.

This is St Ives, a place where ancient history exudes from every rock and grassy mound. Approximately 10,000 years ago, Cornwall began to be occupied, and even today, it retains a uniqueness and a spiritual distance from England. Despite its fluctuating fortunes, since its first settlers moved in, Cornwall has drawn people to live and work, and St Ives, to the north of Penzance, on the coast of the Celtic Sea, has held an enduring attraction for many. Named after a 5th-century Irish princess and missionary called St Ia, St Ives initially flourished through mining and fishing, with its peak in the 19th century, when there was huge demand for tin, copper and locally caught pilchards. In 1877, the extension of the Great Western Railway from Paddington to Penzance made the remote town more accessible, and St Ives became a popular destination for tourists and artists – the latter settling all over the town.

Captivated by the shimmering light and landscape, these original thinkers immersed themselves in St Ives – and thrived, establishing a community of artists and writers. Among the first to travel there were Walter Sickert and Whistler, while the Finnish painter Helene Schjerfbeck and the Swedish artist Anders Zorn spent the winter

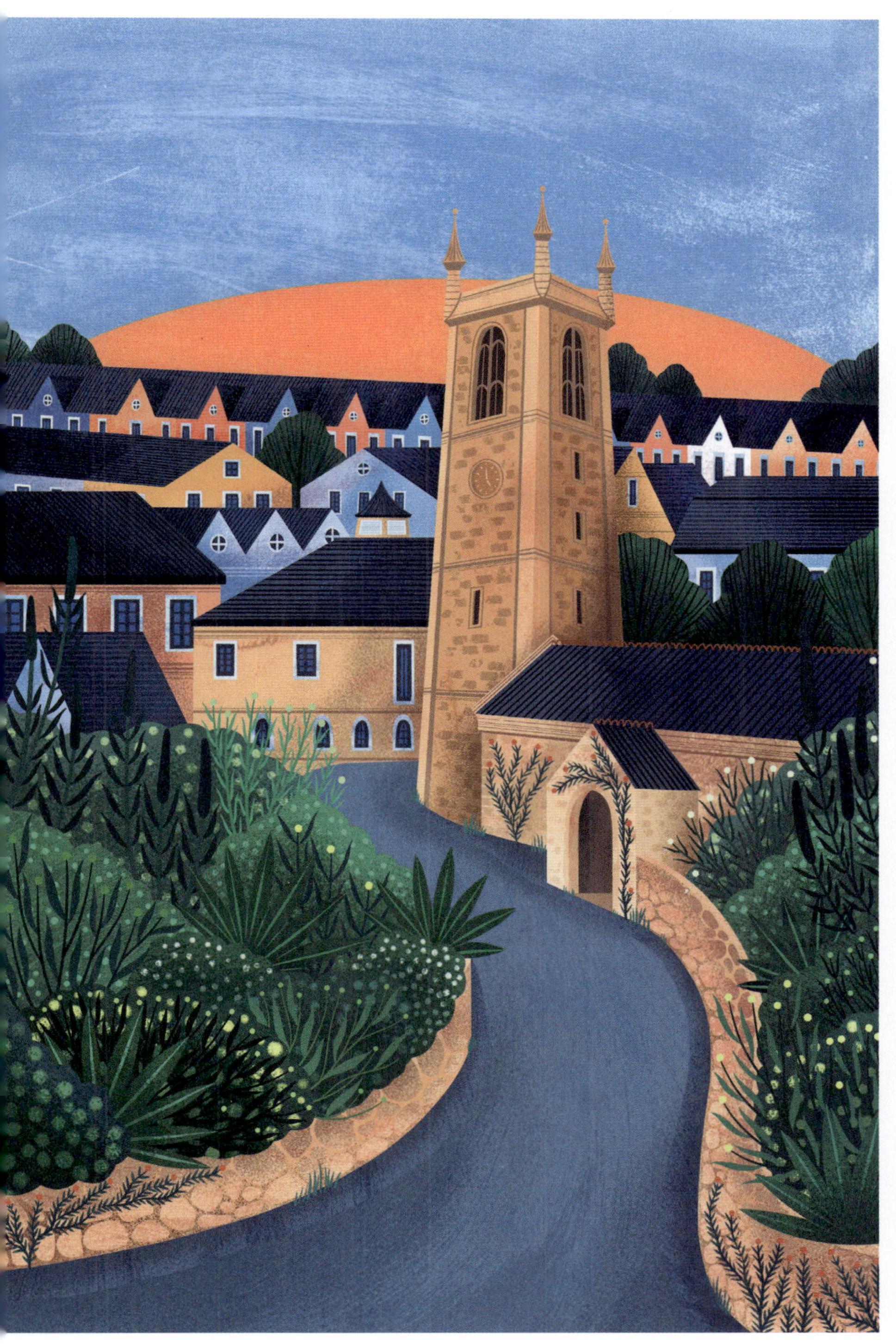

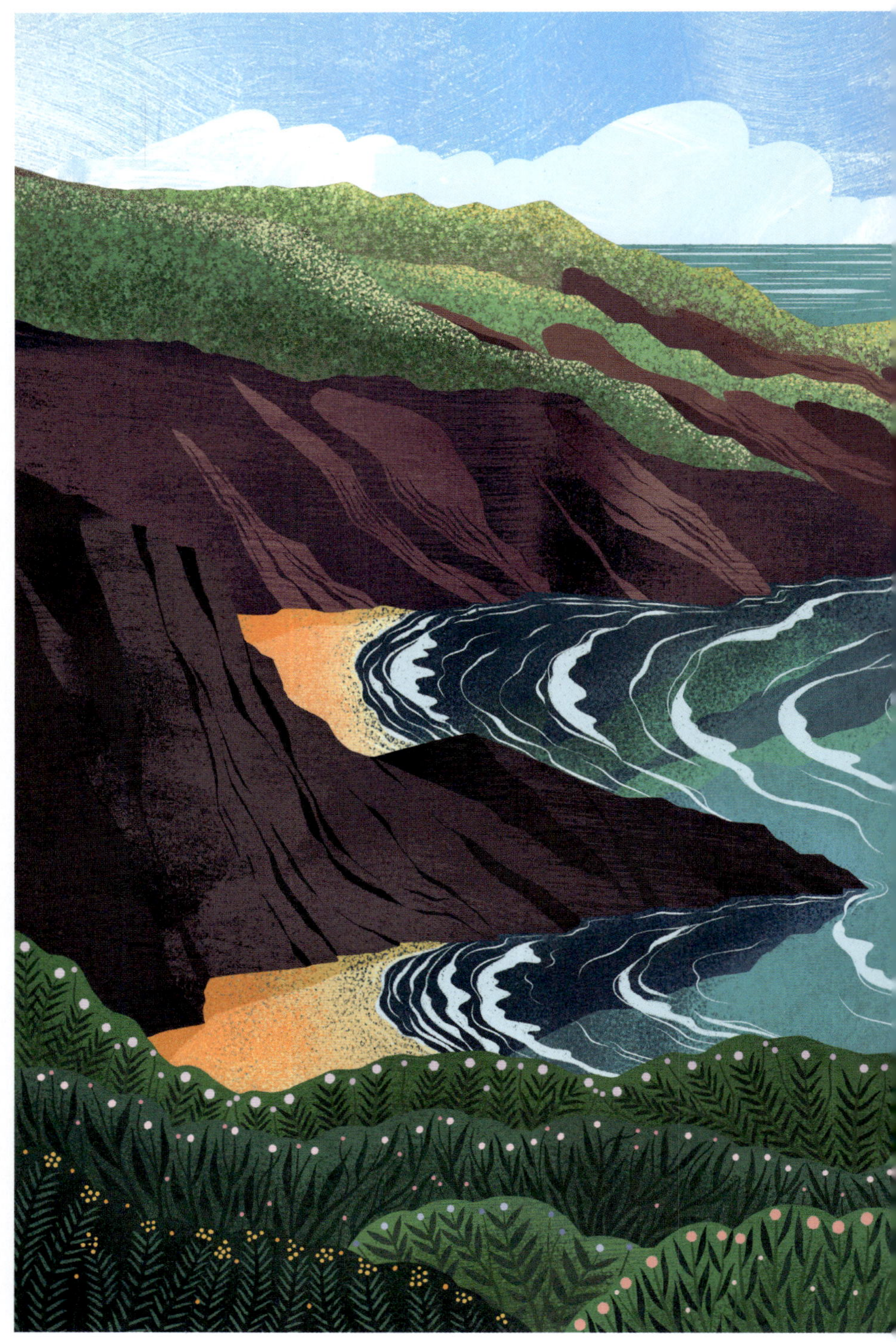

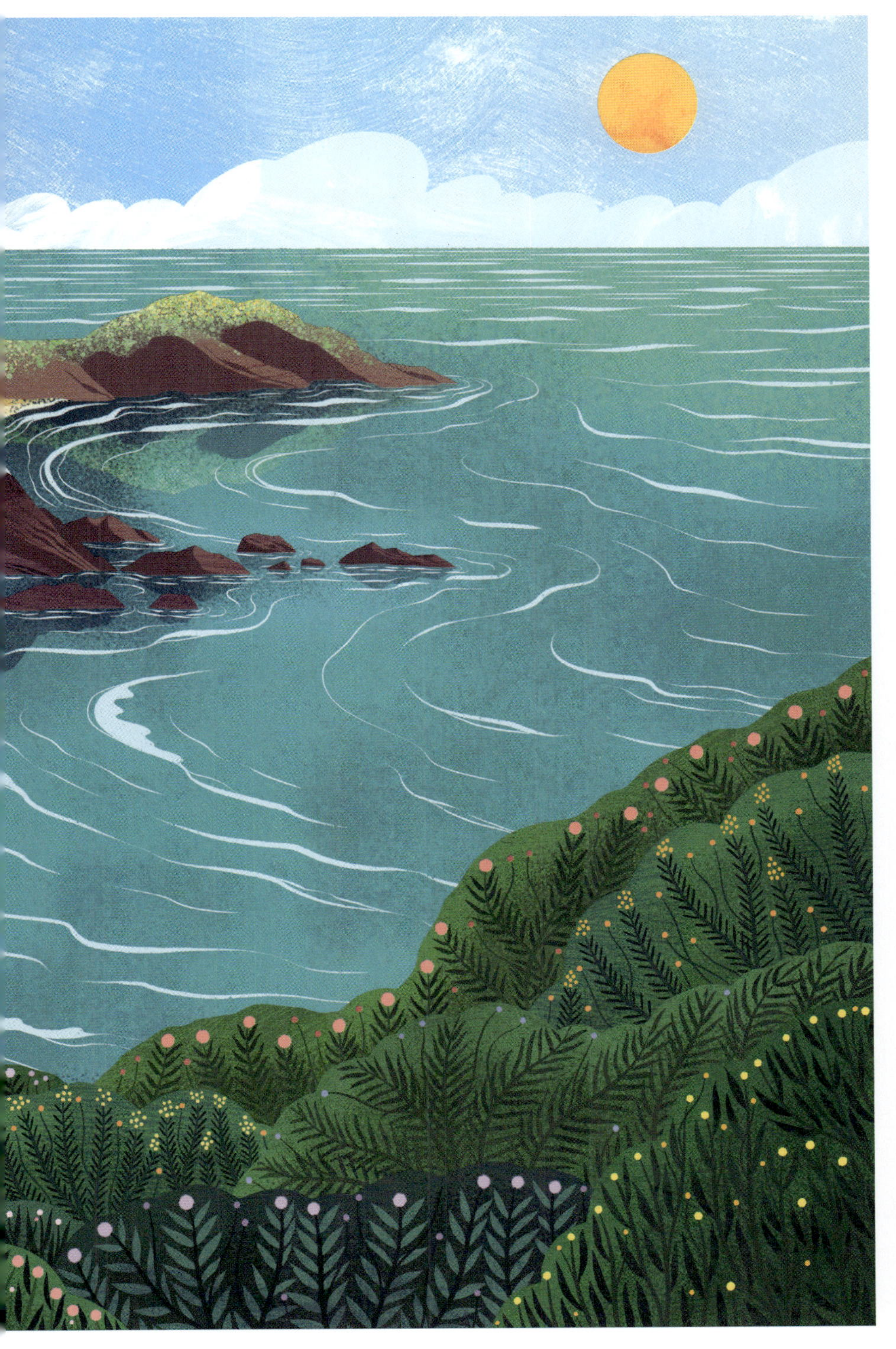

there in 1887–88. Other early settlers established the St Ives Arts Club in 1890 and by the mid-1890s, St Ives was known as a destination for landscape and marine artists. Later it was made more famous by innovative potters Shōji Hamada and Bernard Leach, who opened the now world-renowned Leach Pottery in 1920.

One particular artist to become synonymous with the area was Barbara Hepworth (1903–75) who arrived there with her then husband, the painter Ben Nicholson, in 1939. From the time she moved in, Hepworth's art expressed her surroundings with a passion. In a time when female artists were rare, she evolved innovative ideas, using a wide range of materials, and investigating textures and negative spaces as much as positive shapes in her sculpture, as well as focusing on the relationships of her sculptures to the landscapes around them. Although much of her work was abstract, most referred to aspects of nature. 'All my sculpture comes out of landscape' she wrote, and 'I'm sick of sculptures in galleries ... no sculpture really lives until it goes back to the landscape, the trees, air and clouds.' She also wrote: 'Finding Trewyn Studio was a sort of magic. Here was a studio, a yard and garden where I could work in open air and space.' One of her best-known pieces, *Pelagos* (meaning *sea* in Greek), 1946, is a curving, rounded, spiral wooden sculpture, inspired by a view of the bay, where two stretches of land surround the sea on either side. The hollowed-out sculpture also recalls a shell or the roll of a hill, while the strings suggest music and musical instruments, which Hepworth used to convey 'the tension I felt between myself and the sea, the wind or the hills.'

Other artists added to the legendary status of the St Ives School, and nowadays the town continues to draw artists and art lovers to its many art galleries, including Tate St Ives and the Barbara Hepworth Sculpture Garden, as well as its surrounding scenery. As soon as you experience the sparkling, jewel-bright light, rugged landscape and breathtaking beaches, including the splendid Pendour Cove – with its curved, rocky coastline that inspired Hepworth's 1947 *Pendour* wooden sculpture – and the working port and harbour of Porthminster, you'll be drawn in. With miles of well-marked trails through the countryside and pelagic panorama, St Ives is wonderful for walking or boating from the bay. Old town and new, from narrow cobbled streets to more modern buildings, all appeals to the senses.

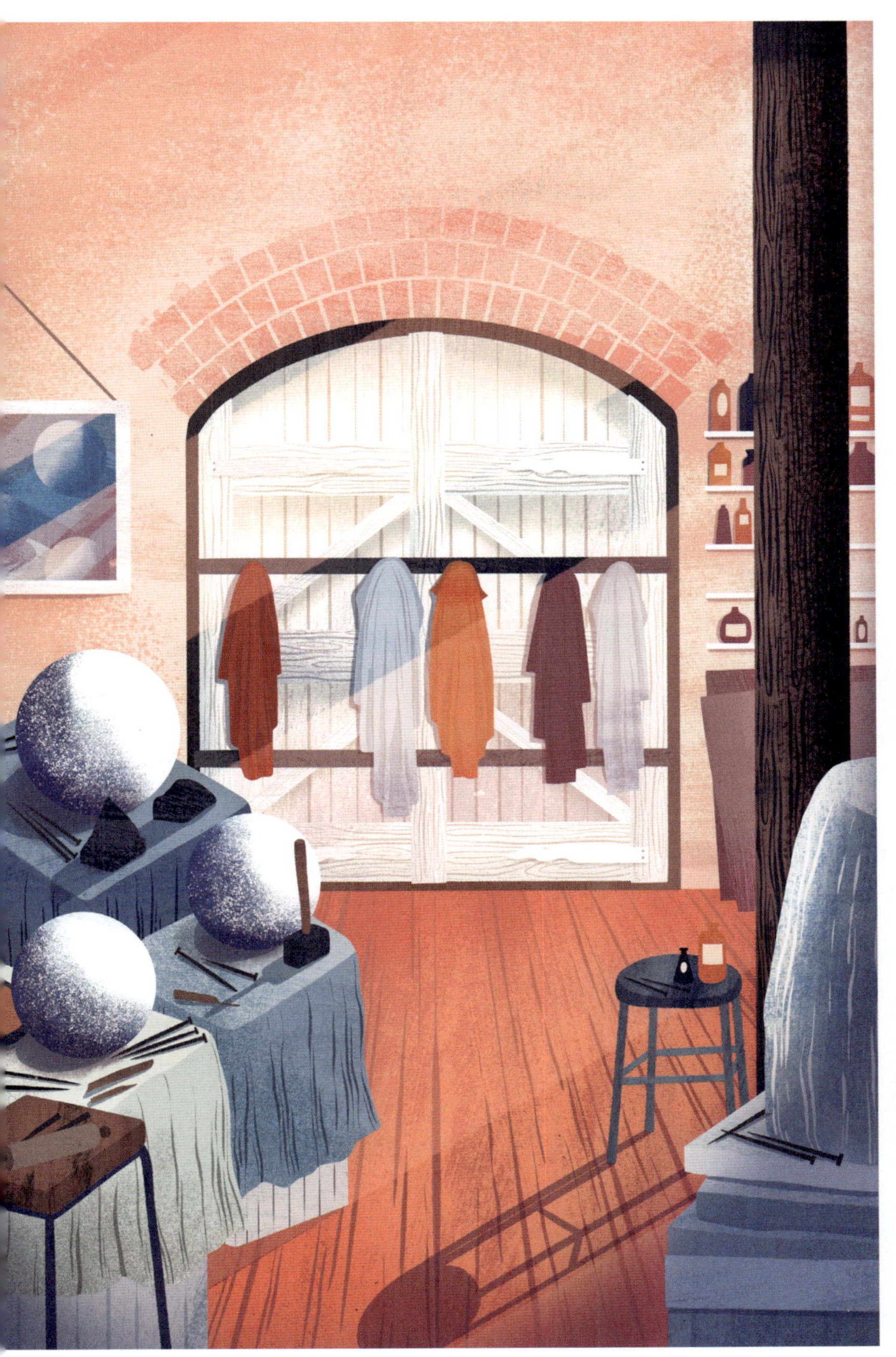

Where?	Cascais and Estoril, Lisbon coast, Portugal
Which?	*The Dance* (1988) by Paula Rego
What?	Rugged coastline with ancient fishing town and royal bay

CASCAIS & ESTORIL

AS THE afternoon moves towards evening, and the sun begins to lower over the distant mountains, the bay of Cascais and Estoril feels calm and relaxed. Golden light slides over the rockroses, heathers, gorse and lavender, and warms the stone of the mansions, built during the 19th and early 20th centuries to house the many wealthy visitors who flocked there. Several of these are now museums, including the Casa das Histórias de Paula Rego (Paula Rego House of Stories), a building with an unusual design that houses several of the works of the expressive Portuguese artist. Also nearby is the Portuguese Music Museum, at Casa Verdades de Faria. Closer to the sea, high on a crag, is the Citadel Palace, the former House of the Cascais governor and once the king of Portugal's summer residence, currently under the authority of the Presidency of the Portuguese Republic.

Directly to the west of Lisbon, the Estoril coastline has remained one of the most popular and cosmopolitan parts of Portugal since the late 19th century, when the king of Portugal spent his summers there and other European royals joined him and his family. The scenic route hugs the coast and the River Tagus, passing several forts that were erected to defend Lisbon. Originally a little fishing town, Cascais now bustles with colourful shops and lively restaurants and bars. A large marina dominates the southern edge of town, frequented by yacht- and catamaran-owners travelling to the Mediterranean, fishermen who take advantage of the deep waters off the coast, surfers and windsurfers, and golfers who come to play on its world-championship courses.

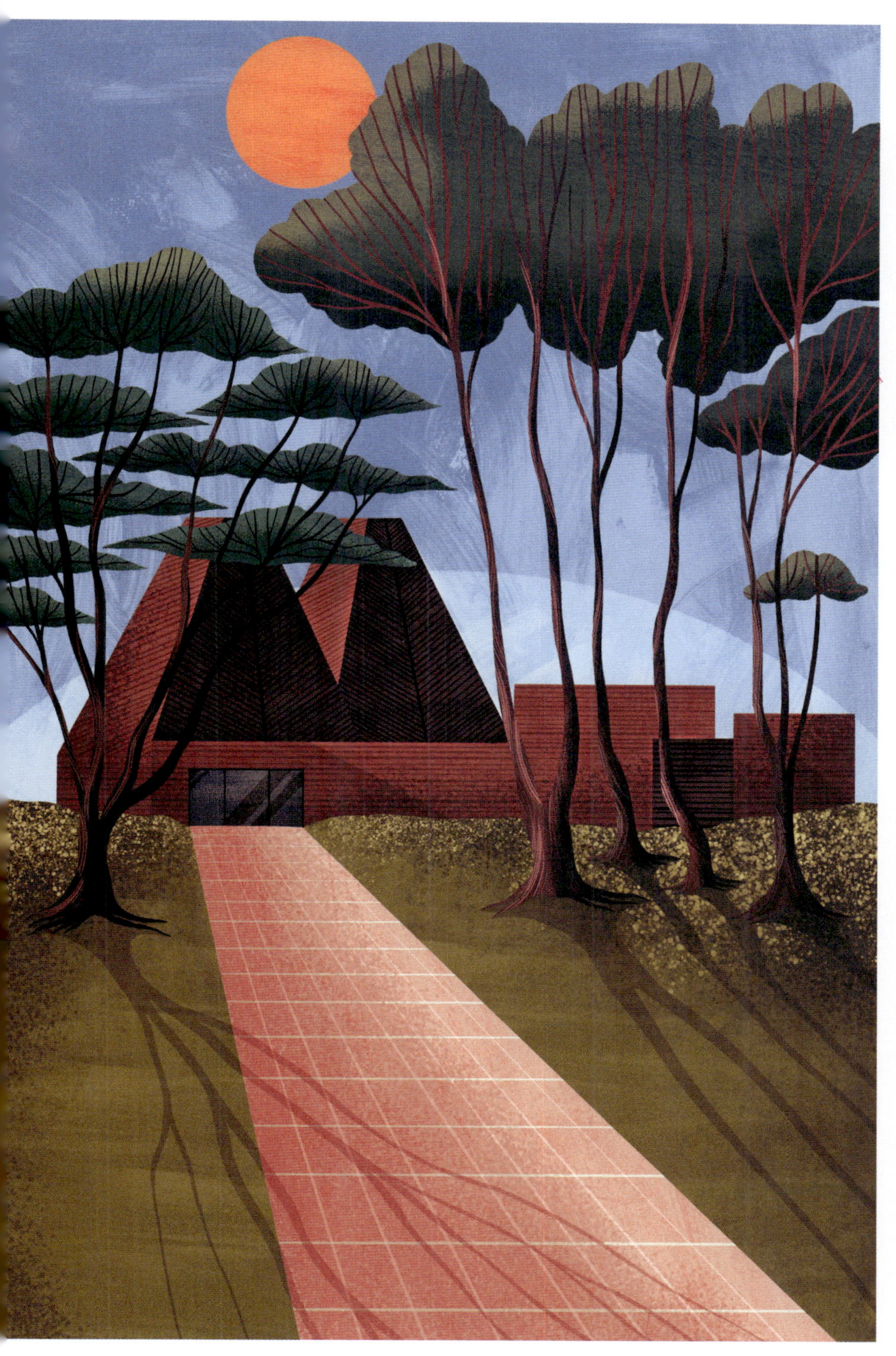

At the northern end of town, Boca do Inferno (Hell's Mouth) comprises a dark and conspicuous rock formation, resembling the steep and craggy cliff that can be seen in the background of Paula Rego's haunting 1988 painting *The Dance*. On the top of this cliff in Rego's painting is the silhouette of an imposing fortress, set against a deep-blue sky filled with ominous dark clouds and a full moon. This fort was used as a prison and torture site during the Estado Novo (1933–74), a period of authoritarian rule in Portugal. With this and its dark, long shadows, the rhythmic, intriguing painting contrasts with the bright holiday atmosphere of the coastal paradise. Born in Lisbon in 1935, Rego moved to Estoril with her family when she was three years old. Yet at the time she painted *The Dance*, she was living in London, having moved there permanently in 1976. The work was the largest painting she had created at that time and represents several of her memories of growing up. She produced 11 preparatory ink drawings for the shadow-filled painting, each exploring various combinations of dancing figures, from 7 young women jumping in the air to a mixed group walking along a beach, all featuring elements of her beloved homeland.

With its balmy climate and rugged shorelines, Cascais is an ideal place for family holidays or for walking or cycling along the promenade between Azarujinha and Nossa Senhora da Conceição beaches. Between June and September, the oldest arts-and-crafts fair in the country, FIARTIL, is held every year, offering an opportunity to discover traditional crafts and to taste the wide variety of regional produce – not least the internationally renowned regional speciality, *Tarte de Natas*. As well as Cascais and Estoril, this coastline is lined with other charming Portuguese resort towns, including Paço de Arcos, Oeiras and Carcavelos. Fishing boats are moored on the sands of the Praia Velha in the picturesque town of Paço de Arcos, while the golden beaches that nestle along this coast include the Praia de Caxias, guarded by two forts, the Forte da Giribita and the Forte de São Bruno de Caxias. These medieval military forts were built at the same time as the Fort of São Pedro do Estoril, or the Fort of Poça, that appears in Rego's *The Dance*. Strolling in the moonlight, past the craggy cliffs and windswept beaches of Cascais, illuminated by the silvery moonlight, you can experience the mystical atmosphere captured in Rego's enigmatic artwork.

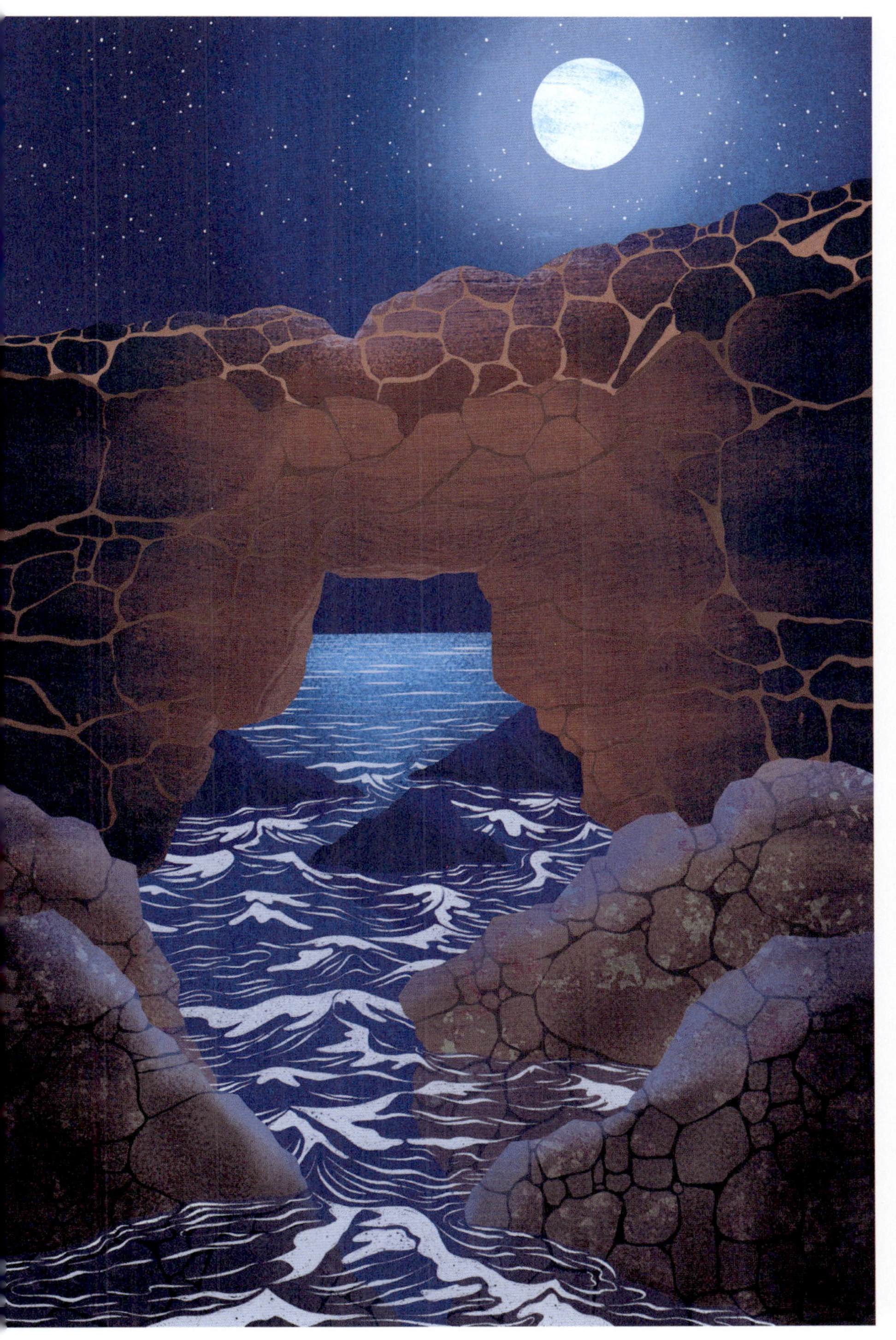

Where?	Guernica, Spain
Which?	*Guernica* (1937) by Pablo Picasso
What?	Spanish town symbolising peace

GUERNICA

ON 26 April 1937, German bombers appeared over the blue skies of Guernica – or Gernika, to use its Basque name – a peaceful market town in the province of Biscay, and launched the first aerial bombing raid of the Spanish Civil War. The defenceless town was razed to the ground by the Nazis, who were allies of General Francisco Franco, the fascist dictator who took control of Spain in 1939 until his death in 1975. The bombing shocked the world, turning Guernica into an everlasting symbol of the atrocity of war – a tragedy that was immortalised in the famous, monumental painting by Pablo Picasso (1881–1973).

Built on the intersection of the roads from Bermeo to Durango, and from Bilbao to Elantxobe and Lekeitio, Guernica was established in the 14th century. On a hillside in the town is an oak tree, Gernikako Arbola, where for centuries, locals have held assemblies to discuss matters affecting the community, laws have been drawn up and generations of Basque leaders and Spanish kings have sworn to respect the region. Behind Gernikako Arbola is the Assembly Hall or Meeting House, its elegant Neoclassical columns echoing the straight oak's trunk, and behind these is the Peace Park, a relaxing oasis that was created after the 1937 bombing, and where nowadays families and couples picnic, and children play, all around a large, semi-abstract sculpture by English sculptor Henry Moore.

Far removed from the horrors of the 1930s now, Guernica is once again a peaceful, thriving town, set in lush hills dotted with old farmhouses, all within sight of the sparkling azure Atlantic Ocean. The local area includes Mundaka, a small seaside resort where

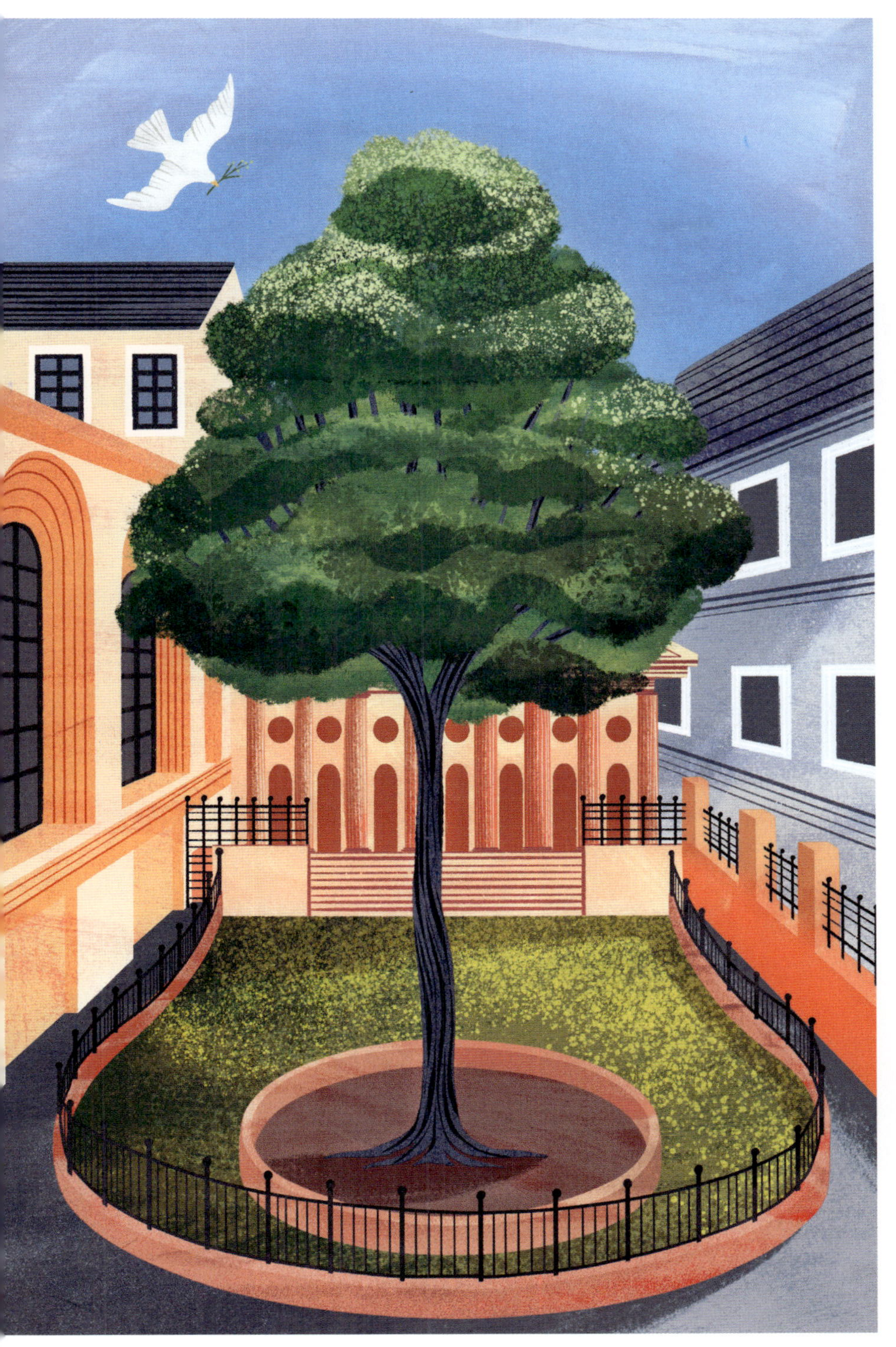

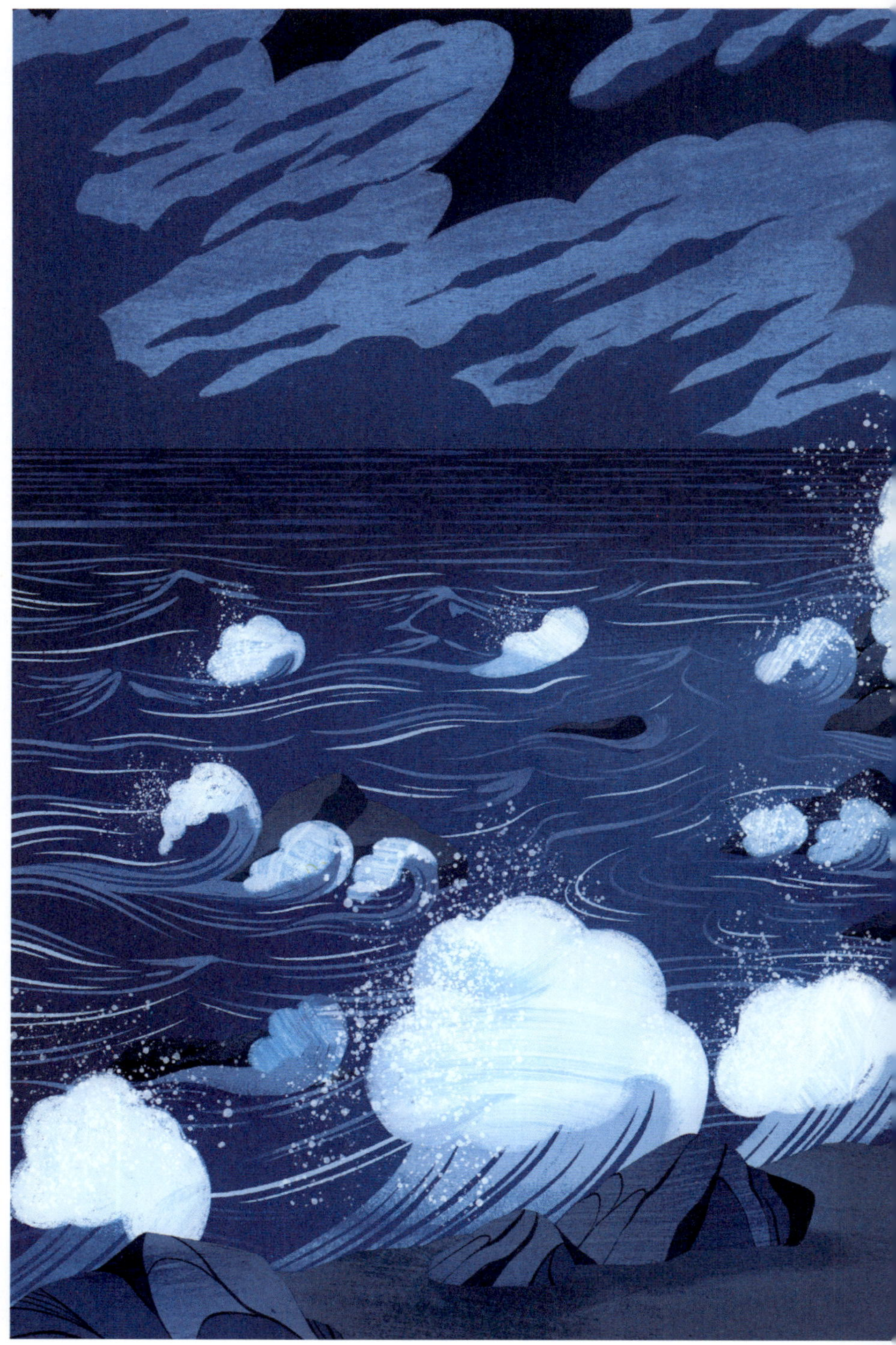

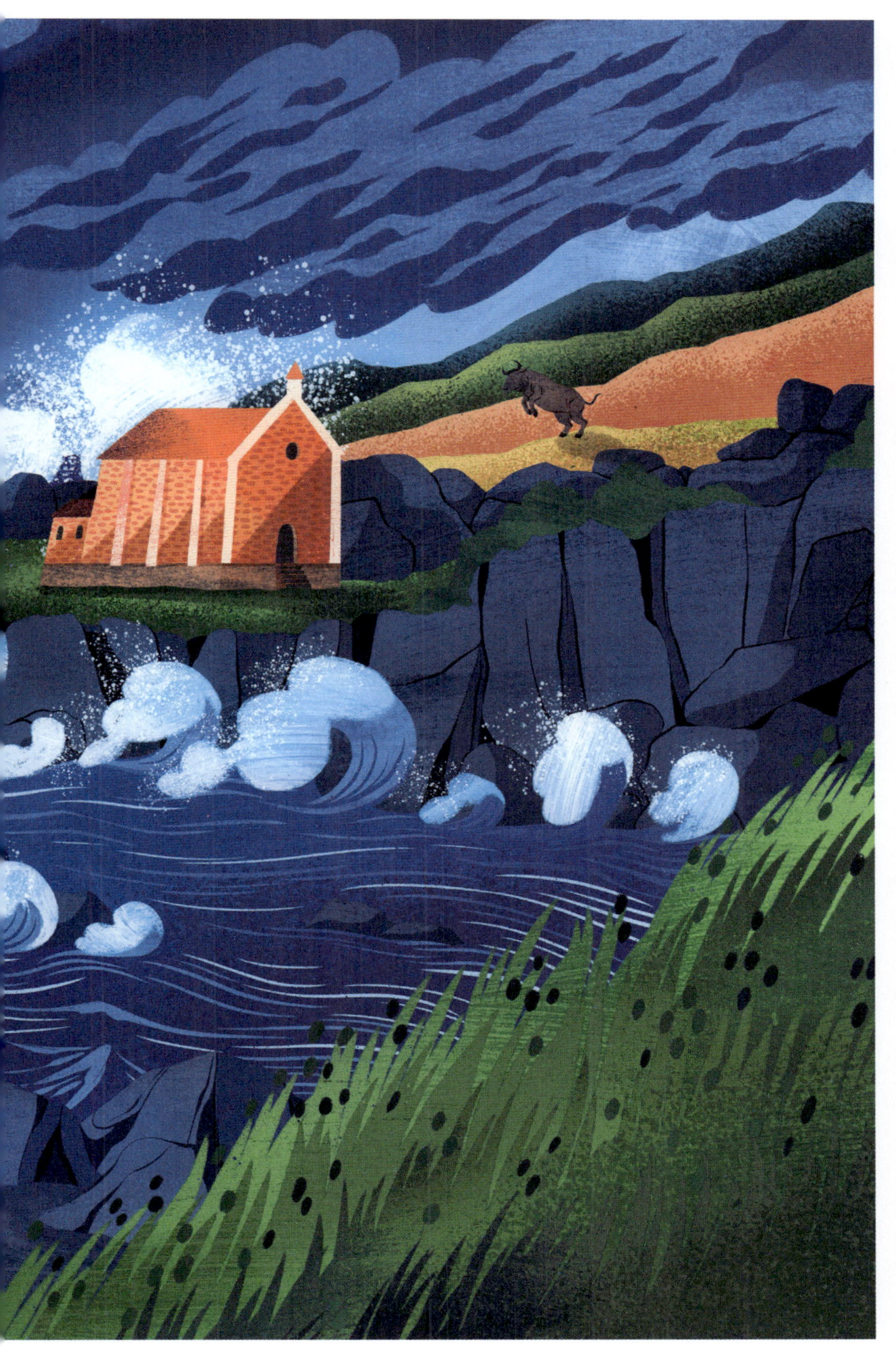

surfers gather throughout the seasons and whitewashed houses cluster, dominated by a Romanesque church that stands proudly by the sea. Outside the church walls, locals play the Basque racket game of pelota. Further west along the coast is the busy fishing port of Bermeo, with a large dry dock and a clutch of colourful houses, connected by narrow streets. Historically, this little port has seen plenty of action since the 14th century, when whalers left to travel as far as Newfoundland for their quarry. Close by is the small hamlet of Elantxobe, where more colourful and whitewashed houses spread, seemingly clinging to the sheer cliff face, and steep alleyways lead down to a tiny harbour.

Then there's the town of Guernica itself. During the Spanish Civil War, Guernica was the northern stronghold of the Republican resistance movement and the heart of Basque culture. Even today, evidence of that April day can be seen in the pockmarks of bullet holes in the stone arcades of the old marketplace. It was market day when the bombing occurred, and women and children were out enjoying the spring sunshine. Then the pounding started, lasting for more than three hours. At the time, Picasso was living in France, and had been commissioned by the Spanish Republican government to create a mural for that summer's Paris Exhibition. He was working on ideas for it when he read a newspaper account of the bombing. Immediately, he abandoned the original idea he had been working on and began painting Guernica in black, white and grey, to reflect that he had learned of the atrocity through newsprint. The painting became Picasso's most powerful political statement, and one of the world's most renowned images of the tragedies of war and the individual suffering it inflicts. Soon after it was completed, the painting was taken around the world on a brief tour, where it became internationally acclaimed and drew attention to the Spanish Civil War. This was not what the Spanish Republican government had intended when they commissioned Picasso.

Picasso had not been back home to Spain for several years when the Nazis bombed Guernica and he vowed that neither he nor the painting would ever return to Spain while Franco remained in power. He began painting the vast work using the distorted approach he had become known for, which created a stronger expression of emotion than realism. He included a bull to symbolise Spain and suggest brutality, next to a sobbing woman holding a dead child. The bull's tail represents a flame or curl of smoke from the bombing. Behind it, a dove holds an olive branch as a sign of peace. A light bulb blazes from the ceiling, its jagged edge suggesting an explosion – or perhaps an all-seeing eye, or the sun, again, a symbol of hope. Although Picasso rarely explained his work, he said that the contorted horse stands for the people. Next to the horse's head, a terrified woman holds a candle. In traditional Christian iconography, a flame is a sign of the Holy Spirit or implies hope. There are two 'hidden' or subliminal images in the horse's body. One is a human skull symbolising death, while a second is below the body; another bull's head, its horn goring the horse's breast. Under the horse is a dead, dismembered soldier with a severed arm that still grasps a shattered sword from which a flower grows. In the soldier's open palm is a stigmata, a symbol of martyrdom from Christ's crucifixion. Of his famous work, Picasso said: 'In the panel on which I am working, which I shall call Guernica . . . I clearly express my abhorrence of the military caste which has sunk Spain in an ocean of pain and death.'

Some 43 years after the bombing, Guernica was rebuilt and declared a global symbol of peace, with its own peace museum, the Museo de la Paz de Gernika, and park. The church bells that once pealed as the first warning that aircraft had been spotted now chime sweetly for weddings and baptisms, celebrating and honouring new beginnings. Visitors of any faith, gender, age or ethnicity will be touched by the serenity and history of this special, reflective place.

Where?	Catalonia, Spain
Which?	*Persistence of Memory* (1931) by Salvador Dalí
What?	Relaxing, chilled, historic and cultural region

CATALONIA

RICH WITH culture and history, Catalonia is part of the Costa Brava, in the north-eastern corner of Spain, comprising the four provinces of Barcelona, Girona, Lleida and Tarragona. Inviting and colourful, several languages are spoken here, including Catalan, Spanish and the Aranese dialect of Occitan. The capital city of Catalonia is Barcelona, with many magical attractions, including the towering, still incomplete basilica La Sagrada Família, Park Güell and Casa Batlló, all created by the visionary architect Antoni Gaudí, and to the north, in the province of Girona, close to Southern France and the Mediterranean Sea, is Figueres, the birthplace of Salvador Dalí (1904–89).

Near Figueres, nestling in a sheltered bay on the southern side of the Cap de Creus peninsula, is Cadaqués, the easternmost port in Spain. Dalí, who later described it as the most beautiful town in the world, used to stay here as a child during family holidays. With its elegant waterfront, narrow, meandering streets, abundance of bougainvillea and dazzling whitewashed houses with blue front doors and windows, Cadaqués sparkles in the sunlight and gleams above the sapphire sea. It became a popular retreat for writers and artists during the 20th century, and visitors included René Magritte, Henri Matisse, Joan Miró, Marcel Duchamp, Luís Buñuel and Pablo Picasso – and, of course, Dalí himself. Aspects of Cadaqués and the surrounding coastline feature in some of Dalí's most famous works, including his paintings *The Spectre of Sex Appeal* (1932) and *The Persistence of Memory* (1931).

The coastal road to Cadaqués winds and dips as it passes picturesque villages on one side and the Mediterranean Sea on the other. Once there, the deep layers of its history can be explored.

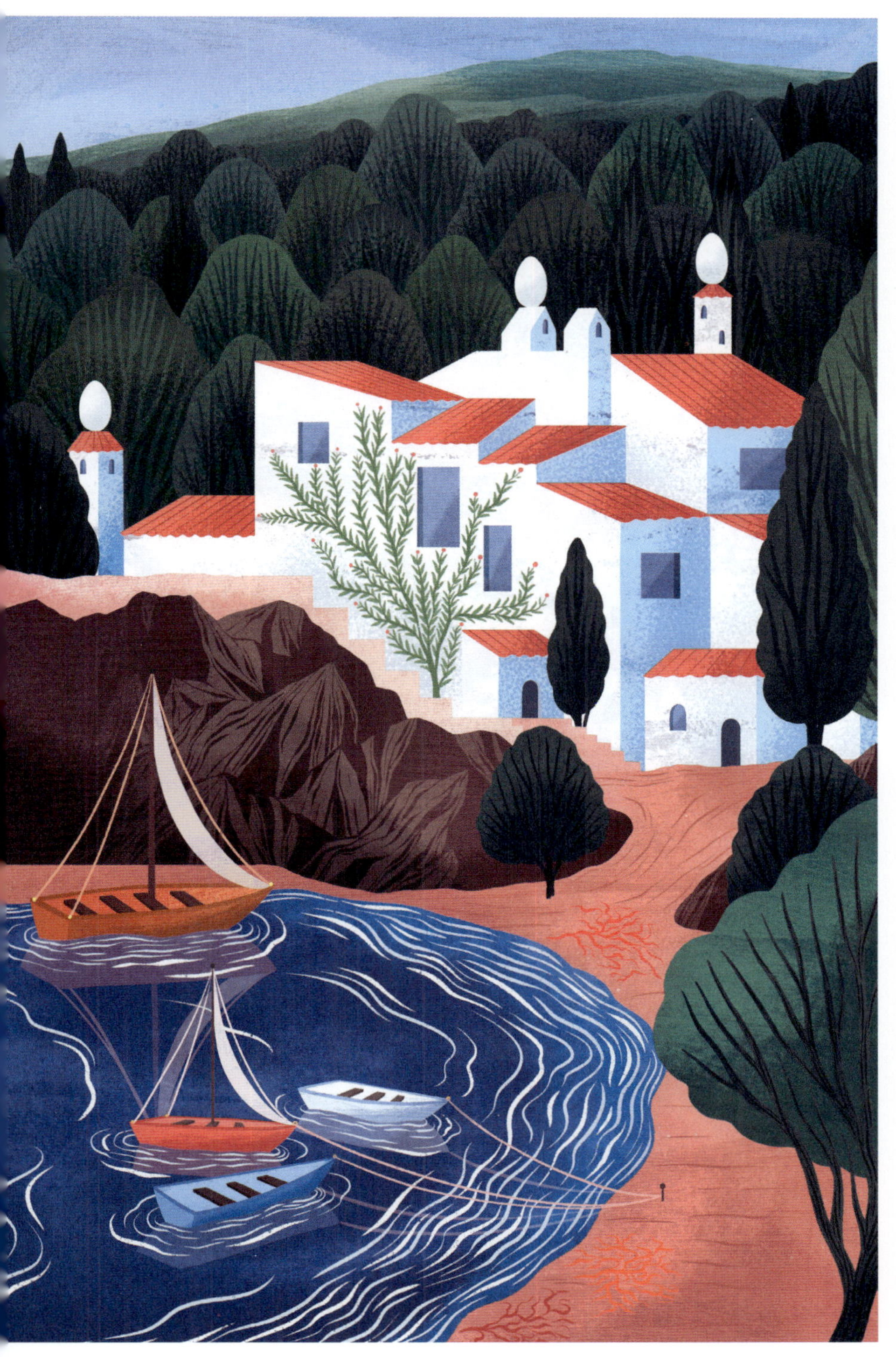

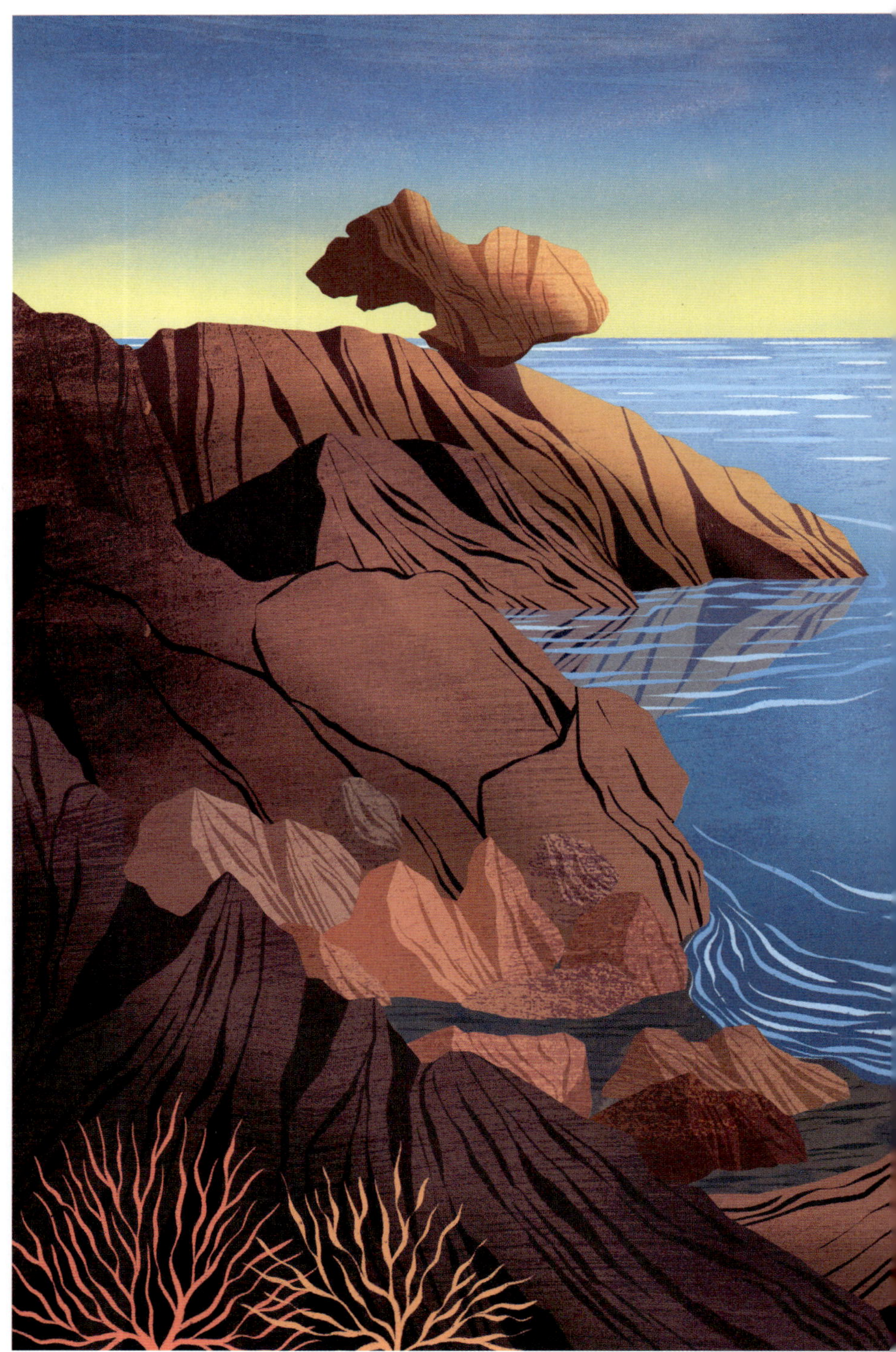

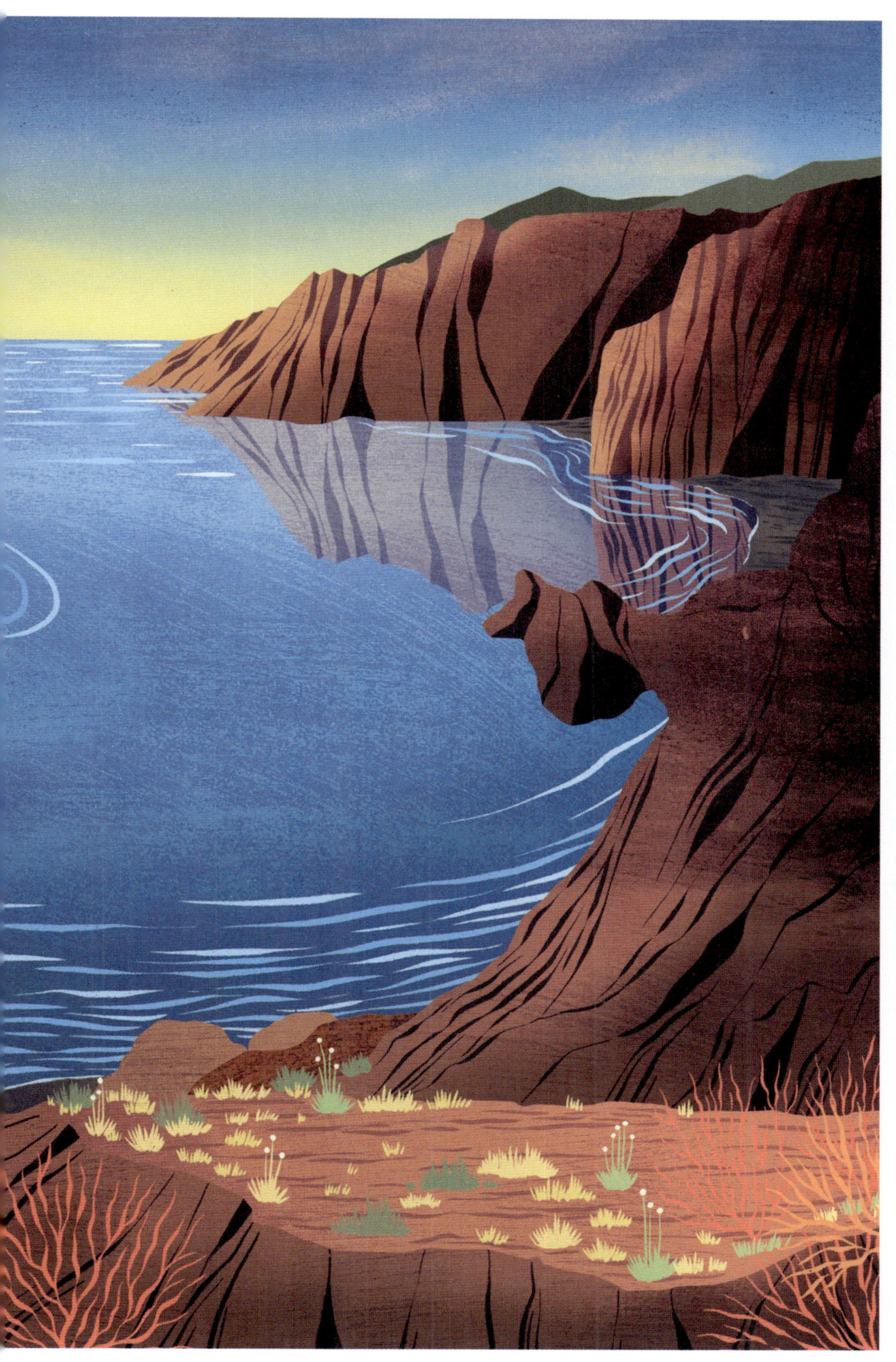

The first settlers were Iberian and ancient Egyptians, Greeks and Romans used the natural harbour as a stopping-off point during voyages around the Mediterranean. Evidence of the fortified medieval town remain in the Torre de sa Fusta des Baluard, an imposing tower overlooking the bay, the Portal de Mar de la Muralla, the arched gateway entrance to the old town, and the Casa del Baró de la Roda, a medieval house built into the old town wall. Throughout the medieval period, pirates frequently attacked, including the infamous red-bearded Barbarossa, who looted the town and torched the church. Situated on the highest point in Cadaqués, this church was replaced in the 16th century with the Santa Maria. Trade routes from the town were established in the 19th century, and in the 20th, several luxurious Modernista-style houses were built along the bay, as the town became a popular destination for tourists.

The background landscape in *The Persistence of Memory* depicts elements of both Figueres and Cadaqués, as well as Portlligat, where Dalí painted this. The craggy Cap de Creus can be seen, while the clear Catalonian light enhances all the colours. Dalí joined the Surrealist movement formally in 1929, and from the start, he imbued his art with a sense of the fantastic, deliberately painting with meticulous precision to create a sense of confusing reality, which he called 'hand-painted dream photographs'. In *The Persistence of Memory* he explored his own psychological issues and phobias, such as his unconscious fear of death and his belief that our unconscious minds are present in all we do in our daily lives. Before joining the Surrealists, Dalí had studied Sigmund Freud's theories on psychoanalysis, which may explain why this work also contains a strangely distorted self-portrait. Overall, the painting suggests the transitory or fluid nature of time.

In the same year in which he joined the Surrealist movement, Dalí met his love, inspiration, muse and future wife Gala (real name Elena Ivanovna Diakonova). Allegedly, his father disapproved of their relationship and told local hoteliers not to rent a room to his son. So, in 1930 Dalí purchased a *barraca* (small fisherman's hut) in nearby Portlligat, where he and Gala lived for over 40 years, gradually extending and adding to it. Dalí lived there until Gala's death in 1982, and it is now a museum, maintained exactly as it was when the couple lived there, housing many of their personal belongings and photographs of famous friends taken there, including

Coco Chanel, Ingrid Bergman and Walt Disney (with whom Dalí collaborated in 1946 on the animated short film *Destino*, and which was finally completed and released in 2003).

If you visit, you will be shown round in groups of up to eight people, who are taken into the house every ten minutes. In this way the tranquil atmosphere, beautiful bay views from every window and the individual exhibits can be fully appreciated. Most of the small whitewashed rooms are decorated with large bunches of Gala's favourite yellow flowers.

A few miles inland from glittering Cadaqués and Portlligat, is Figueres, located between the Pyrenees and the Costa Blanca, the last town before the Spanish–French border, and where Dalí grew up. The name Figueres translates to Fig Tree, as copious numbers of these trees used to grow across the town that comprises a central Old Town, where most of the cultural attractions are located, and a central avenue of La Rambla that connects the old quarter with the newer parts of town that were developed in the 19th and 20th centuries. Across Figueres are various public squares, where people meet, chat, play dominos or just relax. Each square has its own architecture and character – in some, markets are held regularly, others are quieter. There are several cultural attractions to be found here, including the Toy Museum of Catalonia, with more than 4,000 games and toys from different periods, and the Empordà Museum that takes you on a journey through large swathes of fascinating Catalonia. Dalí devotees will want to head to the Teatre-Museu Dalí; a quirky, extravagant, permanent exhibition of his work, which attracts tourists from all over the world. Opened in 1974, the museum was designed by Dalí himself, and it contains work from the entire expanse of his career, from his early beginnings to his utterly ostentatious late works of the early 20th century.

Where?	Giverny, France
Which?	*The Water Lily Pond: Green Harmony* (1899) by Claude Monet
What?	Place of abundant flowers and tranquillity

GIVERNY

AFTER YEARS of struggling as an artist, Claude Monet (1840–1926) became successful and wealthy. By 1883, he could afford to rent a house and large garden in Giverny; a village in Normandy, northern France, where the Rivers Epte and Seine meet, about 75 kilometres (45 miles) from Paris. Seven years later, he bought the house and garden, along with an adjacent plot of land. He hired six full-time gardeners to landscape the area with arbours, archways, colourful shrubs, flowers and climbing plants. The adjoining plot was almost completely taken up with a huge pond, created from of a tributary of the River Epte. They filled the pond with waterlilies, surrounded it with weeping willows and built an elegant Japanese-style bridge to arc over it. Monet once said: 'I perhaps owe it to flowers for having become a painter.' By catching transitory moments and changing light effects with short, broken brushstrokes and bright colours, Monet abandoned accepted artistic traditions. He spent the rest of his life painting in this way in his garden in Giverny and sometimes also in the neighbouring area.

Monet – often described as the Father of Impressionism – had first seen Giverny when he passed through it by train, some years before. With its country-feel and proximity to Paris, he determined to live there, and once he did, he rarely left. His passion for gardening, as well as for colours and the effects of light, can be seen in his flowers and pond that are an extension of his paintings of art, and visitors to his house and garden can still see these arrangements of blooms and shrubs – including graceful wisterias and flamboyant azaleas – and drink in the atmosphere. Now the Fondation Claude

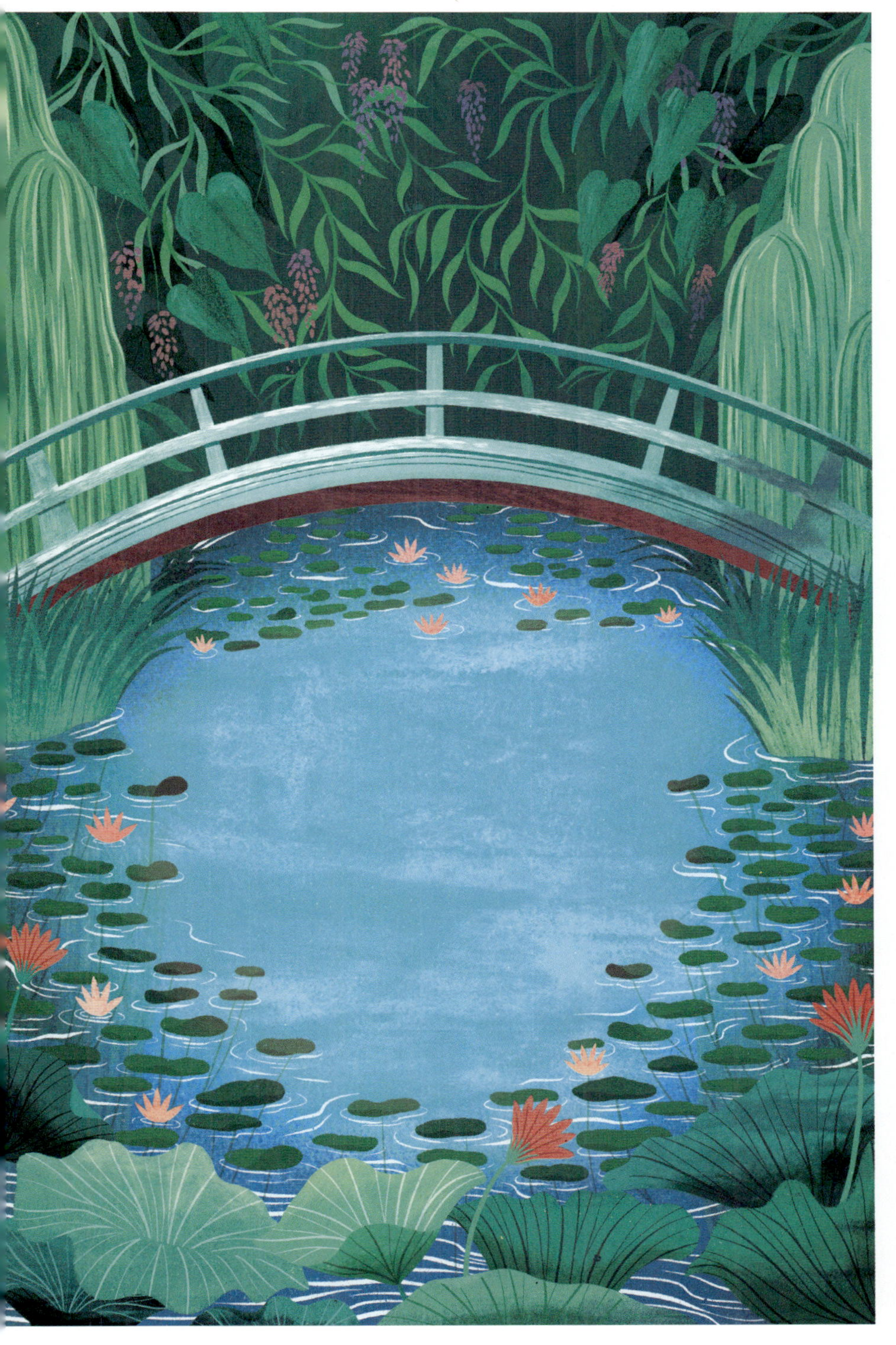

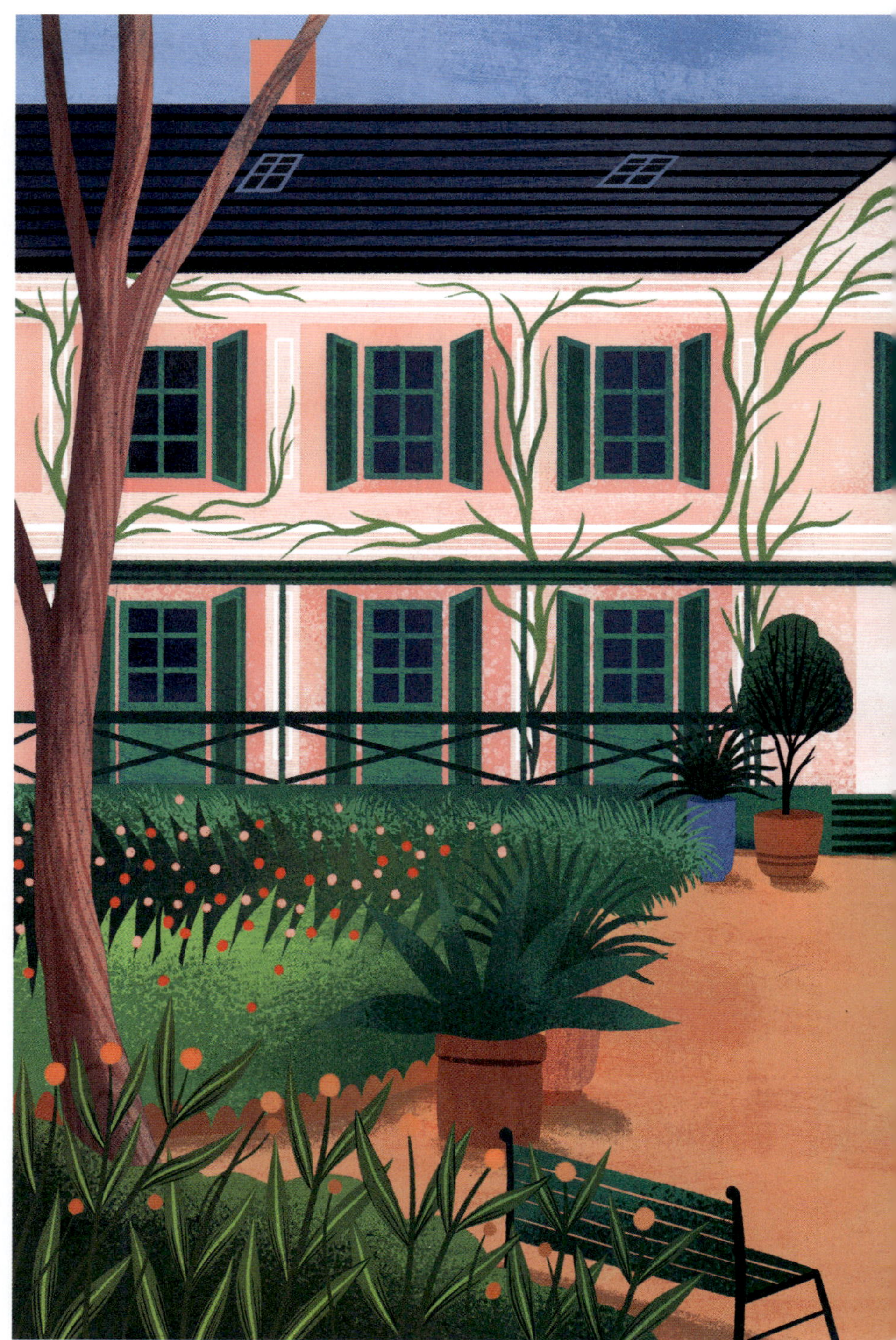

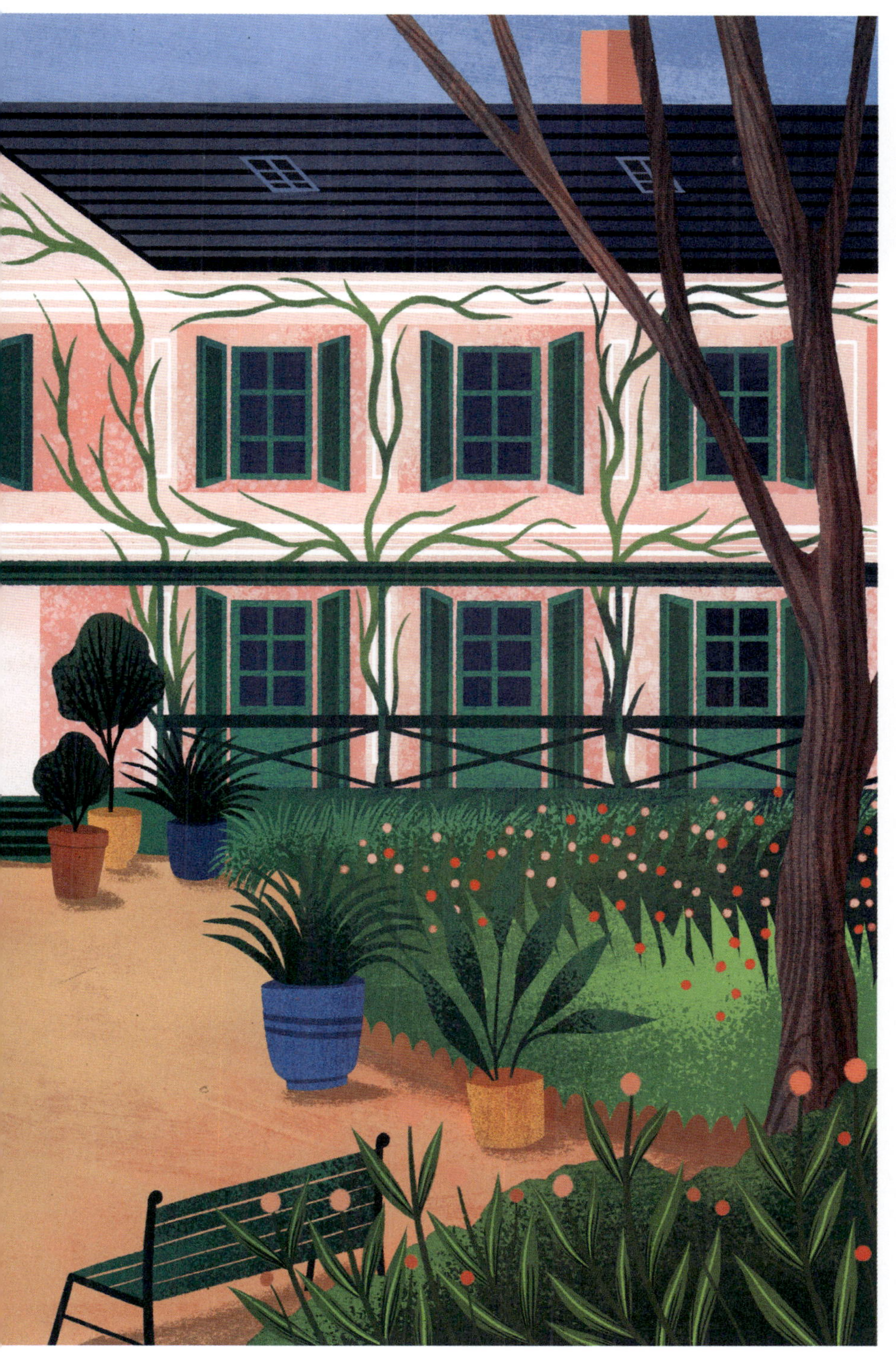

Monet museum, Monet's house and garden are beautifully preserved as he designed and lived in them. You can visualise him everywhere; in the house, the gardens and even the studios that he built on the plot. Stroll around and spot the familiar aspects of the garden and house that you recognise from countless paintings, then walk through the underpass that connects you to the water garden. Once there, you can look for the reflections that Monet saw, take a selfie on the Japanese Bridge, or even better, get someone else to take one for you. The pond – one of Monet's greatest sources of inspiration that he recorded in countless different light effects – is breathtaking. From the end of the 19th century until his death, Monet painted views of this pond over and again, from *The Water Lily Pond: Green Harmony* of 1899, to his vast *Grandes Decorations*, which he undertook between 1914 and 1922. The pond became the principal preoccupation of the last 26 years of his life.

Near Monet's house is the Musée des Impressionnismes Giverny, which showcases more of the Impressionist art movement. Giverny is most easily reached from Paris by a 45-minute train that runs from Saint-Lazare station several times a day. Shuttle buses run into the village from the station every 15 minutes – or you can walk it, it's not far. The hills surrounding Giverny are dusted with wildflowers throughout the spring and summer months, creating the perfect setting for walks and rambles. Pick up a Tourist Board route map or follow the old railroad path and, even if you get lost, you can trace your steps back to Vernon. Historical buildings to explore in Vernon include the Old Mill and the church Collégiale Notre-Dame, both of which Monet painted, as well as the Château des Tourelles, a 13th-century castle.

Although most famous as Monet's home for 43 years, and where he created his home, garden and monumental waterlily paintings, a settlement has existed in Giverny since Neolithic times, recorded in ancient deeds as 'Warnacum'. In around 1887, drawn by Monet's example, several American Impressionists also settled there – staying at the Hôtel Baudy, which is now a convivial and stylish restaurant – and Giverny became something of an artists' colony until the First World War broke out in 1914. Even today the village is home to many contemporary artists who have established their own small private galleries. Monet himself is buried in the place he loved, in the picturesque cemetery of the Romanesque-style Église Sainte-Radegonde.

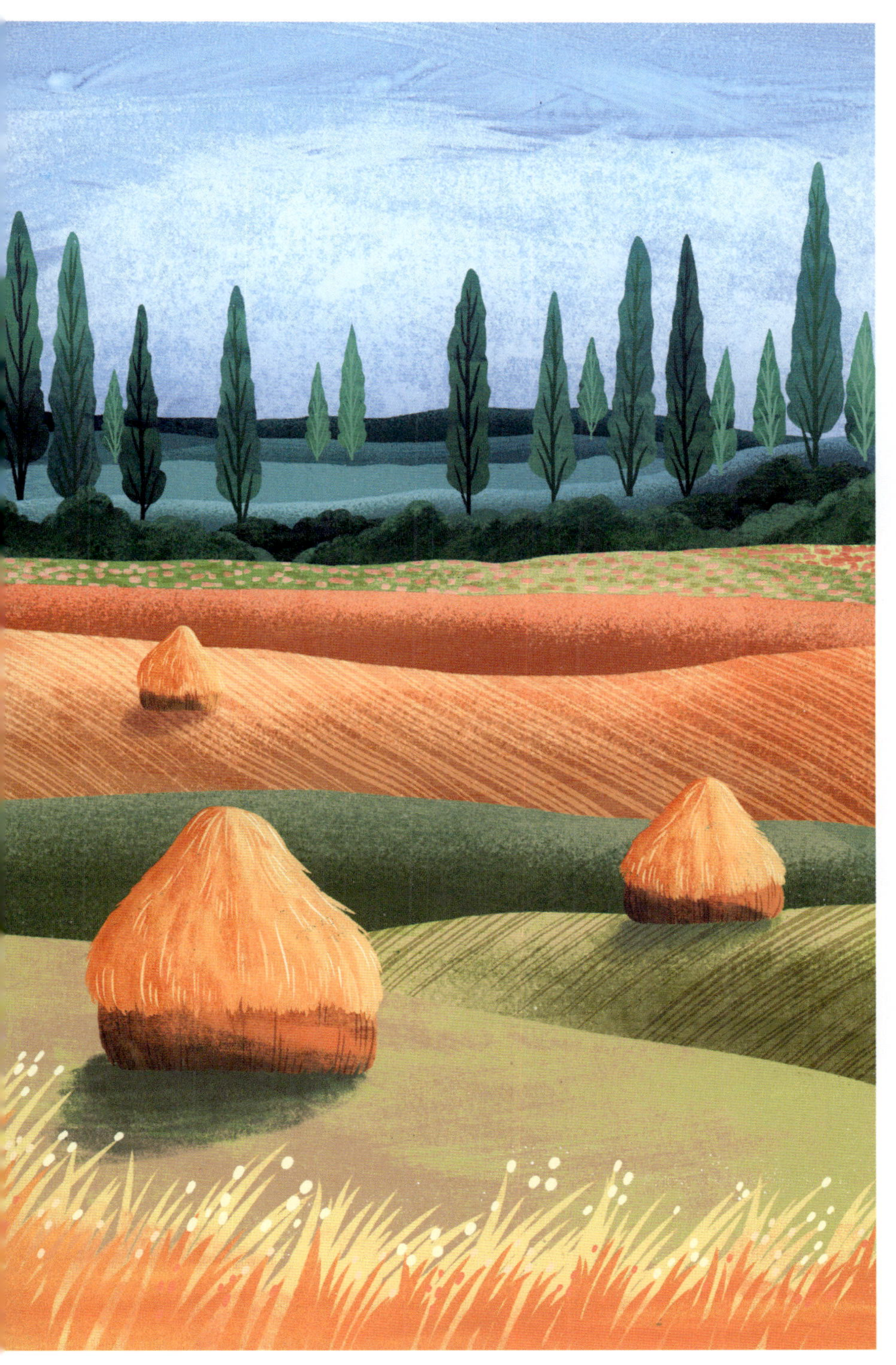

Where?	Arles, France
Which?	*Café Terrace at Night* (1888) by Vincent van Gogh
What?	Ancient Roman city of swirling skies and artistic legends

ARLES

LONG BEFORE Vincent van Gogh (1853–90) produced approximately 300 paintings here, Arles in Provence on the River Rhône was a Greek colony, established in the 6th century BC. Five centuries later, Julius Caesar occupied Arles, turning it into the flourishing gateway to Roman Gaul, transforming the area into an imposing civilisation and one of Gaul's most venerated cities. Featuring aqueducts, canals, roads, pavements, sewers, latrines, thermal baths, a forum, a hippodrome, a theatre and an arena, from 308–12 AD it became home to Emperor Constantine, who brought Christianity with him. These days, several charming classical antiquities and examples of Romanesque stonework remain, while the rest of the town boasts shady, restful streets and squares, and shuttered houses basking in golden sunlight.

Every Saturday there is a colourful market in Arles, brimming with local produce, clothes, trinkets and household items for sale. Most famous, of course, for the dramatic events and vibrant works of art produced by Van Gogh, Arles is a popular city for tourists, many of whom follow in the artist's footsteps on the Van Gogh Walking Tour. Maps are available from the Visitors Centre on Boulevard des Lices, or in the smaller Visitors Centre at Arles train station, and this free, self-guided tour takes you around the city, exploring all the major sites that Vincent himself saw and painted during his time living there. At each key point, there is a reproduction of the scene that he painted on that spot, so you can fully immerse yourself in Van Gogh's world and see through his eyes.

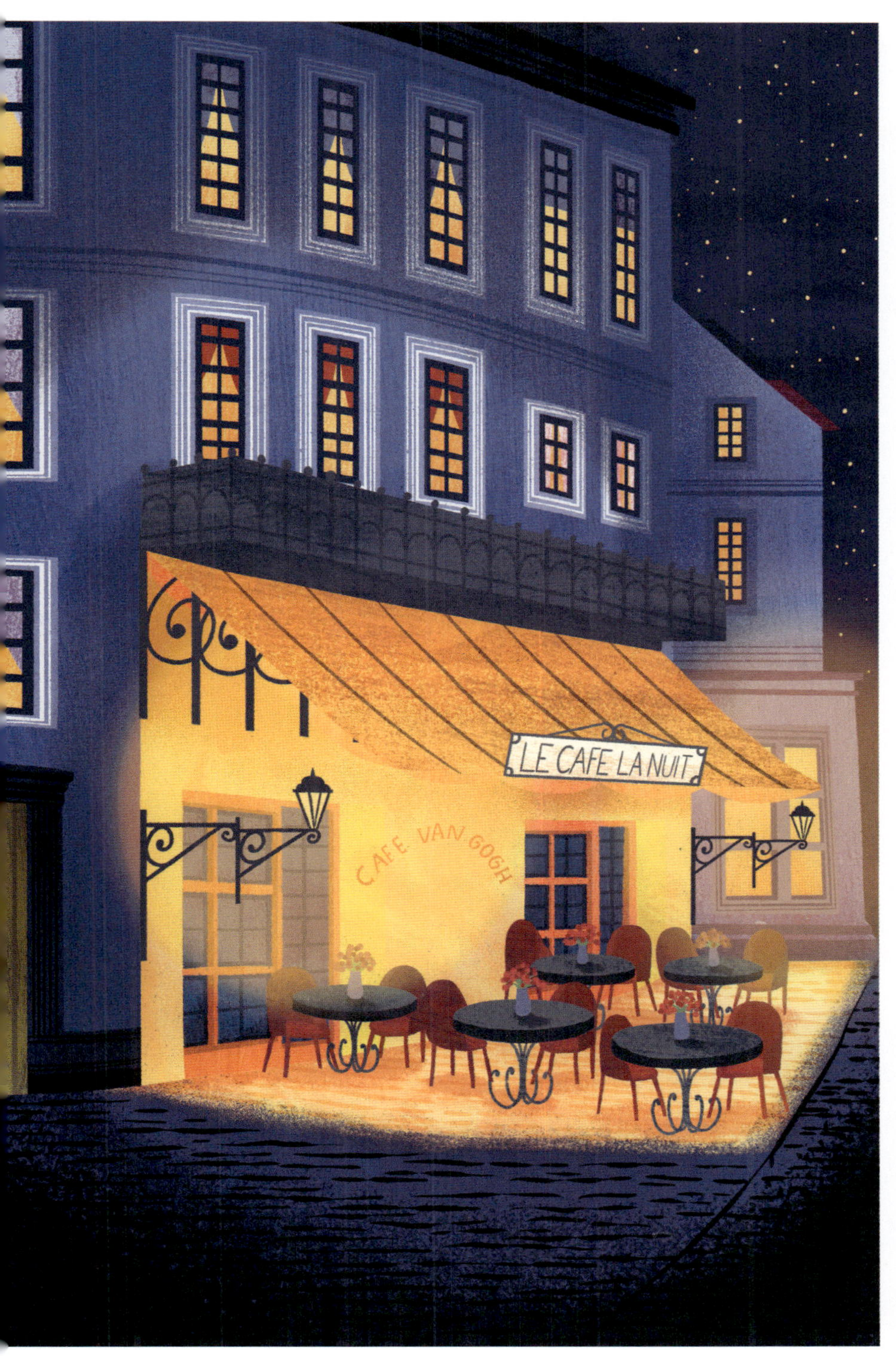
LE CAFE LA NUIT
CAFE VAN GOGH

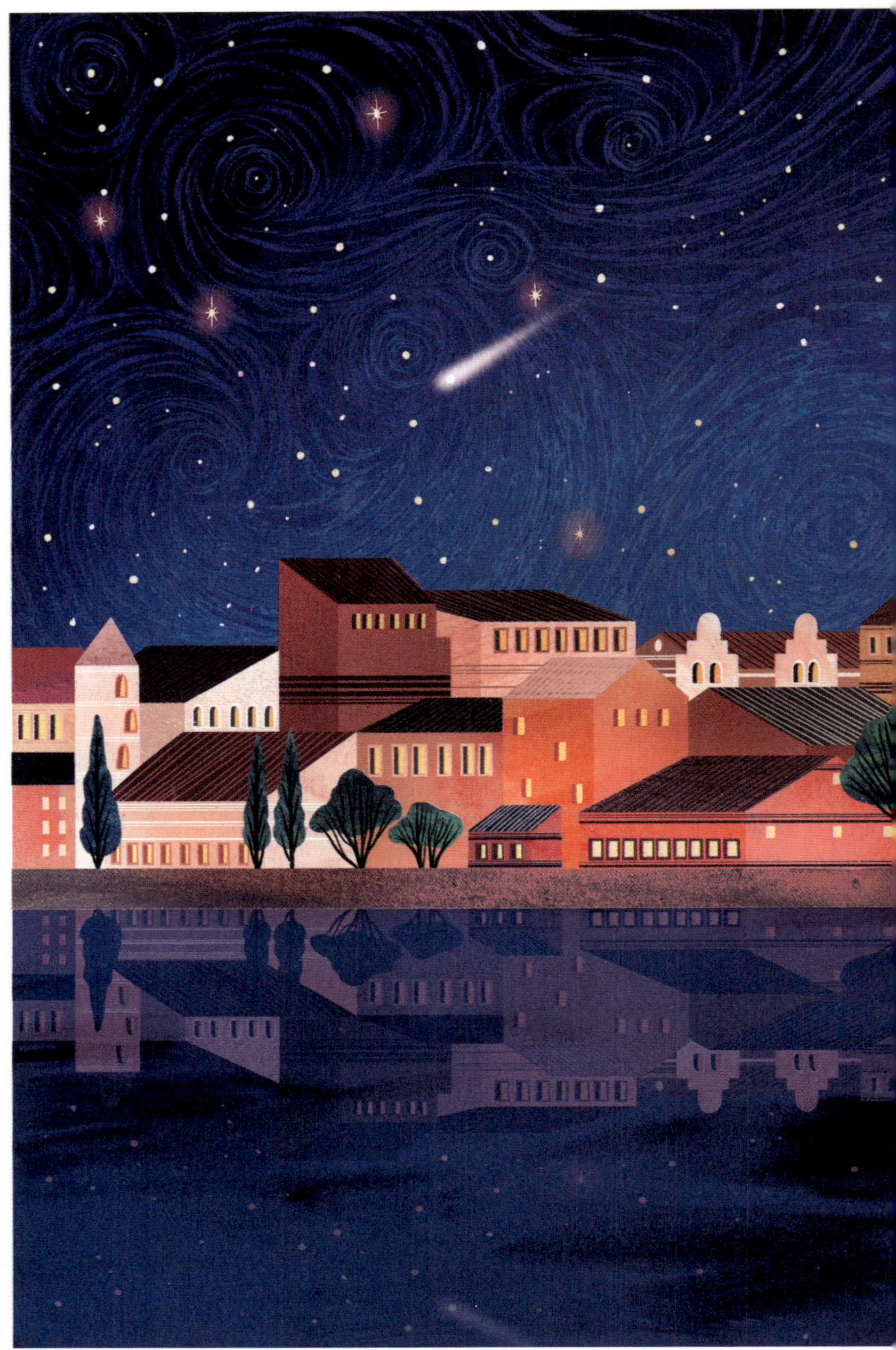

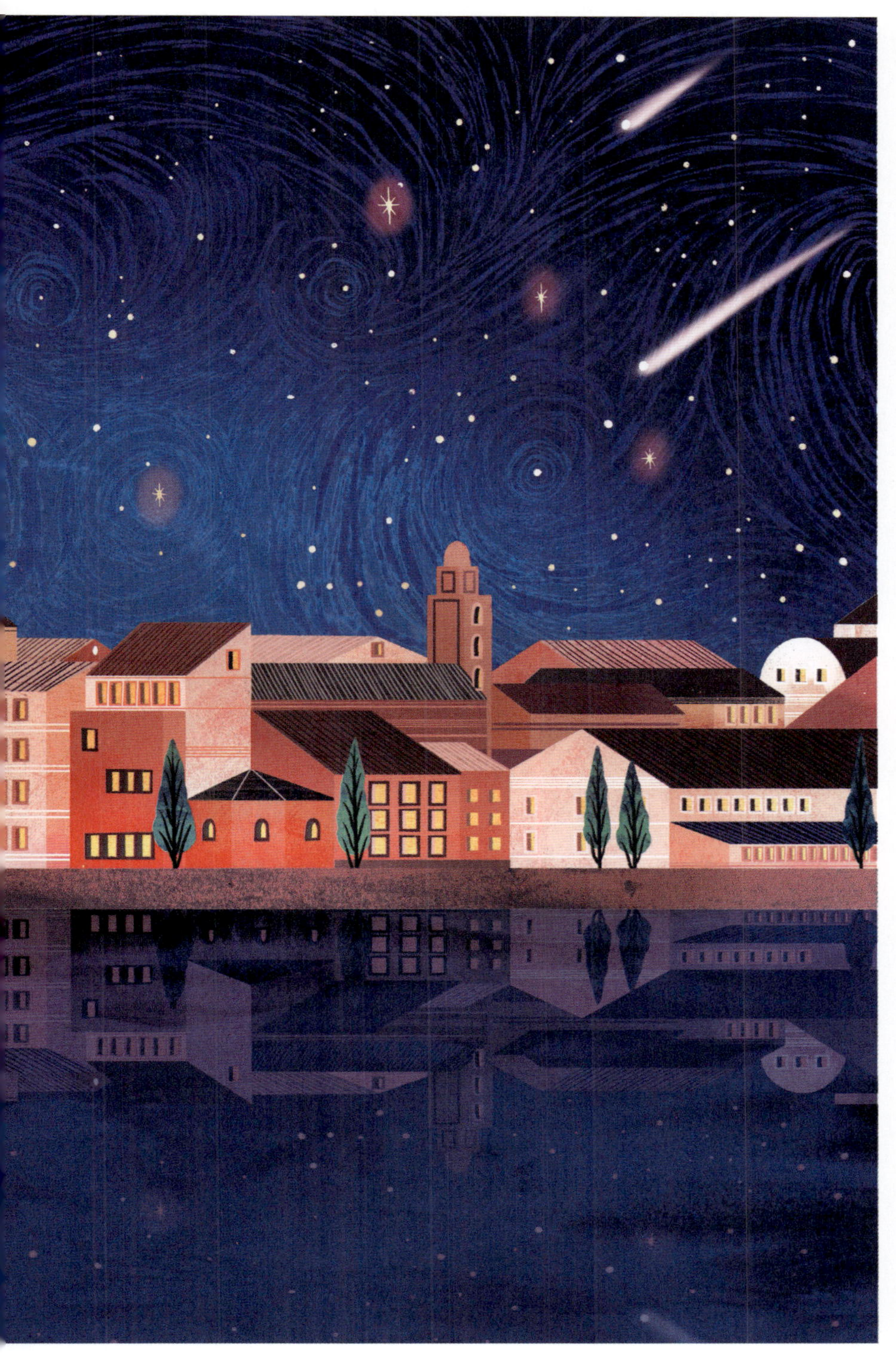

When Van Gogh arrived in Arles in February 1888, he was yearning for the sunshine and glowing colours of the south of France, so was shocked and disappointed to discover it had recently snowed. But for most of the year – around 300 days – the city and surrounding countryside are illuminated by dazzling yellow sunlight or peppered with sparkling silver stars and a glowing moon. So once the snow had melted, he made the most of it. Van Gogh first checked in at the hotel-restaurant Carrel, and later at Café de la Gare. After six months, in early September, he moved into the Yellow House at 2 Place Lamartine, which he had been using as a studio since the beginning of May and where he lived for a time with the artist Paul Gauguin. It was here that Van Gogh severed his own ear in December 1888, allegedly after a row with Gauguin, who had announced he was leaving Arles. Van Gogh ended up in the local hospital, where he was treated by assistant physician Dr Félix Rey, who believed that Van Gogh was suffering from a form of epilepsy brought on partly by too much coffee and alcohol and too little food. A few weeks later, he voluntarily entered an asylum in nearby Saint-Rémy, from where he painted his famous work, *The Starry Night*, in 1889.

Although the famous Yellow House, which he painted in 1888, was destroyed during the Second World War, many other vistas that Van Gogh painted in Arles, such as *Starry Night Over the Rhône*, *Café Terrace at Night* and *Les Alyscamps* (all painted in 1888) remain remarkably unchanged. The whirling skies really are as Van Gogh painted them; clear and blue by day, deep and velvety by night.

In the first century AD, the Place du Forum, where Van Gogh later painted *Café Terrace at Night*, was the centre of the city. The part that remains today is only a segment of the Roman original, but because of Van Gogh's painting, it is now more associated with him than with its connection to antiquity. Now called the Café Van Gogh, the café still looks as it did when he painted it, and visitors can while away a few hours here, soaking up the atmosphere of a place the artist loved. Near the Place du Forum, in the restored 15th-century Hôtel Léautaud de Donines, the Fondation Vincent van Gogh was established in 2014 to present aspects of his time in Arles and reflect on his impact on art today.

Other features of the Roman settlement in Arles can still be seen today, including the Arles Amphitheatre, constructed during the reign of Emperor Augustus. Built for 20,000 spectators, it once showcased gladiators and chariot racing. Next door is the Théâtre Antique, which also dates from the 1st century AD and is now used in the summer for dance, film and music performances and festivals. Also remaining is the Thermes de Constantin – the Roman baths of the Emperor Constantine, which were built in the 4th century as part of his palace.

In the Arles Museum of Antiquity, just outside the city centre at Rue du Cirque Romain, among other fascinating objects is the oldest known bust of Julius Caesar that was made during his lifetime, and unearthed in 2008 in the River Rhône. Also found in the River Rhône, having spent 2,000 years under water, is a remarkably well-preserved ancient Roman wooden barge. More history can be uncovered at the Hôtel Nord Pinus, where bull fighters, Pablo Picasso, Ernest Hemingway and Henry James all either socialised or stayed. The building contains two embedded Corinthian pillars from a temple that was once part of the ancient Roman Forum, while the Hôtel Jules-César, that was once a convent, was designed by renowned French fashion designer Christian Lacroix, who was born in Arles.

Meanwhile, just beyond Arles is the mythic Camargue, an astonishingly beautiful area featuring salt flats, small saltwater lakes, lagoons, marshlands and farmland, and roamed by black bulls, white horses and pink flamingos. Not far too, is the Alpilles, a small, rocky mountain range that runs between the Rivers Rhône and Durance.

Arles, however, will forever be primarily renowned for its connections with Vincent van Gogh as a place where he was happy – for much of the time – and where he produced some of his brightest works, such as *Wheat Field with Cypresses* (1889), *Pont de Langlois* (1888) and his series of Sunflower paintings (1888–89). Even today, long after he left it, Arles epitomises Van Gogh's vision. So briefly touched by a brush of genius, the town has become iconic.

Where?	Brussels
Which?	*The Empire of Light* (1953–54) by René Magritte
What?	Belgian region of innovative architecture that inspired a surreal image

BRUSSELS

WITH ITS mild climate, Brussels is perfectly designed for walking. There's so much to see: parks, buildings and squares such as Grand Place; a beautiful central square surrounded by Gothic-style buildings, including the Town Hall and the King's House; open-air antique markets, bars and cafés that spill on to the streets, and the elegant street where the Surrealist painter René Magritte (1898–1967) lived for nearly 30 years. Visitors today can soak up the atmosphere so familiar to Magritte in Greenwich café, Rue des Chartreux, where his paintings were once rejected and where he often met friends and sometimes played chess, at least once with Marcel Duchamp.

Known for its culinary specialities, including artisan beers, velvety hot chocolate and hot, sweet waffles, Brussels is a region like no other, comprising 19 municipalities, with 2 native languages spoken: Dutch/Flemish and French, and English, spoken by nearly a third of the population. The city's artistic tradition goes back to the Middle Ages, when it became notable for its innovative artists. These included Rogier van der Weyden, one of the most influential painters of the northern Renaissance, famed for his expressive, naturalistic images; Jan Brueghel the Elder, who worked alongside Peter Paul Rubens; and the Expressionist James Ensor, who, in 1888, painted a scene of Christ entering Brussels in a rather unnerving Mardi Gras parade. Long known as a meeting place for artists, writers and intellectuals travelling across Europe, today, Brussels continues to attract a vibrant community of artists.

Located in the north-central part of Belgium, about 110 kilometres (68 miles) from the coast, Brussels has many different

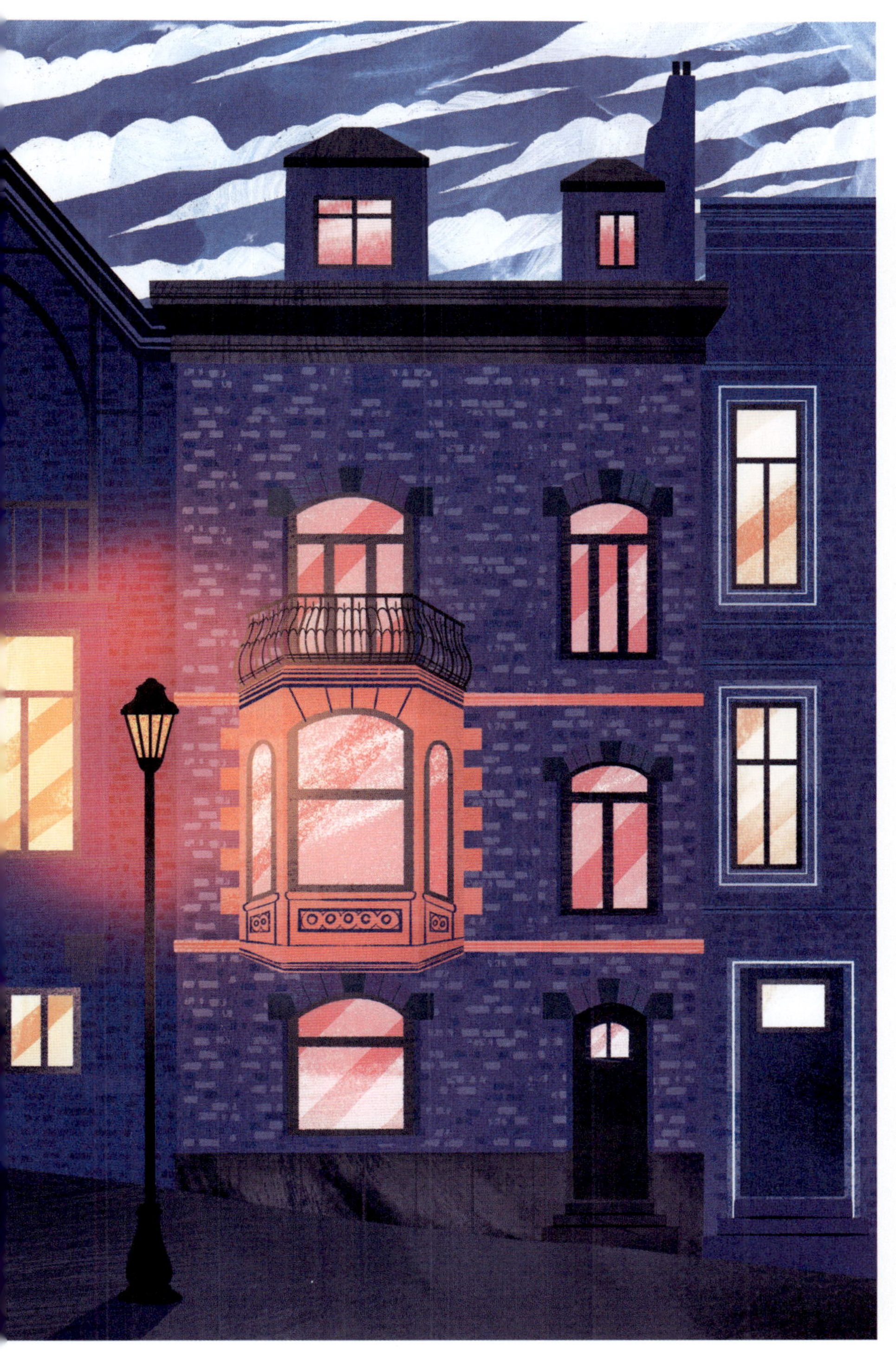

architectural styles standing adjacently, including Art Deco, Gothic and Baroque. Some examples to look out for include the steel-and-glass Art Nouveau Musical Instrument Museum, the opulent La Monnaie opera house, the Gothic church of Notre Dame du Sablon and the Baroque Eglise Saint-Jean-Baptiste au Béguinage. The city is also famous for its Art Nouveau town houses designed in the 1890s by the innovative architect Victor Horta, who, although born almost 40 years before René Magritte, was similarly inventive, as is apparent with his use of iron and glass.

From its beginnings in the Stone Age as a small rural settlement on the river Senne, Brussels rose to a prominent position in Europe by the second half of the 20th century. German forces occupied it during the two world wars, and René Magritte lived through both. At the end of the First World War in 1918, he graduated from Brussels' Royal Academy of Fine Arts, four years later, he married his childhood sweetheart Georgette Berger, and he lived in ten different places in the capital. Apart from a brief period living in Paris – where he became part of the Surrealist group – Brussels remained a constant in Magritte's life. His home in Jette at 137 rue Esseghem – now the René Magritte Museum – became his artistic headquarters, and he and Georgette lived there for 24 years.

Magritte made almost half of his entire output of work while living in Jette and many of his paintings were executed there at his easel in his living room. Everywhere in and around the apartment you can see his inspirations – from the windows to the fireplace, and from the garden aviary to the staircase. From outside the house, you can picture his mysterious paintings *The Empire of Light* (1953–54) that present an unexpected juxtaposition. He painted several versions, all depicting a dark street at night, showing his own house in shadows, but illuminated brightly from the inside and from the outside by a single street light. Above is a pale daytime sky with scudding clouds. The disconcerting paradox of day and night together deliberately confuses our understandings about time and existence. The painting explores Magritte's fascination with the workings of the mind, showing that the inexplicable can be found in even the most conventional of places. In a radio interview in 1956, he explained, 'This evocation of night and day seems to me to have the power to surprise and delight us. I call this power: poetry.' Standing across the street and looking back at his house, you can visualise Magritte's *The Empire of Light* and contemplate this poetry.

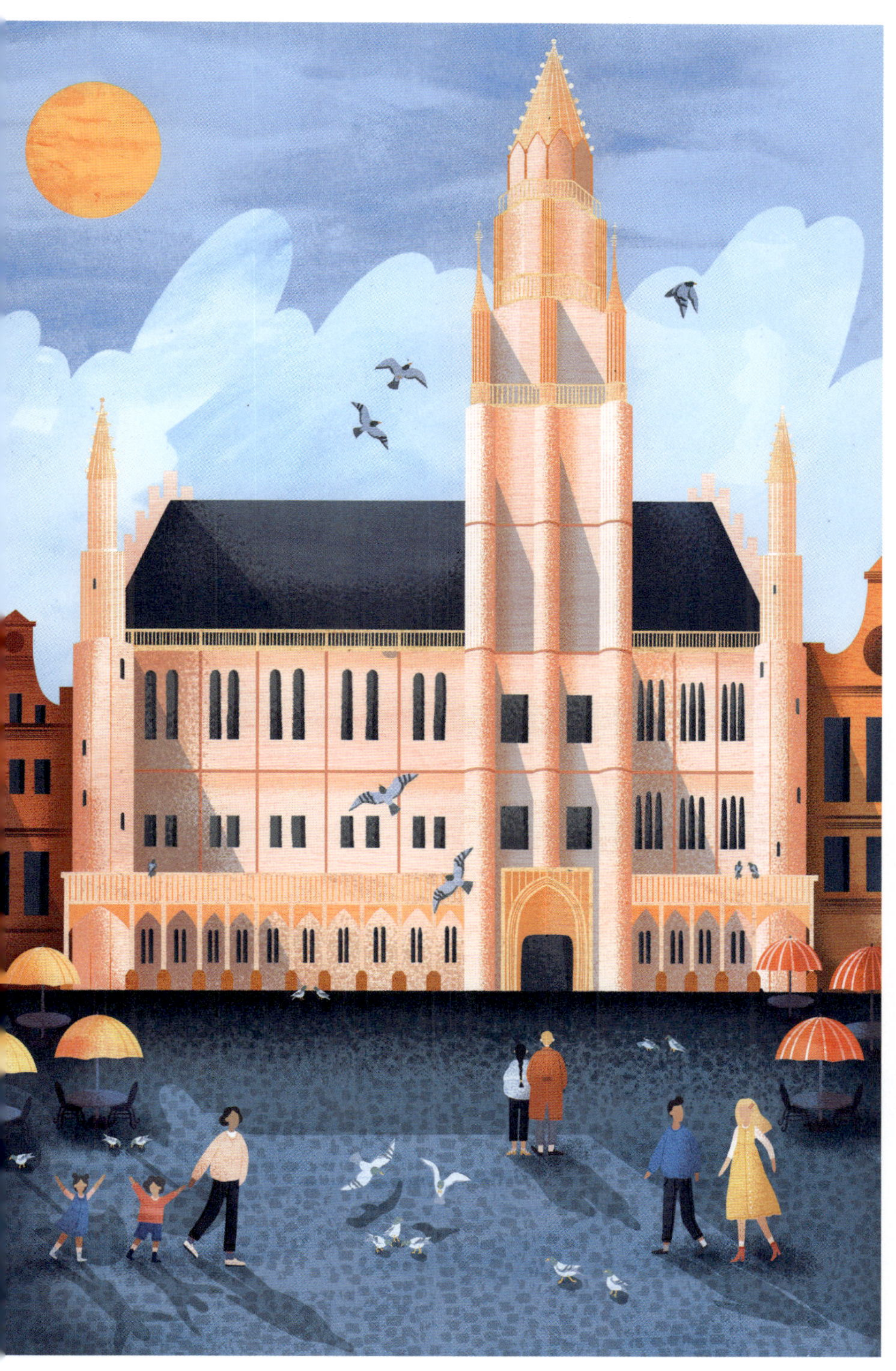

Where?	Bern, Switzerland
Which?	*Mount Niesen, Egyptian Night* (1915) by Paul Klee
What?	Ephemeral city surrounded by snow-capped mountains

BERN

EVERYWHERE IS cool and crisp. Glistening, snow-capped mountains of the Bernese Alps encircle the city, creating a calming, almost mystical presence. On clear days, from certain vantage points, you can see across the panorama of the city and all the way to the Eiger, Mönch and Jungfrau mountains. Although Bern is one of Europe's smallest capitals, its heart is anything but diminutive. Here, among many other things, you will find superlative art galleries, first-class urban swimming and the smoothest chocolate in the world.

All around Bern, the clear mountain air glitters in the sunshine. Powdery white distant peaks are the source of the meltwater that flows down to the astonishingly blue River Aare, where hardy swimmers gather daily for a bracing dip.

At one of four Gelateria di Berna across the city, you can tempt your tastebuds with homemade Swiss gelati, in delicate flavours such as lavender, hibiscus flower or luxuriantly moreish raspberry and ginger. Popular among local workers is the Turnhalle café and bar in the centre of the city – which is also frequented by artists and designers who rent studios in ProGR (the attached cultural centre). Sip a steaming coffee, nibble on a melt-in-the-mouth pastry and browse for books at Apfelgold, then buy hunks of chocolate at Läderach, where every flavour you can imagine is displayed in huge slabs on the counter and sold by weight. Or you can visit two especially famous landmarks, the 13th-century clock tower (Zytglogge) and the cathedral with its 100-metre (328-foot) spire.

Elsewhere in this sparkling city are some of the most mesmerising, world-class art galleries and museums, including the

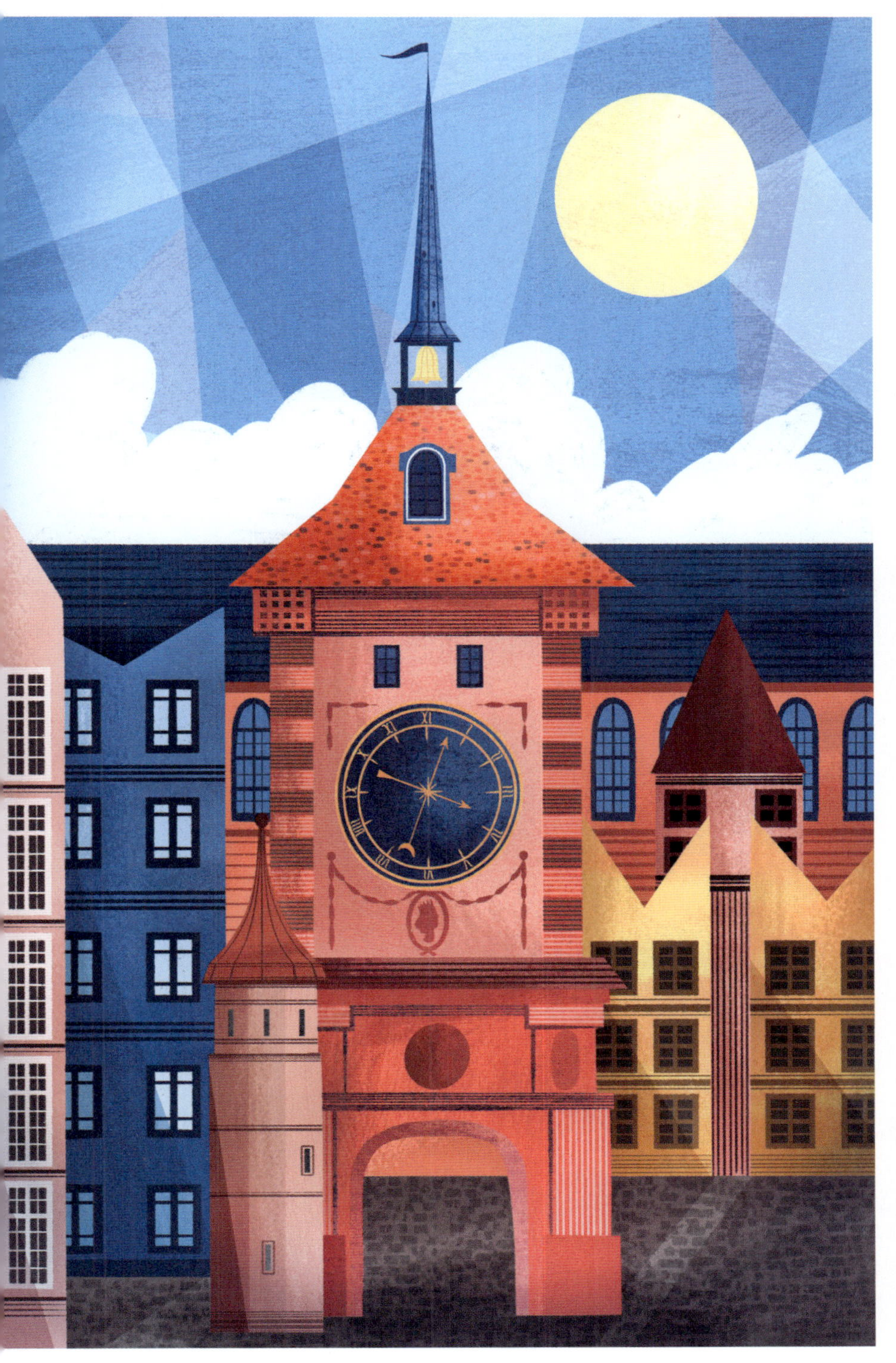

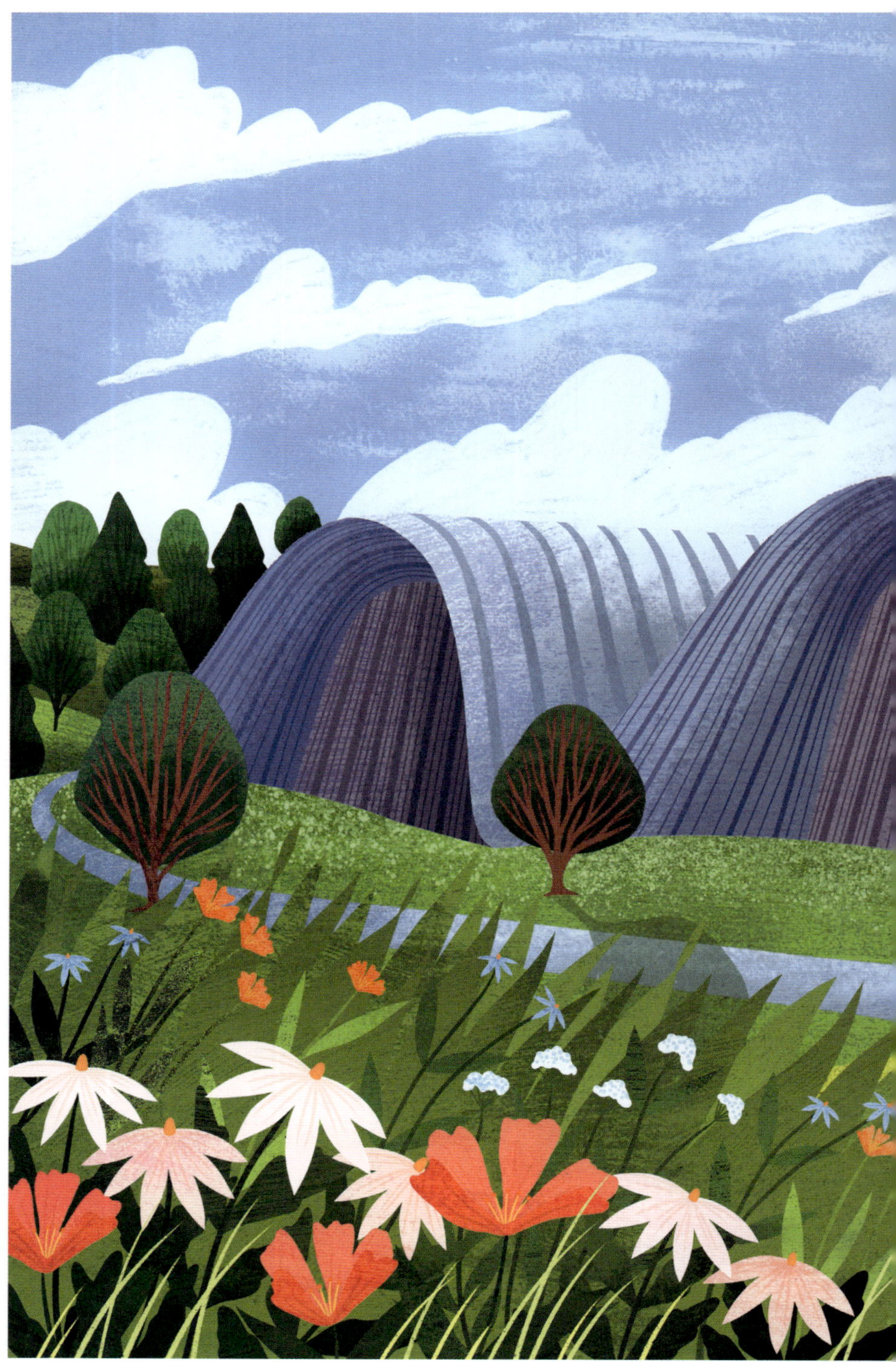

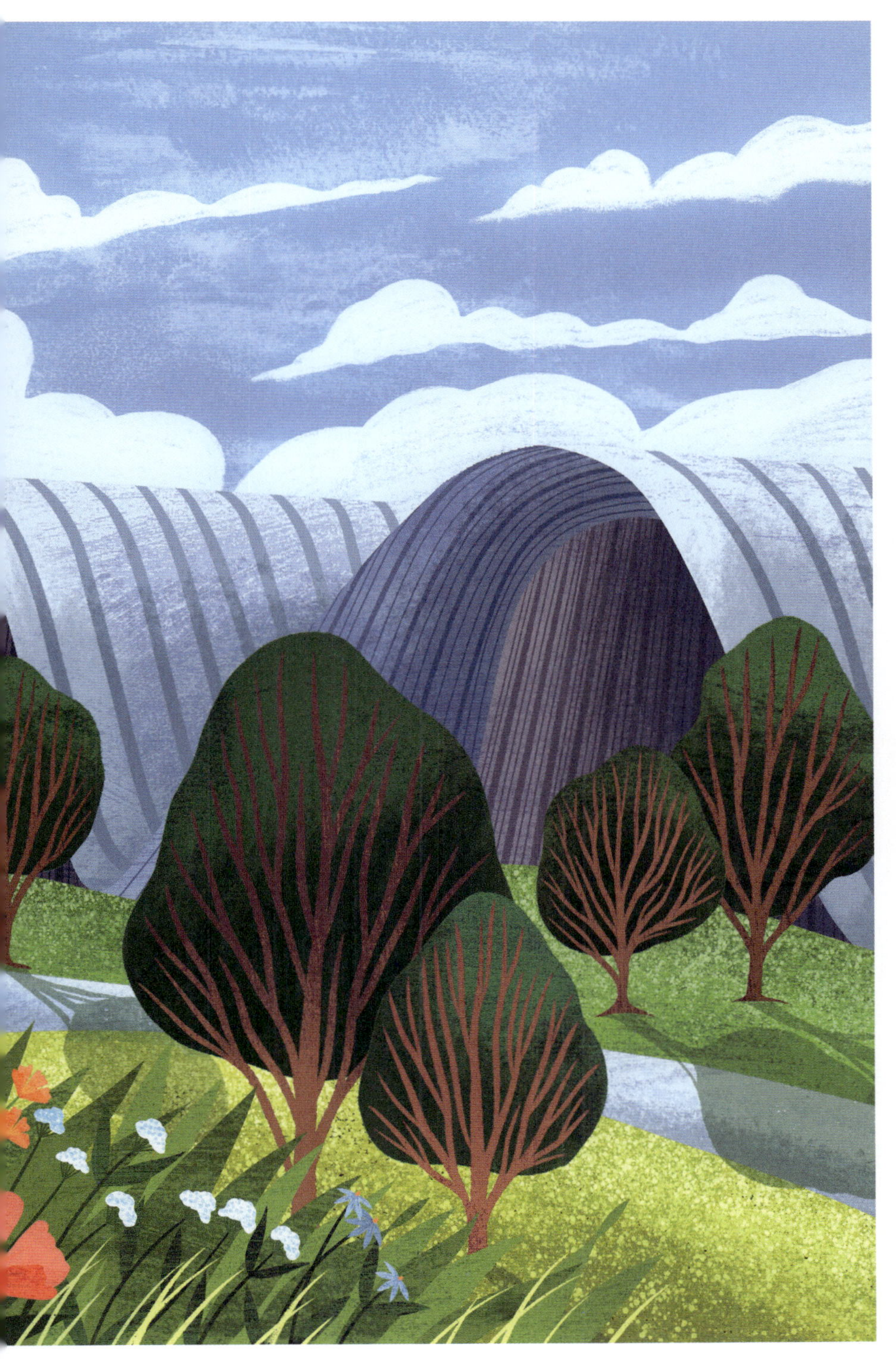

Kunstmuseum Bern, with its permanent collection of over 50,000 masterpieces, covering 800 years of art history. On the outskirts of the city is the Zentrum Paul Klee that houses some of the finest works by Bern's most famous artist, as well as hosting regular international exhibitions. Although he spent much of his life in Germany, Paul Klee was born in Bern in 1879, and died there in 1940, having been forced out of Germany by the Nazis. Klee's Swiss mother and German father spent most of their lives in Bern too, and it was largely at their home that Klee developed his highly innovative style, influenced by several avant-garde art movements as well as his fascination with colour, his dry humour, his love of animals, his outstanding musical talents and his natural draughtsmanship.

Approximately 60 kilometres (37 miles) from the city, overlooking Lake Thun in the Bernese Oberland region, is Mount Niesen, which forms the northern end of a ridge stretching north from the Albristhorn and Mannliflue mountains, and separates the Simmental and Kandertal valleys. Although the translation of the German word *niesen* is 'sneeze', the shape of the mountain has traditionally earned it the nickname 'The Swiss Pyramid'. This famous pyramid shape has captured the eye of numerous artists but most notably, it was painted several times by Paul Klee – usually depicted as a triangle or pyramid and often linked to ancient Egypt, as in his 1915 painting *Mount Niesen, Egyptian Night*. Variously associated with Expressionism, Cubism, Futurism, Surrealism and Abstraction, Klee's art cannot be categorised, so it remains elusive, but through his original interpretations, his use of different media, his extensive writing and lecturing about his inventive methods, and his theories, he became exceptionally influential to other artists and designers.

Take the funicular railway – the red Niesenbahn train – from Mülenen to the summit of Mount Niesen, or, if you prefer, take the 11,674 steps that flank the funicular, the longest stairway in the world. However you get there, the spectacular views at the peak over the Bernese Alps will not fail to inspire you, just as they did in the early 20th century for Paul Klee.

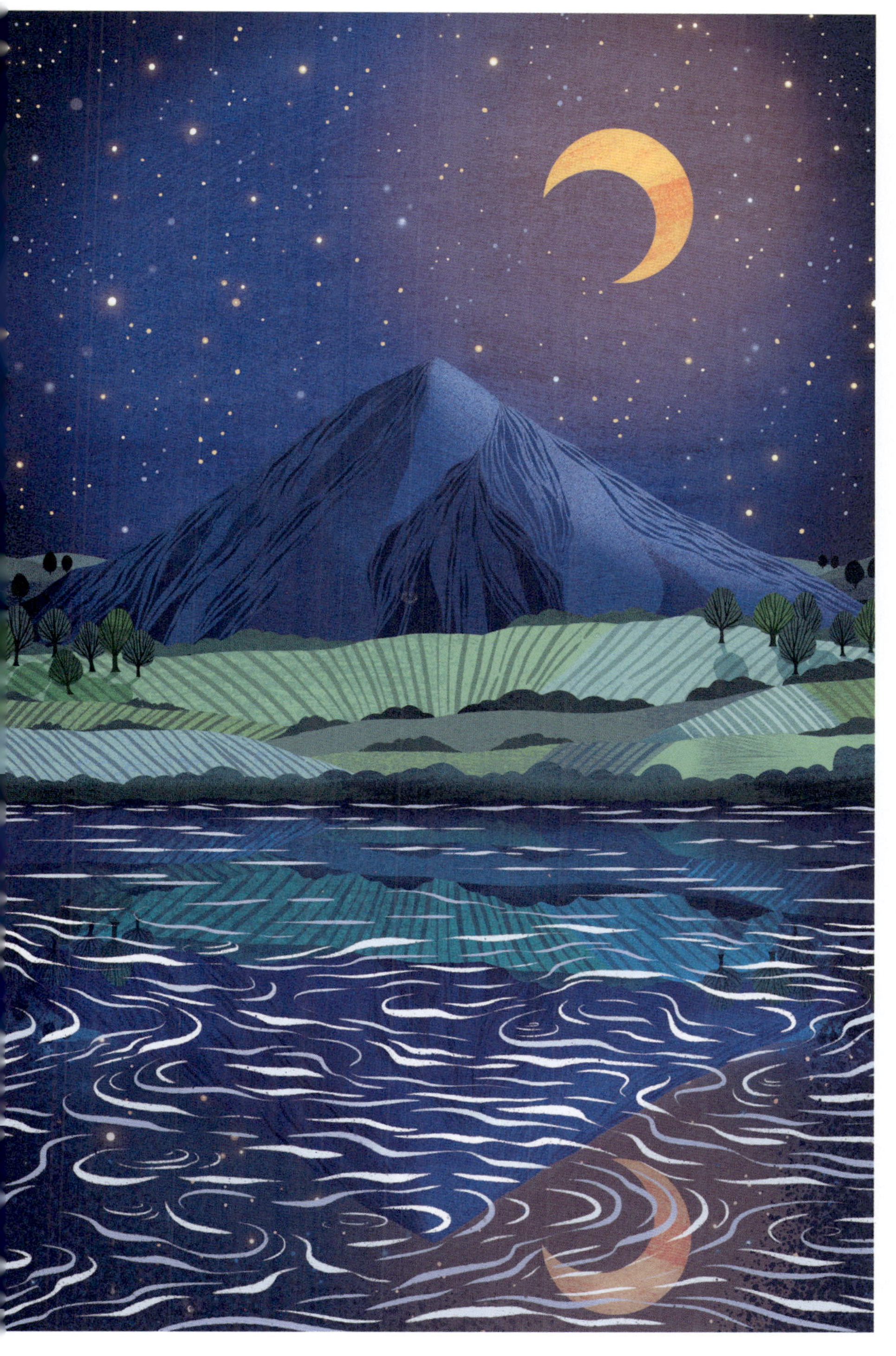

Where?	Florence, Italy
Which?	*David* (1501–04) by Michelangelo
What?	Iconic Renaissance city, home to countless masterpieces

FLORENCE

THE CRADLE of the Renaissance, Florence is a beguiling city, bathed in architectural beauty and artistic charm, and steeped in history. Set on either side of the banks of the River Arno in Tuscany in the north-west of Italy, the small city with its cobbled streets lined with medieval and Renaissance palaces and churches has changed little since the 16th century. At different times of day, the light changes from pink and gold to blue and silver, and the stone buildings either glow in response or stand in cool silhouette, while from almost every area, Florence Cathedral (Santa Maria del Fiore) can be seen with its striking green, pink and white marble façade, its imposing brick dome designed by Filippo Brunelleschi and the slender, marble-faced campanile designed by Giotto di Bondone. Throughout the day across the terracotta rooftops, church bells ring out, while the Arno snakes along, attached on both sides by a series of bridges, including the Ponte Vecchio with its Vasari Corridor, a long passageway that connects the Uffizi Gallery on the north side to the Pitti Palace on the south.

A treasure chest of art, Florence surprises and delights at every turn, teeming with charming vistas, quiet courtyards, atmospheric places of worship, bustling streets and piazzas, while almost everywhere are magnificent works of art, produced by some of the greatest masters, including Giotto, Lorenzo Ghiberti, Donatello, Filippino Lippi and Botticelli. According to UNESCO statistics, 60 per cent of the world's most important art is in Italy and half of that is in Florence. Probably the most famous of all its works of art is the huge marble sculpture of David made by Michelangelo

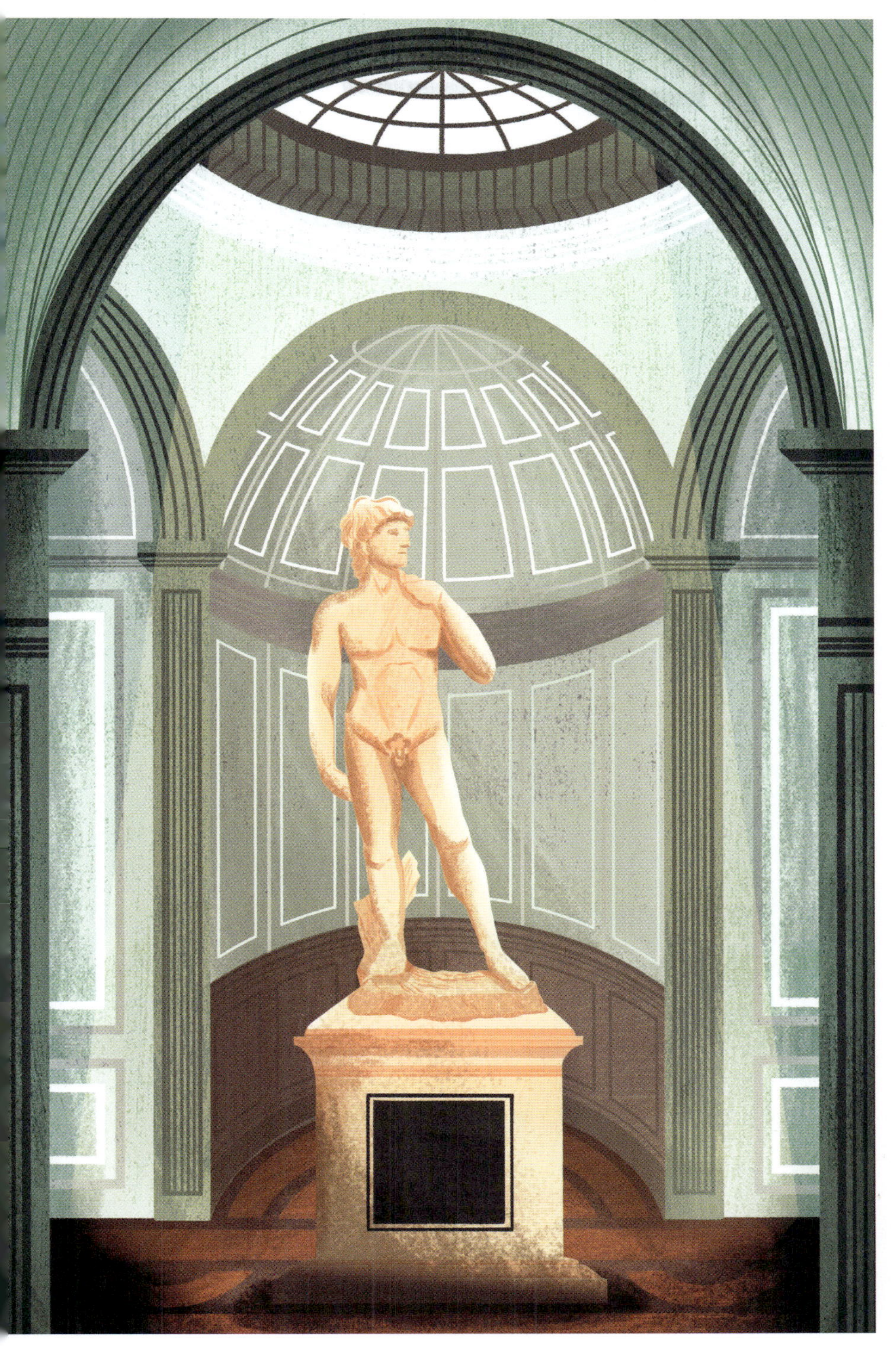

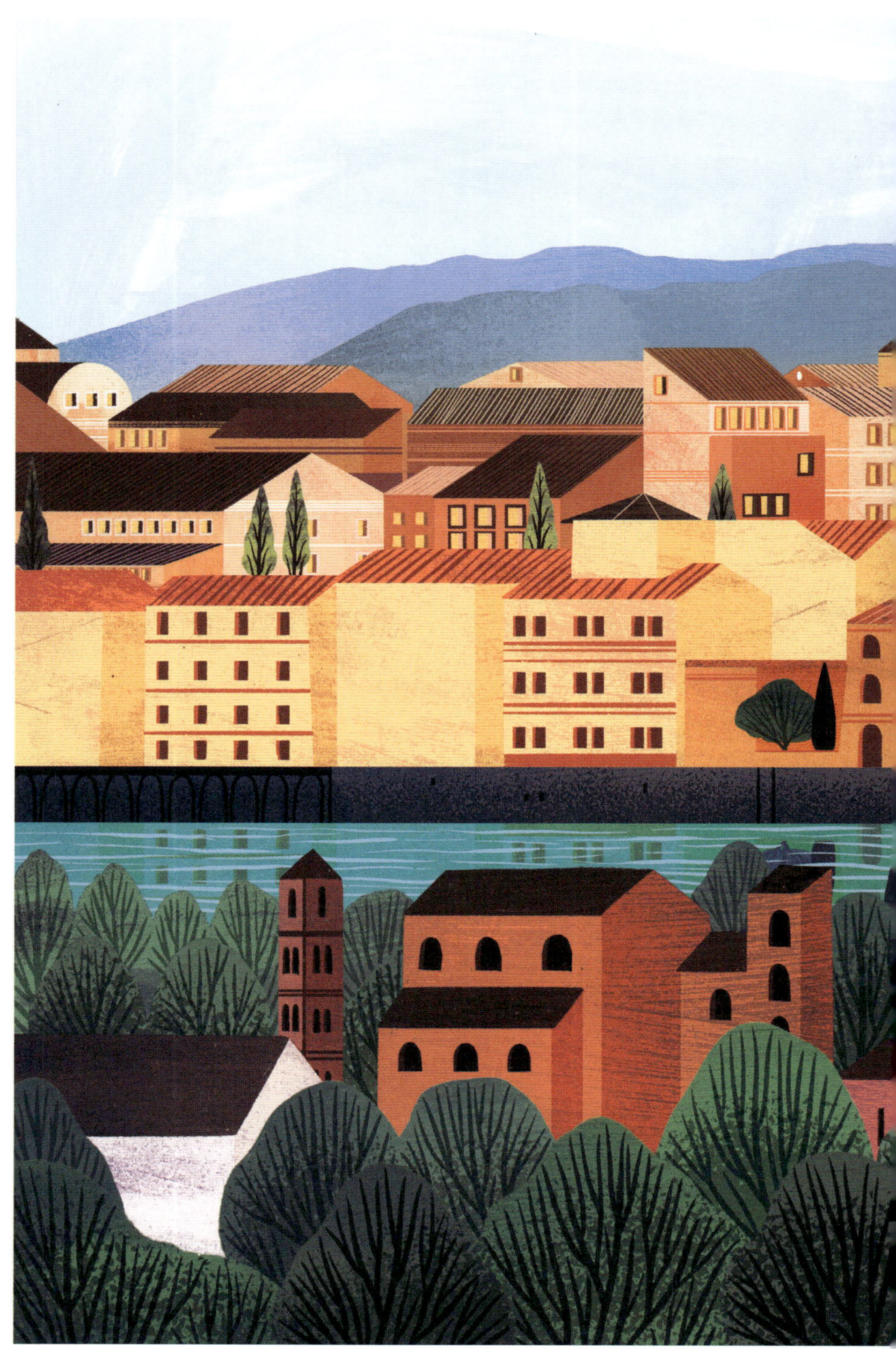

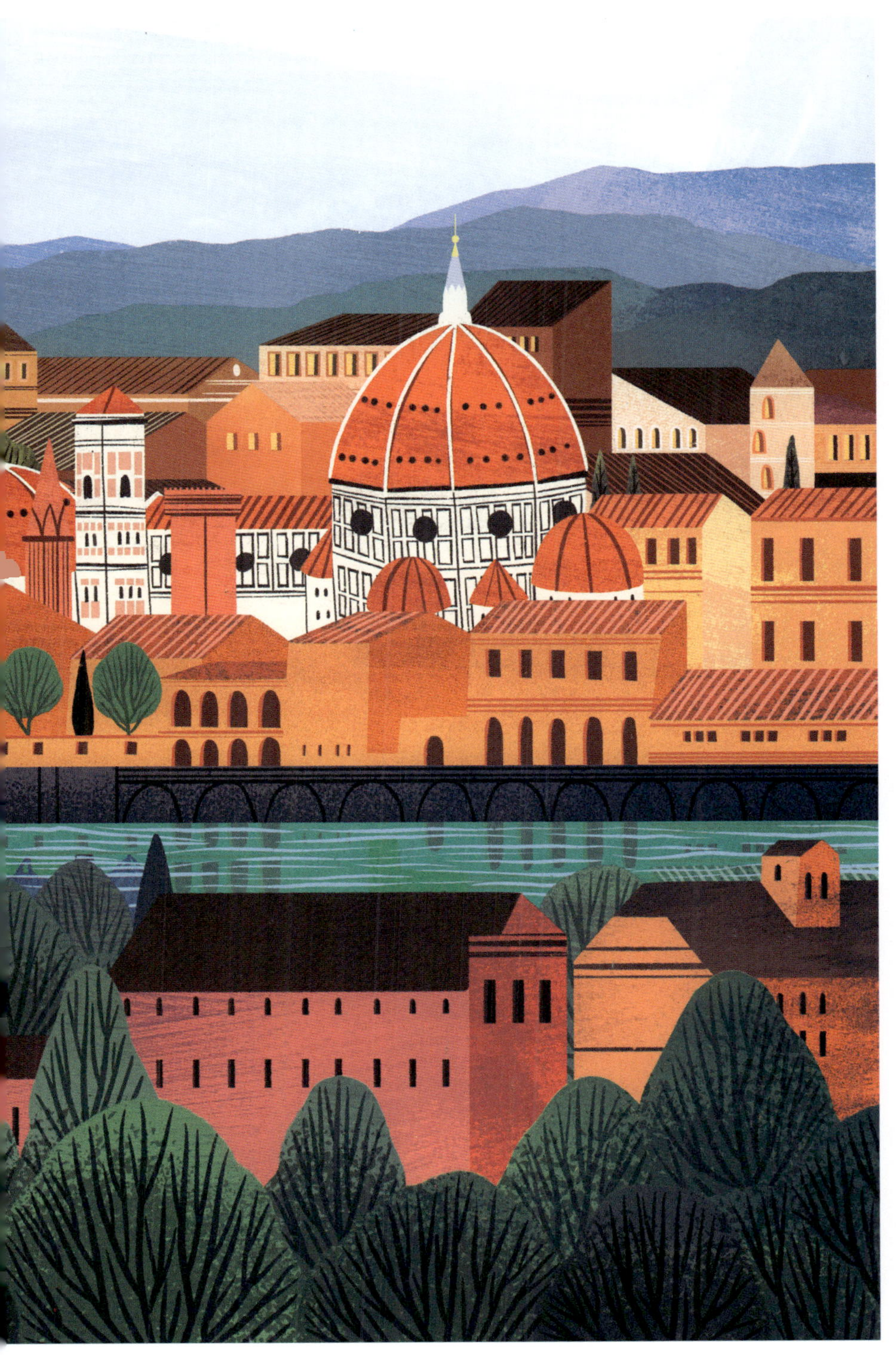

Buonarroti (1475–1564) between 1501 and 1504. Although his frescos in the Sistine Chapel and his *Pietà* in St Peter's Basilica in Rome are as well-known as his statue of David, Michelangelo is linked above all with his beloved birthplace – and place of burial – the city of Florence.

From the Old Testament, David was a courageous young shepherd who with one shot from his sling killed his people's enemy Goliath. For his bravery, strength and spirit, and for being initially overlooked as insignificant, David became the emblem of Florence, and in 1501, Michelangelo was commissioned to make the statue from a block of marble that another sculptor had previously abandoned. When he completed the 5.17-metre (17-feet) high statue, it was deemed too wonderful for its intended destination – a buttress high up on Florence Cathedral. Instead, the Florentines wanted it to stand in the city's main square, in front of the Palazzo Vecchio. It took four days and forty men to move it the half mile from Michelangelo's workshop behind Santa Maria del Fiore to the Piazza della Signoria. An archway had to be pulled down to accommodate it as it was rolled along, strapped upright in a large wooden cart. Today a replica stands in the Piazza della Signoria, with the original in the nearby Galleria dell'Accademia, and another copy in the Piazzale Michelangelo, a hilltop square in the Oltrarno district on the south bank of the Arno. One of Michelangelo's early biographers, Giorgio Vasari, wrote: 'Without any doubt, this figure has put in the shade every other statue, ancient or modern, Greek or Roman . . . anyone who has seen Michelangelo's *David* has no need to see anything else by any other sculptor, living or dead.'

Over the course of his 88 years, Michelangelo, a sculptor, painter, architect and poet, changed western art beyond compare. At the age of 13, he became an apprentice in the Florentine workshop of the fresco painter Domenico Ghirlandaio, but within a year, he had moved into the house of the ruler of Florence, Lorenzo de' Medici. Using their wealth to govern and commission art, the powerful Medicis helped to shape Renaissance Florence. With its huge cornice, arched doorways and an internal garden perfumed with the scent of orange trees, the Medici palace in Via Cavour was the earliest Renaissance building erected in Florence, and where Michelangelo first saw the Medici collection of ancient Greek and Roman sculpture and mixed with some of the most learned men of the times. Lorenzo had established a school for young sculptors, and there Michelangelo studied the basics of sculpture and carved several works. Now called the Palazzo Medici Riccardi, the place where Michelangelo began to sculpt is open to visitors.

Michelangelo became one of the first artists to be renowned as a celebrity, nicknamed 'Il Divino' (The Divine One). To view some of his works, start at the Galleria dell'Accademia, where you will see the statue of David and four unfinished marble 'prisoners' that appear to be trapped in the stone; metaphorically conveying the struggle of the soul to free itself. Also in the Accademia is one of Michelangelo's last works, the *Pietà di Palestrina*, depicting Christ's crucified body being held by the Virgin Mary, Mary Magdalene and Nicodemus, whose face is probably a self-portrait of Michelangelo himself.

As you make your way towards the Arno, stop at the Basilica di San Lorenzo. During the Renaissance, artists also often worked as architects, and Michelangelo designed the Sagrestia Nuova (New Sacristy) as part of the Medici Chapel attached to the Basilica of San Lorenzo. As well as designing the building, he created seven sculptures inside, including four allegories of time: *Day* and *Night* and *Dawn* and *Dusk*. He also designed the adjoining Laurentian Library, one of the first examples of Mannerist architecture. Closer still to the River Arno is the Gallerie degli Uffizi. There you will find Michelangelo's famous painting known as the *Doni Tondo* (1504–06), a Holy Family in a circular, pyramidal composition and one of only three panel paintings known by him.

Once you have left the Uffizi, cross the river, either over the Ponte Vecchio or the Ponte Santa Trinita, to the Oltrarno district, where, in the Basilica di Santo Spirito, you can discover one of the earliest examples of Michelangelo's astonishing anatomical accuracy; in his teenage years, he created a wooden Crucifix – still there – in thanks for being allowed to study human cadavers in the Santo Spirito hospital. Once run down, the Oltrarno neighbourhood now buzzes with craft shops, restaurants, bars and piazzas, including the Piazzale Michelangelo, which can be reached by a steep but picturesque climb, or by bus or car. Once there, you can admire a copy of the statue of David and a magical panorama of Florence.

Where?	Venice, Italy
Which?	*The Entrance to the Grand Canal, Venice* (c.1730) by Canaletto
What?	Magical jewel-box city, steeped in history

VENICE

HOW MANY feet have tramped this magical, floating masterpiece? Romantic, ancient and enchanted, Venice is unequalled; a glittering city of canals, gondolas, jewel-box architecture, endless waterways and domed cathedrals. Sail a little further and you reach the colourful towns of Murano and Burano or the peaceful, laid-back Giudecca. Nothing could be grander than the Grand Canal that mirrors the splendours of centuries of Venetian pride and power, while rising up all along the canal, glittering in marble and glass, are decadent palaces and churches that hold the secrets of time.

As well as churches and palaces, Venice is home to several remarkable art collections, including the Peggy Guggenheim Collection, the Galleria dell Accademia, Museo Correr and the Punta della Dogana. Everywhere are works of architecture that resemble decorative pieces of wedding cake, such as the Bridge of Sighs, a white limestone masterpiece that connects the interrogation rooms of Doge's Palace to the prison, or the Rialto Bridge, an ornate structure that crosses the Grand Canal, connecting San Polo to the *sestiere* (district) of San Marco. In the narrow back streets, even the tiniest churches are filled with breathtaking paintings by Venetian natives, such as Veronese, Titian, Jacopo, Gentile and Giovanni Bellini, and Tiepolo and Andrea Mantegna, as well as magnificent statues and dazzling stained-glass windows that sparkle like gemstones, making this city a treasure trove for aesthetes. Many artists have captured its beauty with great success, such as Claude Monet and John Singer Sargent, who both captured its special atmosphere in their own individual ways.

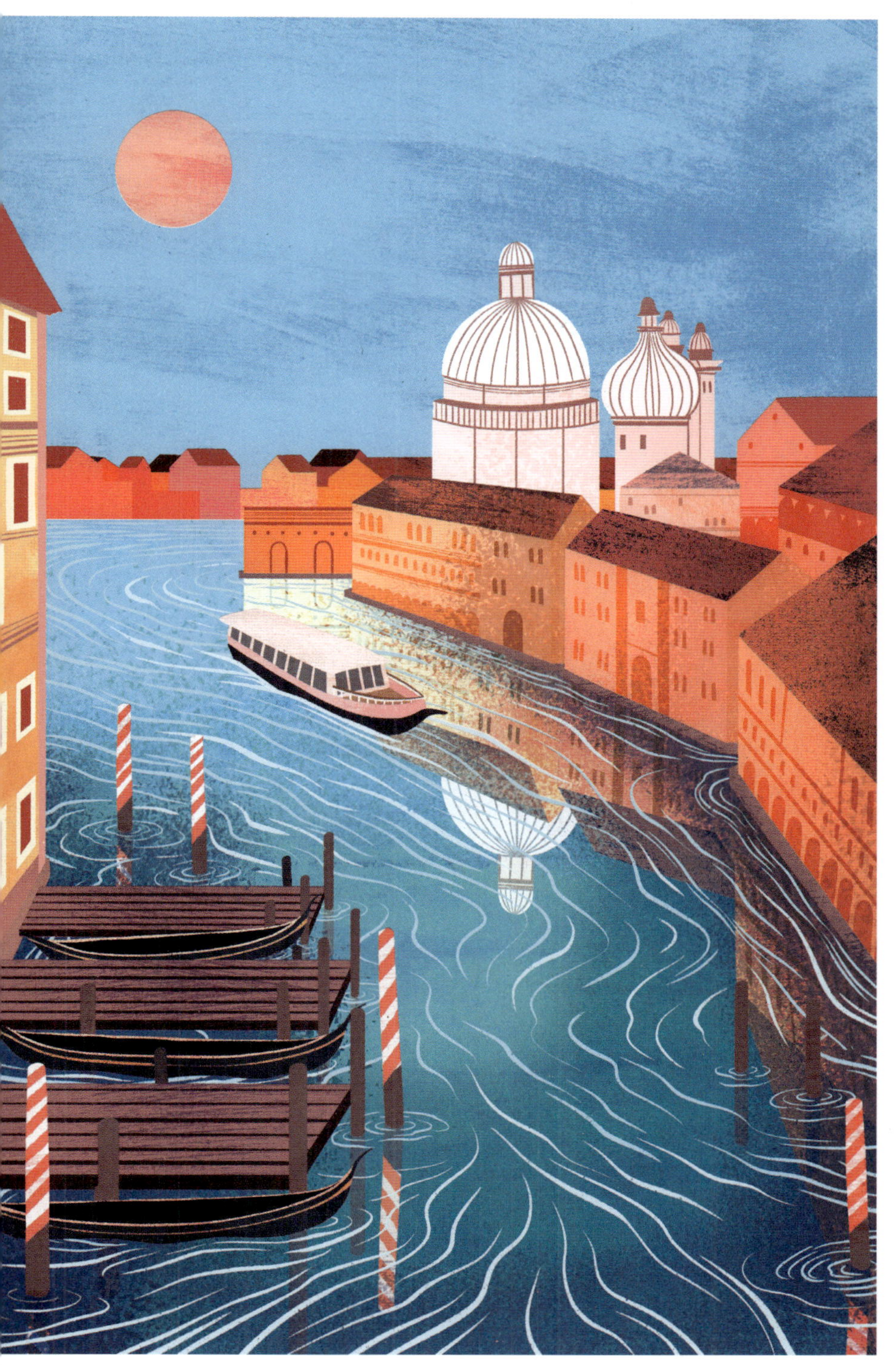

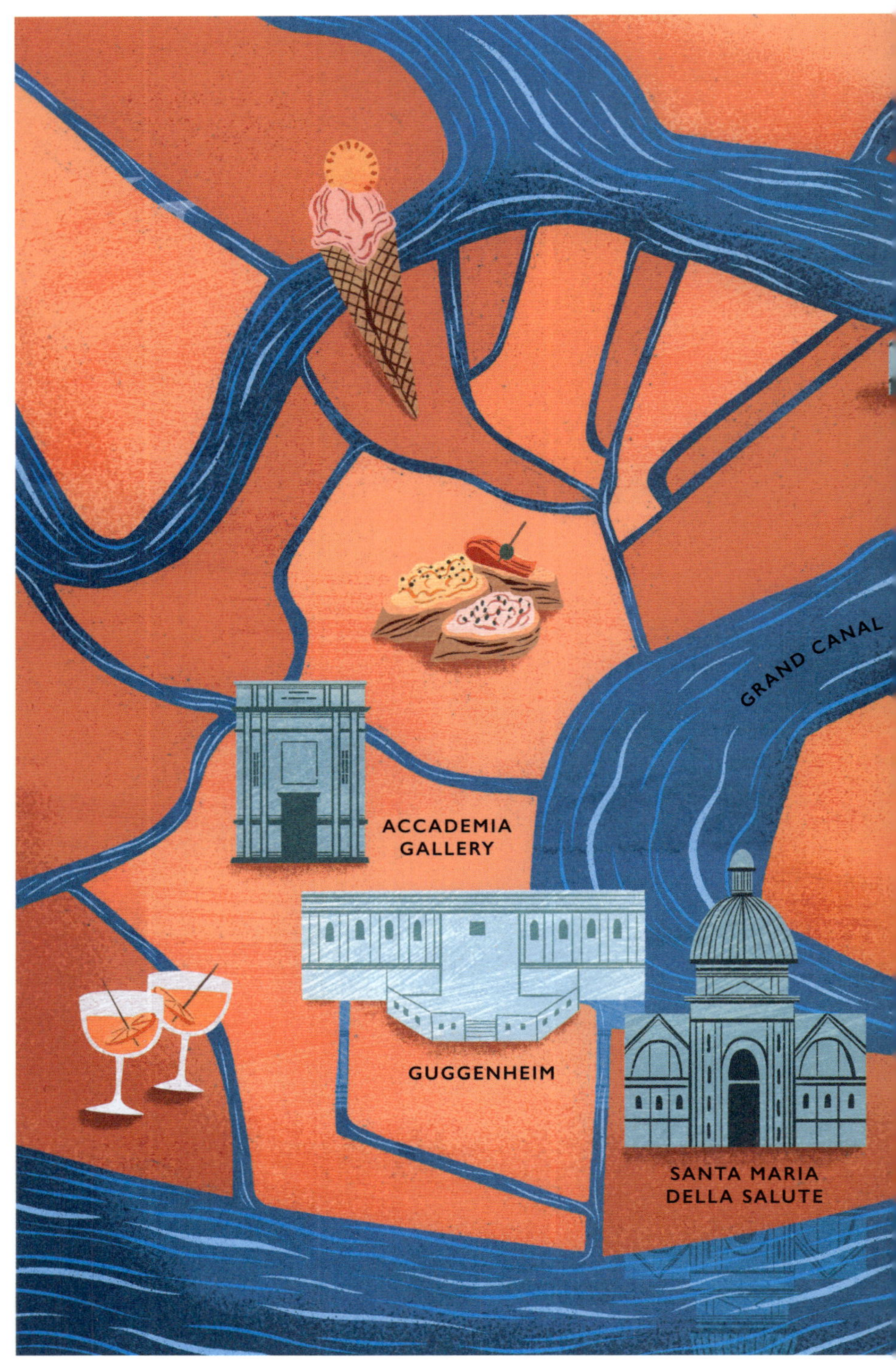
GRAND CANAL
ACCADEMIA GALLERY
GUGGENHEIM
SANTA MARIA DELLA SALUTE

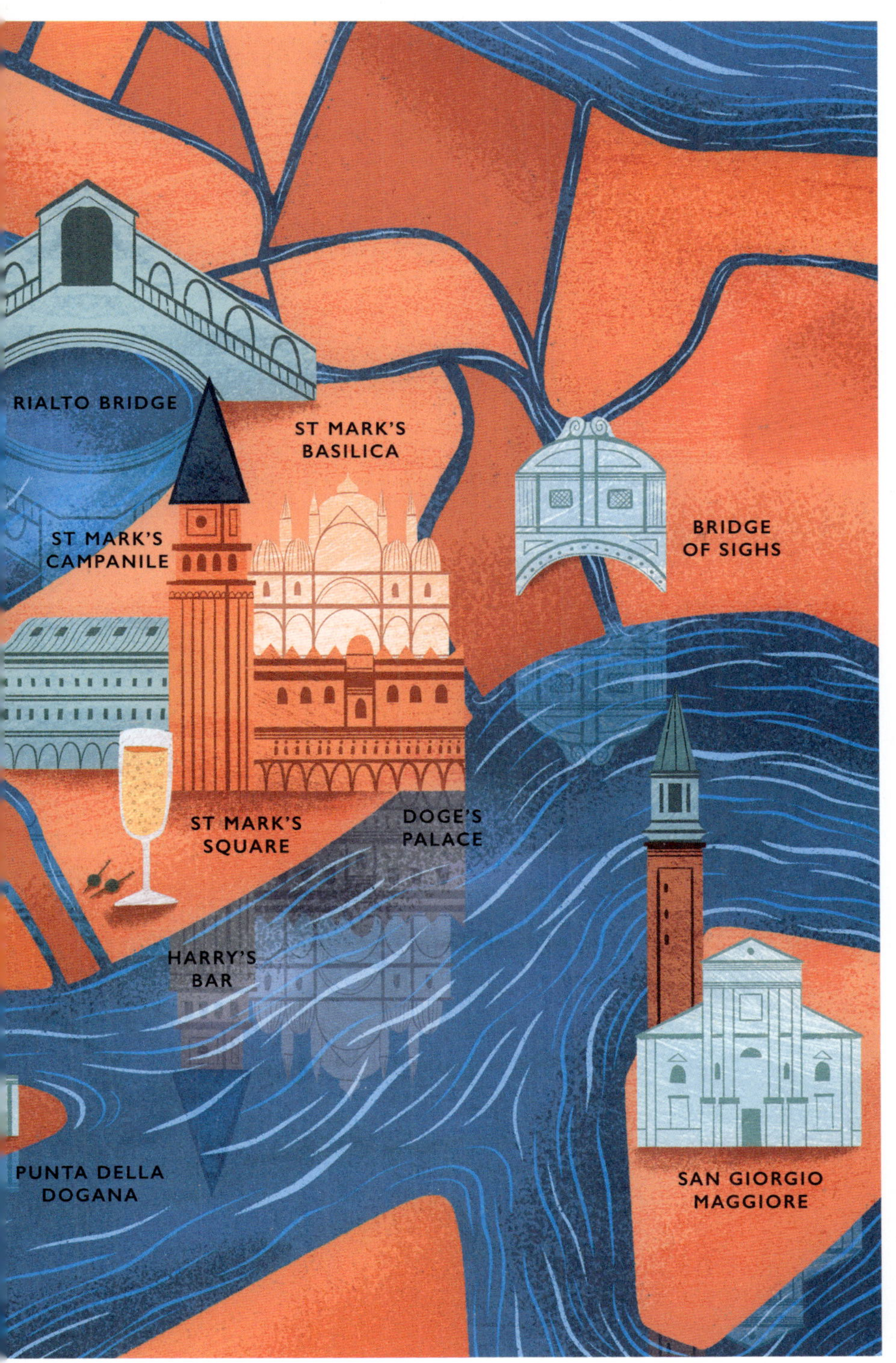
RIALTO BRIDGE
ST MARK'S BASILICA
BRIDGE OF SIGHS
ST MARK'S CAMPANILE
ST MARK'S SQUARE
DOGE'S PALACE
HARRY'S BAR
PUNTA DELLA DOGANA
SAN GIORGIO MAGGIORE

But one artist above all is synonymous with this dazzling city. If you're facing west, you might be lucky enough to find yourself bathed in one of Venice's spectacular red–gold sunsets. Made famous by Giovanni Antonio Canal (1697–1768), known as Canaletto, Venetian sunsets are known the world over. Canaletto also made many other views of Venice renowned. During the 18th century, long before postcards or photographs existed, Canaletto's skill at capturing the atmosphere of Venice gained him great success among tourists, many of whom were young aristocrats on their Grand Tour – an educational journey through Europe.

These wealthy young things purchased Canaletto's paintings as mementos of their travels, of the theatricality and feast for the senses that Venice has always been. At the time, Canaletto became the ultimate postcard painter on a huge scale. To achieve accuracy, he perfected his skill of painting with almost photographic likenesses by using a tool called a camera obscura. Despite the exacting likenesses, he often moved some elements within his paintings to create harmonious compositions. Taking home a painting from this most esteemed local artist was a prestigious memento, and in time, almost every British aristocrat had a Canaletto on their walls. Over his career, Canaletto produced more than 1,000 paintings and drawings in total, but although he travelled elsewhere, his depictions of Venice were his most popular.

Art is not the only draw here – with its tantalising traces of ancient spice routes, Venetian cuisine is inventive while retaining the elements of traditional Italian fare. Pop into any one of the warm and welcoming bars at happy hour and find lavish spreads of cicheti (Venetian tapas), or go to Harry's Bar to sample the original Bellini – prosecco and peach purée, invented sometime between 1934 and 1948 by Giuseppe Cipriani, who named it Bellini because its pale pink colour reminded him of the toga of a saint in a painting by Giovanni Bellini. Make sure you leave room to also sample the lagoon seafood at any of the canal-side bistros – washed down with Veneto's signature bubbly prosecco.

Venice became established in around 400 AD, when the Roman Empire collapsed and refugees settled there after escaping successive waves of barbarian invaders in their original homes in Roman cities such as Padua, Aquileia, Treviso and Altino. By the Byzantine, Renaissance and Baroque eras, Venice had become a major city, with some of the most opulent architecture along its waterways and in the central Piazza San Marco. Here, you can discover sumptuous Byzantine mosaics, elegant statues, the splendid Gothic Doge's Palace, lively cafés and bars, the towering red-brick Campanile and, of course, spectacular St Mark's Basilica itself, one of the best-known examples of Byzantine architecture in Europe.

Architectural shapes are unmistakably Venetian. For instance, in the Dorsoduro sestiere of the city between the Grand Canal and the Giudecca Canal, is Baldassare Longhena's magnificent basilica, Santa Maria della Salute, its white stones and high domes gleamingly visible from Piazza San Marco. Yet before building could even begin on this landmark, at least 100,000 pylons had to be driven deep into the *barene* (mudbanks) to shore up the tip of Dorsoduro. Distinctive and uniquely Venetian, the architecture draws on several influences, including Greco–Roman pagan temples and Jewish Kabbalah diagrams.

Few cities can claim such a priceless artistic and historical heritage. Built on mud, sand, slime and continuous water, the city itself was formed on a group of 118 small islands in a shallow lagoon. Separated by canals that are now linked by over 400 bridges, this city, in the Veneto region of north-eastern Italy, remains a miraculous testament to creativity, human endeavour and genius architectural engineering. With his innovative technique, strong colours and atmospheric effects, Canaletto's landscapes captured this city's famed originality, and even today, three centuries later, when travelling down the Grand Canal, it is like stepping into a Canaletto painting.

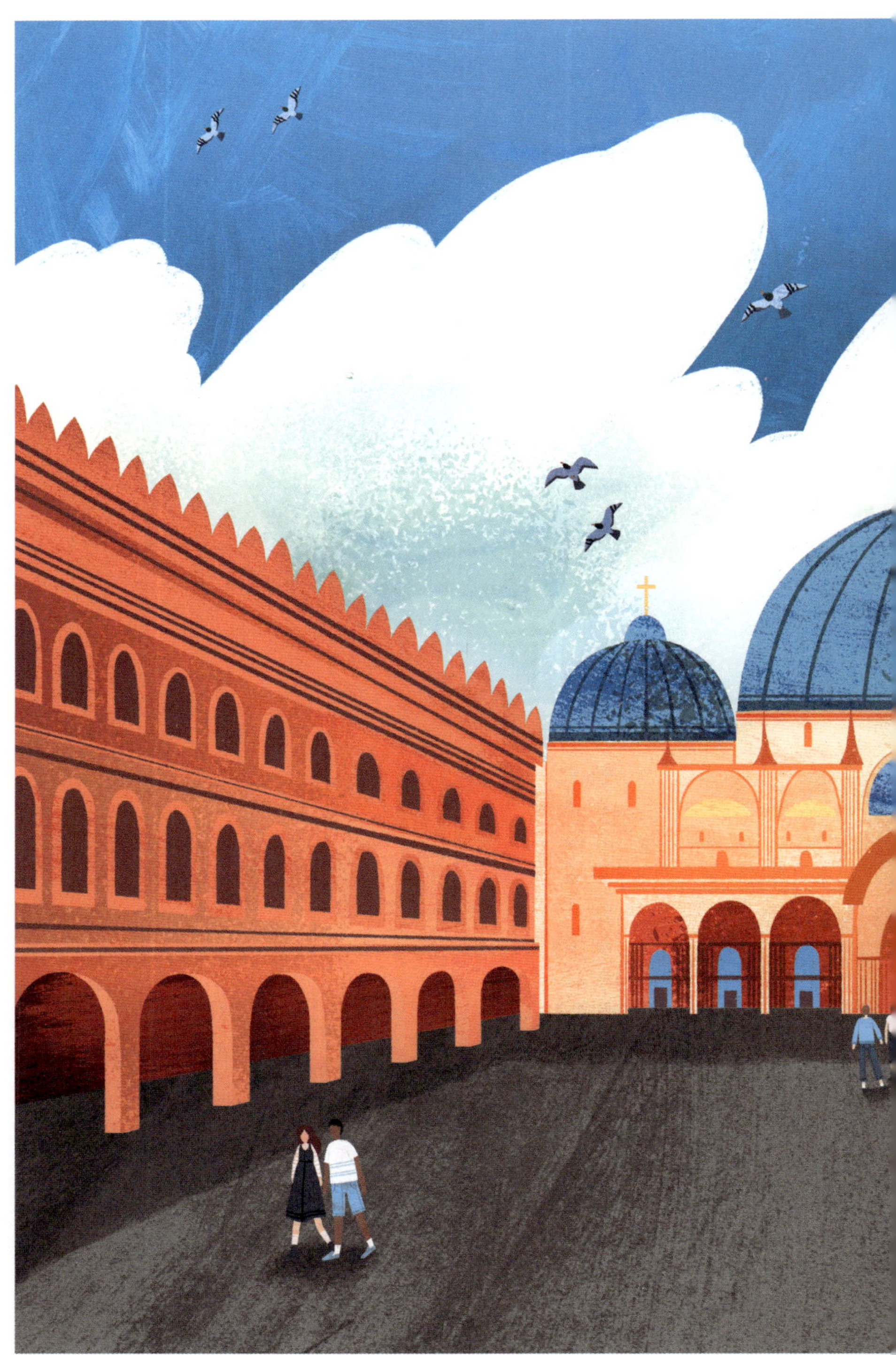

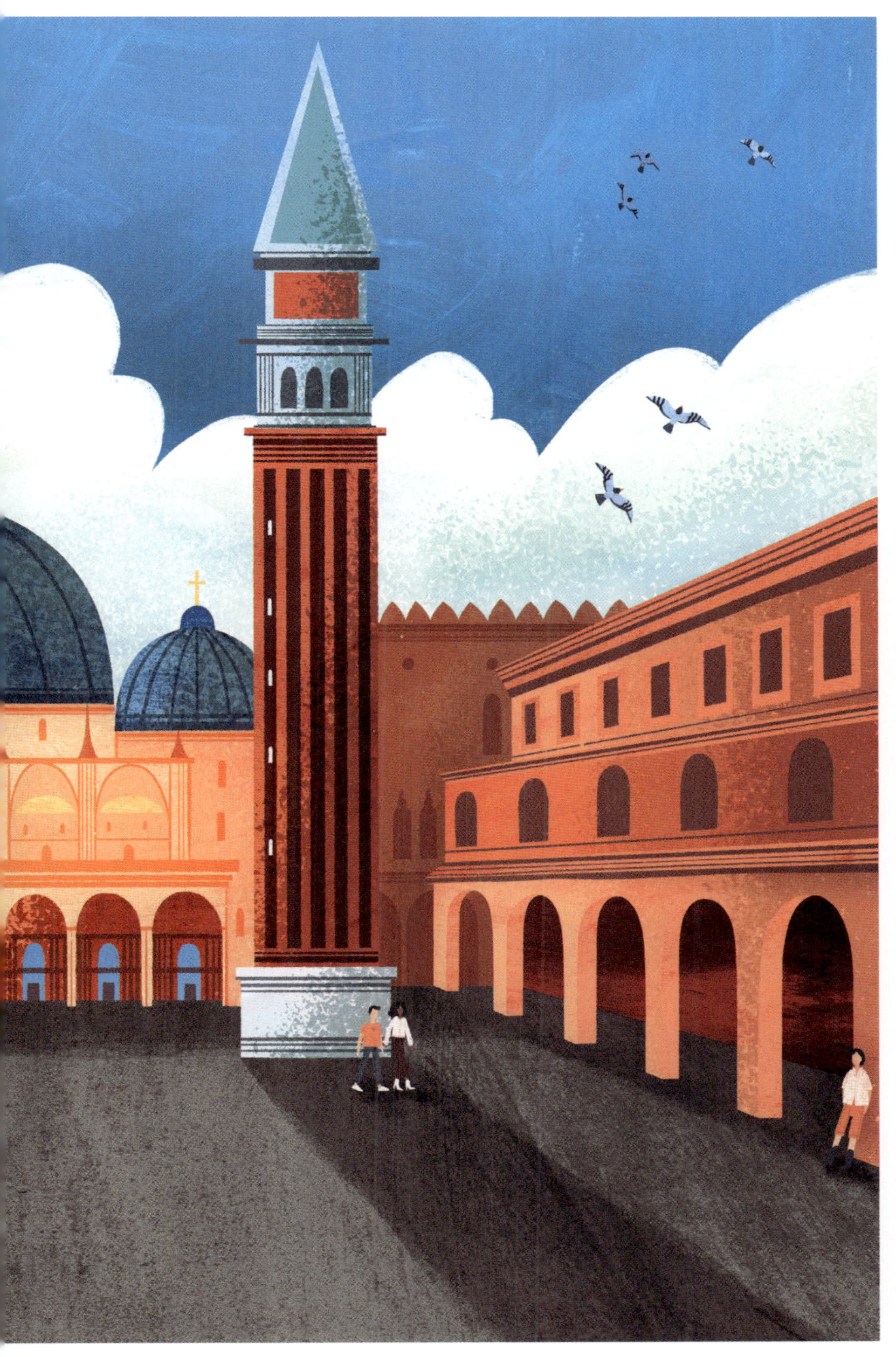

Where?	Delft, Netherlands
Which?	*View of Delft* (c.1660–63) by Johannes Vermeer
What?	Charming city of soft, fluid light

DELFT

THE WORD 'Delft' itself is derived from delven, meaning 'to dig', as a great deal of digging led to the intricate network of canals that hold this charming city together, rather like a painting by famous Dutch artist Piet Mondrian. Part of the original city planning, the canals of Delft were built to serve as both defence systems and lifelines for the inhabitants. Even today, the canals – or *grachten* – are the veins of the city, keeping its heart beating.

Suffused with artistic imagery through its connections with the glowing, meticulous paintings of Johannes Vermeer (1632–75) and the delicate blue patterned pottery that has been made there since the 16th century, Delft is a visual feast. Small enough to walk around, much of it is closed to cars, so the peaceful canals, bridges, churches, mansions and courtyards can be enjoyed alongside the livelier museums, markets, pubs and bars. In close up, the elegant splendour of the place conveys the pride of a nation that had fought for – and gained – its own autonomy. Officially a city since 1246, Delft is nestled between The Hague and Rotterdam. When, in 1572, William of Orange (often called the 'Father of the Fatherland') moved to Delft, it served as headquarters for the Dutch resistance against Spain during the Eighty Years' War (1568–1648). Ultimately, this resulted in Dutch independence, which in turn led to the cultural zenith of the Dutch Golden Age in the 17th century, when the Netherlands rose politically and economically. Everywhere you walk in the city, you can feel the allure of that gilded period, and recall the paintings of the Dutch Golden Age, particularly the light-filled works of Vermeer.

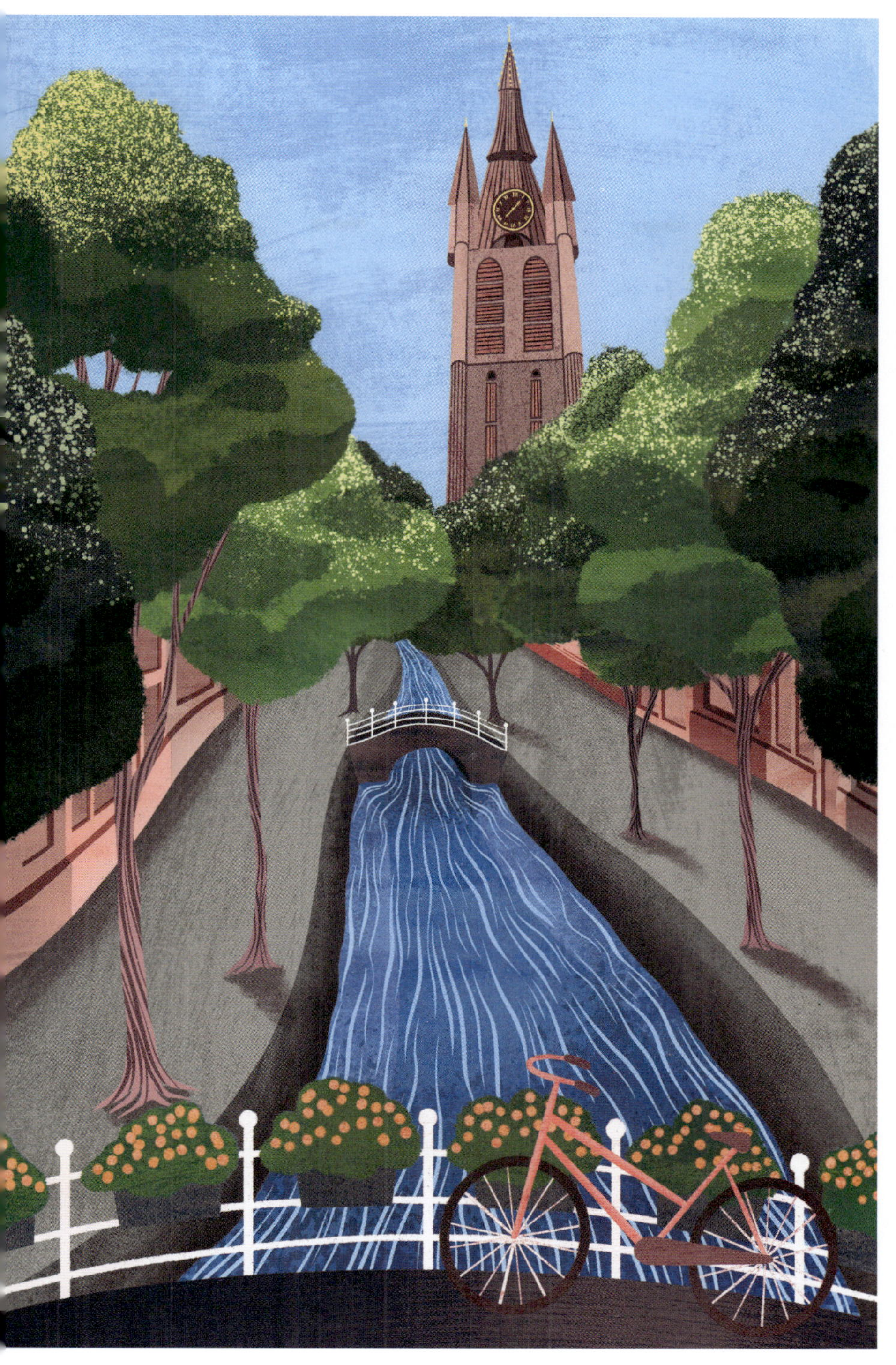

While strolling around Delft, be sure to admire the beautifully preserved, mostly 17th-century buildings that look just as they did when Vermeer was painting there, alongside other great artists of the Dutch Golden Age such as Pieter de Hooch, Carel Fabritius and Jan Steen. The Oude Kerk (Old Church, consecrated in 1306), nicknamed Oude Jan (Old John) or Scheve Jan (Skewed John), has a 75-metre-high (246-feet-high) brick tower that leans about 2 metres from the vertical. Climb to the top and marvel at the glorious panorama of the city beneath you, watching boats glide along the canals. Among other notable Delft residents, such as the painter Hendrick Cornelisz van Vliet and scientist Antonie van Leeuwenhoek, Vermeer is buried in the Oude Kerk, while he was baptised in the Nieuwe Kerk (New Church, built in 1496).

Born in Delft in 1632, Vermeer spent his entire life in the city. Now one of the best-known Dutch artists, he experimented endlessly to create the illusion of three-dimensional space and render the effects of natural light in paint. While not a single drawing by him has survived, his compositions are complex and accurate in scale and perspective. To begin a work, he drew, then applied 'dead colouring' or underpainting; a monochrome version of the final painting. Colour was applied next in layers and glazes to achieve a variety of effects, and his insight into how the eye registers optical effects can be seen in his careful rendering of textures and tones. His two paintings *The Little Street* (c.1657–58) and *View of Delft* (c.1660–61) portray the city that he knew and loved so well, while his *Girl with a Pearl Earring* (c.1665) and *The Milkmaid* (c.1660) are studies of (anonymous) Delft residents. The Vermeer Centrum Delft brings together life-size reproductions of all 37 of Vermeer's paintings that have survived (it is thought that he painted around 50 in total), with information about each work and about his life. From a high vantage point, looking down on the calm waterfront, *View of Delft* shows both how little and, contrastingly, how much the city has changed. Vermeer included the area of river that had been widened to serve as the harbour, the distant tower of the Oude Kerk and the dazzlingly sunlit Nieuwe Kerk. His painstaking approach of precise details, diffused highlights and lustrous light effects appear to have sunk deep into the psyche of the city – *View of Delft* is probably the most recognised cityscape in western art – and visitors to this charmed city can still admire this same view in the soft, fluid light of Delft today.

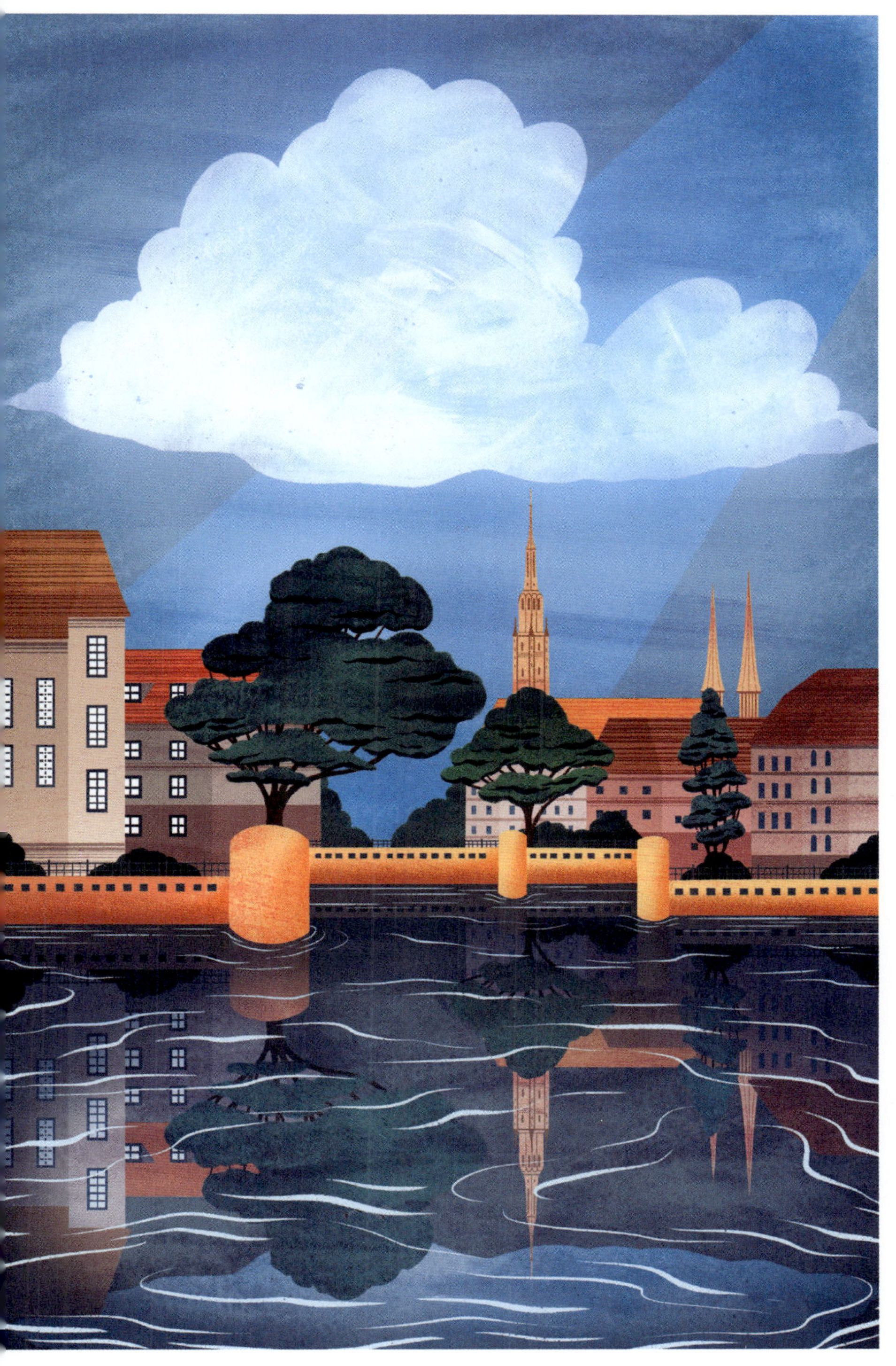

Where?	Bauhaus, Dessau, Germany
Which?	*Untitled Wall Hanging* (1926) by Anni Albers
What?	Industrial city of functional beauty and practicality

DESSAU

RATIONAL AND disciplined, the Bauhaus buildings in the industrial city of Dessau are icons of modernist architecture. Even today, long after the people who designed and worked in the buildings have left, the place exudes calm confidence and a sense of purpose. In its uniting of art, craft and technology in the years following the First World War, the Bauhaus was established to improve people's living conditions through modern design. It became the most influential modernist art school of the 20th century.

Founded in 1919 in the city of Weimar by the German architect Walter Gropius, the Bauhaus was named after a German word meaning 'house of building'. It was a unique and outstandingly successful school that existed in three German cities: Weimar, from 1919 to 1925; Dessau, from 1925 to 1932; and Berlin, from 1932 to 1933. Even after it closed because of Nazi pressure, the staff and students continued to spread its idealistic principles as they emigrated all over the world. Long after its closure, its approach to teaching, and to the relationship between art, society and technology, had a major impact on art and design. With his vision of unifying all of the arts, Gropius developed a craft-based curriculum that would produce artists, artisans and designers who could create beautiful and practical objects. It was a radical concept. By amalgamating fine and applied art, Bauhaus students – who came from wide-ranging backgrounds – learned practical, technical and creative skills and theories in order to be able to make and market their designs. From 1923, the school adopted the slogan 'Art into Industry.' Responsible for the design and delivery of the curriculum

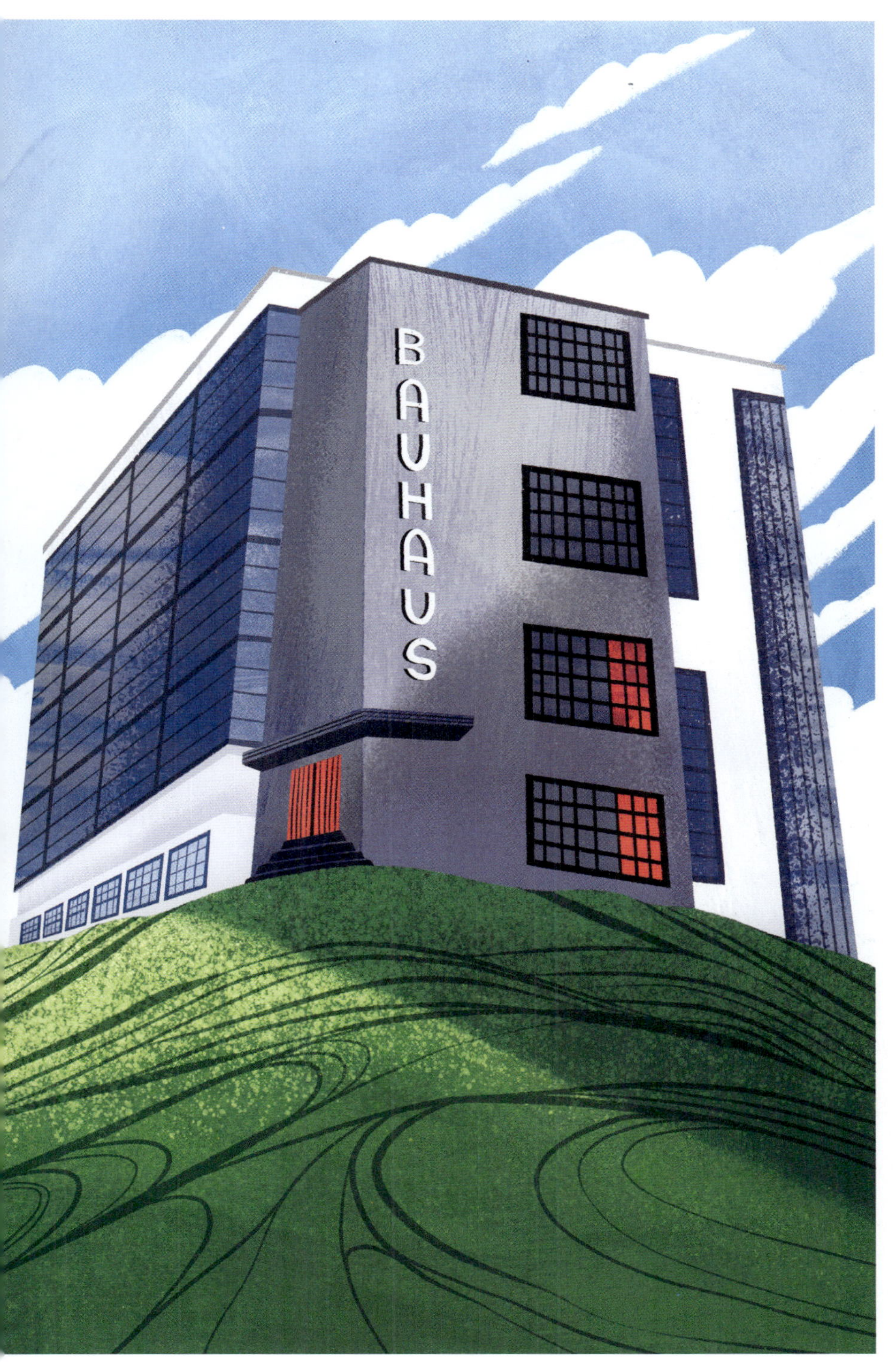
BAUHAUS

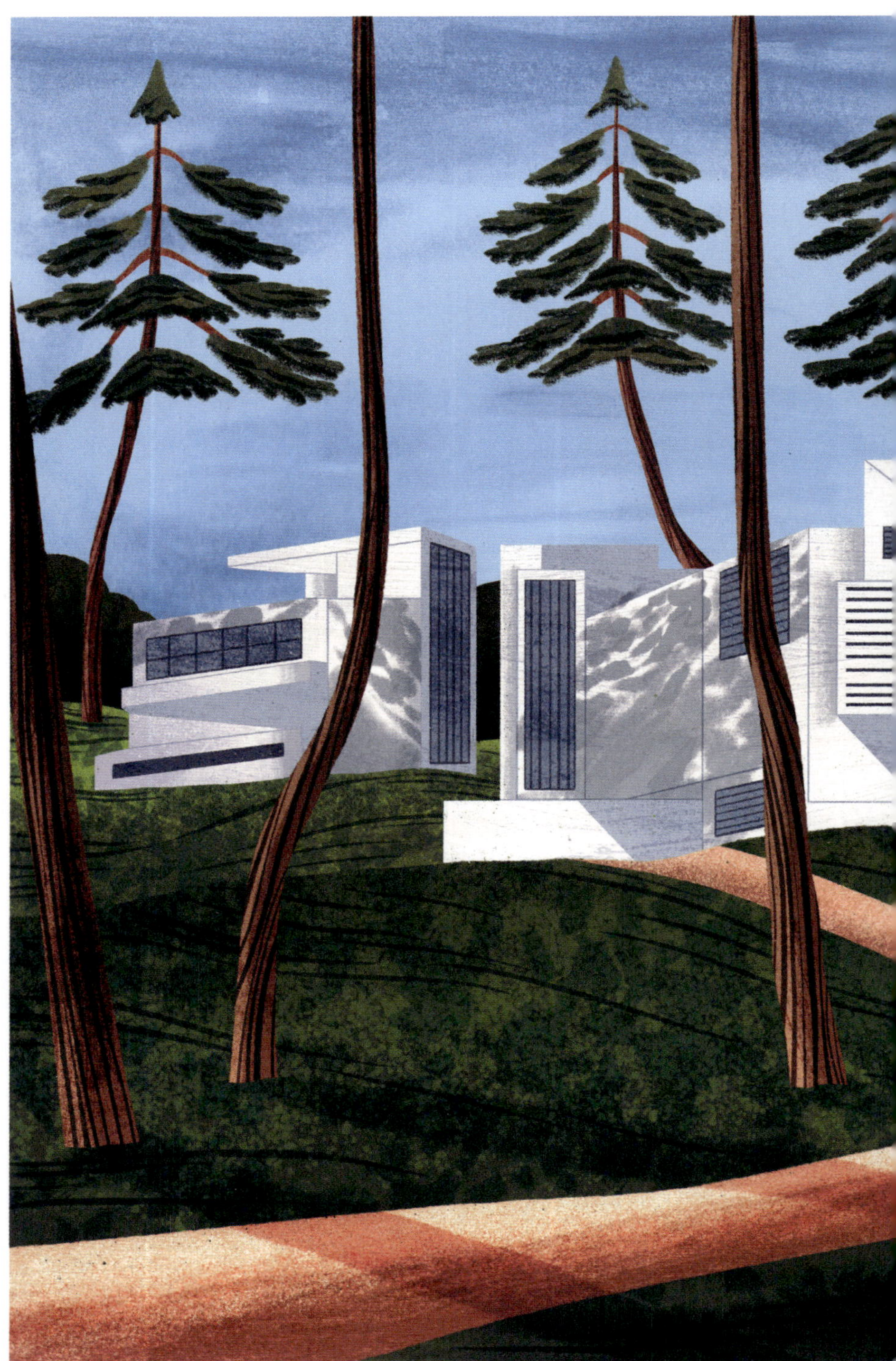

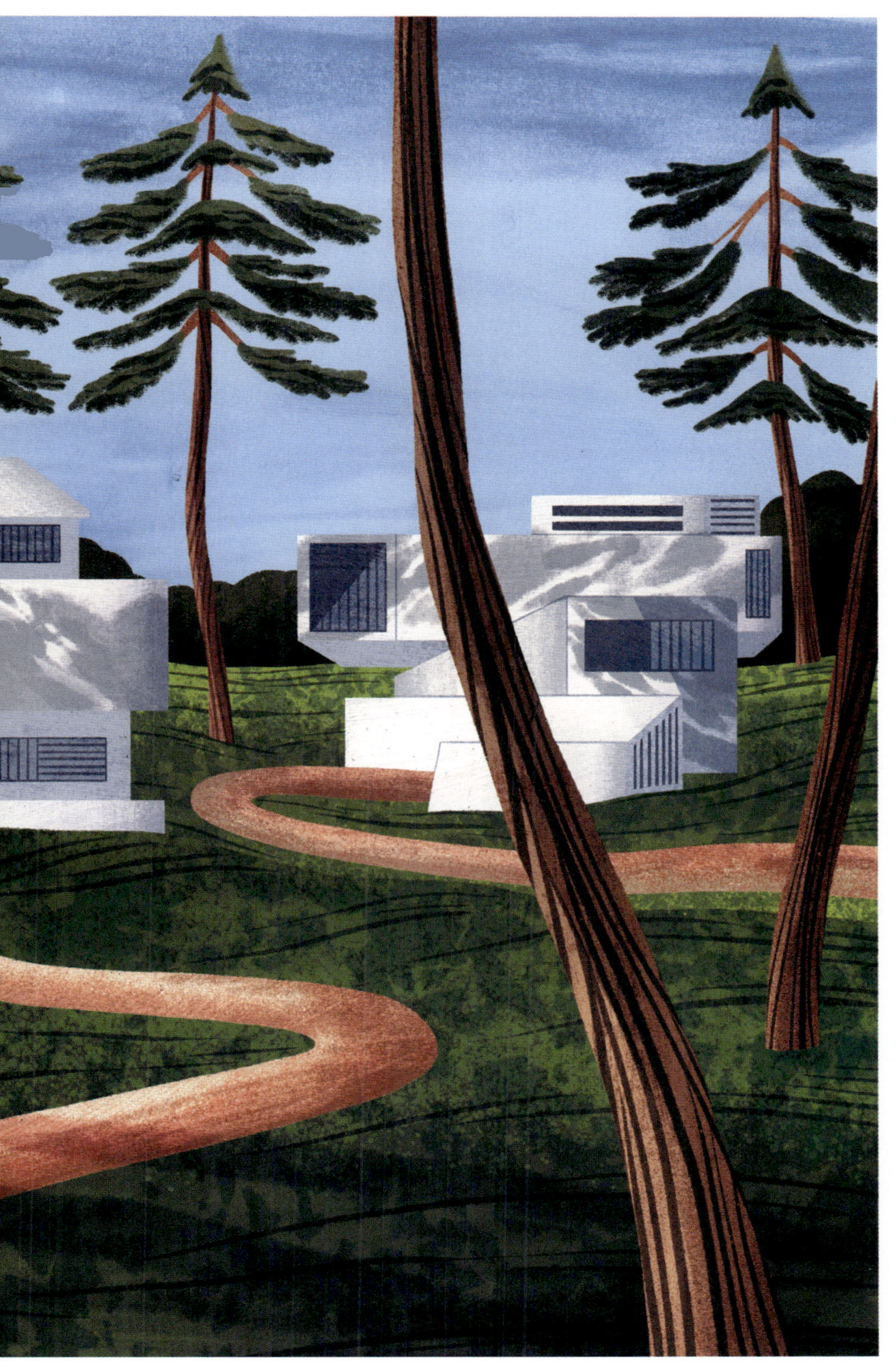

were exceptionally talented masters who were also successful artists and designers in their own right. The innovative curriculum included a six-month preliminary course for all students that concentrated on the essential aspects of design; intermediary three-year courses that included technical, workshop-based instruction, and then each student studied a specialist subject, such as metalworking, cabinetmaking, weaving, pottery, typography, wall painting and, after 1927, architecture.

Anni Albers (1899–1994) joined the Bauhaus as a student at Weimar in 1922. Although it aspired to equality between the sexes, the Bauhaus nonetheless discouraged women from learning certain disciplines. So, following the other female students there, Albers joined the weaving workshop and largely through Paul Klee's teaching, she learned that shapes, colours and marks could connect with viewers on subconscious levels. Independently, she began creating innovative weaving methods and techniques, seeking to create fabrics with 'a drawing power' to 'make you look again and again'.

In April 1925, when the Bauhaus moved from Weimar to Dessau, south-west of Berlin and north-west of Dresden, Albers went with it. The school remained there until October 1932, its longest and most productive period. Even today, Dessau is often described as the 'Bauhausstadt' – or Bauhaus City – because of the impression the school left. In 1925, Dessau commissioned and financed the design and construction of the Bauhaus building and the Meisterhaus estate (the Masters' homes). Designed by Gropius, they had an enduring influence on architecture for the rest of the 20th century and beyond. With their steel-frame construction, glass façades, flat roofs, large windows, horizontal emphasis and asymmetrical plans, the school buildings broke with all previous architectural designs. Gropius and his wife lived in the largest, detached house, while three semi-detached houses nearby were named after the tutors who lived in them, including László Moholy-Nagy, Lyonel Feininger, Wassily Kandinsky and Paul Klee. The buildings contrast and complement their pine woodland surroundings.

Officially known as Dessau-Rosslau since a 2007 merger with its neighbour across the Elbe, the Bauhausstadt remains a fascinating place to visit, not least for the contrasts of architecture; from the utilitarian Bauhaus buildings, the opulent splendour of the various palaces in the nearby Garden Realm and the lushness of the surrounding countryside. Today, regular tours are held throughout the Bauhaus buildings, and because of the school's legacy, Dessau can be described as the city where Modernism began. In the popular cabinetmaking workshop, the master Marcel Breuer created his pioneering lightweight metal chairs that were inspired by the steel tubes of his bicycle. Under Gunta Stölzl in the textile workshop, students created innovative abstract textiles, often using unorthodox materials such as cellophane, fibreglass and metal. Albers began as one of Stölzl's students, but by 1931, in Berlin, she was in charge of the weaving workshop herself. Throughout her life she created and wrote about modernist textiles, including reflecting on how she came to weaving: 'In my case it was threads that caught me, really against my will. To work with threads seemed sissy to me. I wanted something to be conquered. But circumstances held me to threads and they won me over.' Her striking geometric patterned designs with their radical use of materials and colour made her one of the most influential textile artists of the 20th century.

Unlike many of her colleagues, Albers usually used a palette of neutral-coloured threads and focused her attention on complicated weaving techniques and linear designs as she created textiles that could be mass produced on an industrial scale. One pattern for a wall hanging, *Untitled*, that she produced at Dessau in 1926, is based on repeating and interlocking stripes and blocks, using a triple-weave technique. Two years earlier, she had published an essay, *Bauhaus Weaving*, which noted how little had changed structurally in textile weaving since it was first invented, but that also in the mass production of the day, designers and weavers were producing low quality designs. She offered solutions to these problems, and in her 1929 *Untitled* wall hanging, she used new synthetic fibres, including artificial silk, which were advanced then, but which later became standard materials for mass-produced textiles.

Albers' work and the wider legacy of the Bauhaus school can be further explored at the new Bauhaus Museum Dessau, which was opened in 2019 to celebrate the centenary of the school opening. Dedicated to showcasing designs associated with Bauhaus, the museum contains approximately 49,000 exhibits, the second largest collection in the world of Bauhaus exhibits. It is the perfect venue to reflect on the far-reaching influence of this unique city and those who lived, learned and worked here.

Where?	Elbe Sandstone Mountains Germany
Which?	*Wanderer Above the Sea of Fog* (1818) by Caspar David Friedrich
What?	Mountainous region of magnificence and mystery

ELBE

THE RIVER Elbe flows through a steep, narrow valley of sandstone, carved by erosion through mountains on the border of the state of Saxony in south-eastern Germany and the North Bohemian region of the Czech Republic. Formed of forested areas, plains and ravines, the breathtaking scenery of the region attracts hikers, cyclists and rock climbers – as well as writers and artists. The varied terrain is also home to a broad range of flora and fauna. Predominantly comprised of sandstone, the mountains were formed millions of years ago, when rivers carried deposits of minerals including sand, clay and other eroded debris and deposited them on the seabed. Over millennia, these deposits hardened together in layers, building up to create the dramatic mountainous region so loved by artists such as Caspar David Friedrich (1774–1840).

Best known for his allegorical, atmospheric and often ambiguous landscapes with enigmatic figures, Friedrich frequently depicted the Elbe Sandstone Mountains. Rather than objectively capturing the drama and contrasts of the scenery however, his underlying themes were commonly spirituality and the contemplation of nature, and he often featured anonymous figures and ruins silhouetted against moonlit or misty skies in his work. Through his expressive, introspective approach, he conveyed the infinite power and timelessness of nature, reminding viewers of their frailty and insignificance within the universe. Nowhere was this more apparent than in his 1818 painting *Wanderer Above the Sea of Fog*.

Friedrich was working as the Romantic movement was evolving in art and literature, and he infused his landscapes with deep

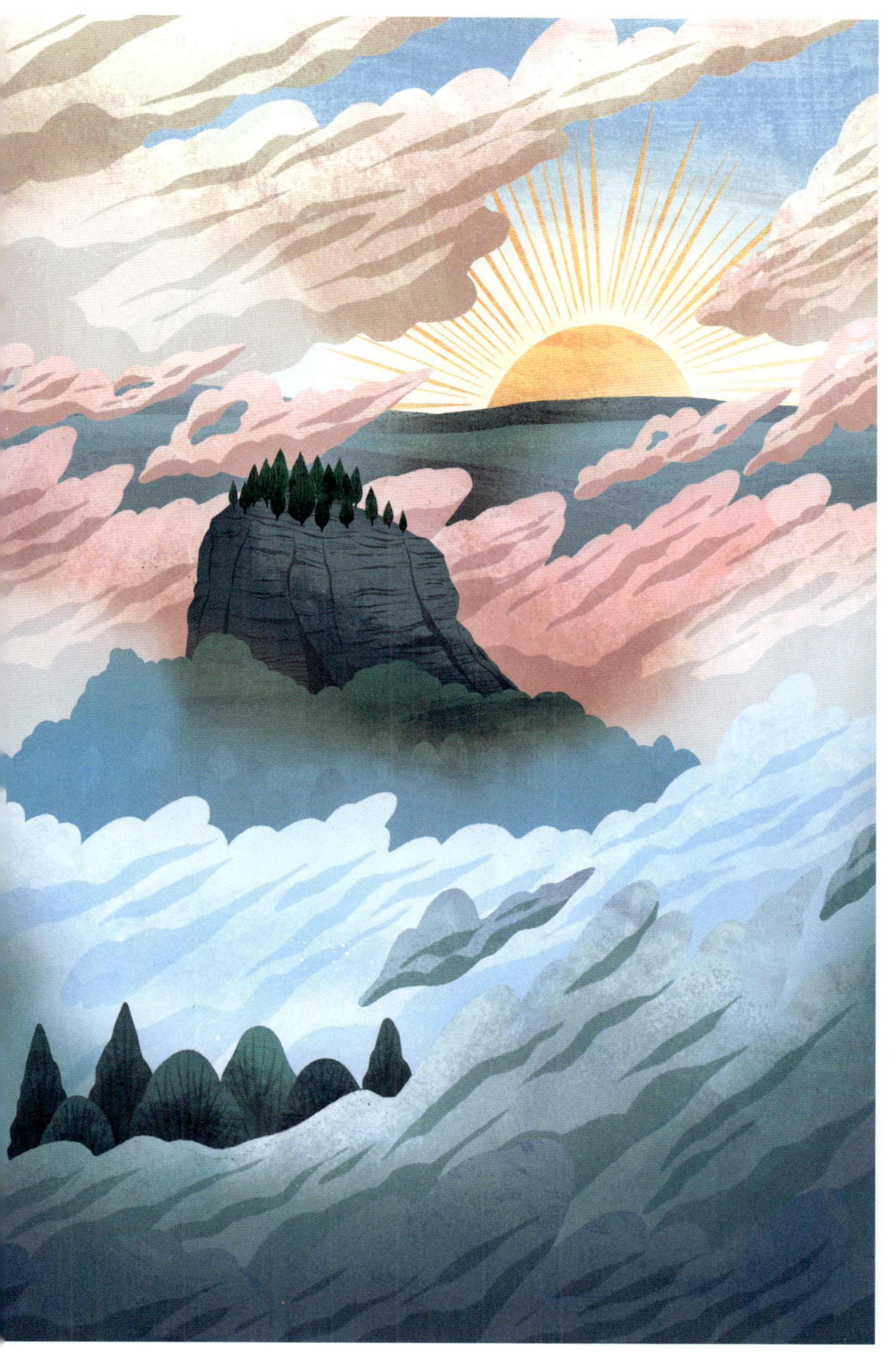

religious and mystical significance, conveying the power and magnificence of the divine through the natural world. Inspired by the Elbe Sandstone Mountains, Friedrich's inventive portrayal of landscape was his major innovation. He did not just capture the grandeur and extraordinariness of the vista, but suggested through it that close contemplation of nature enables us all to achieve an appreciation of spirituality. In this way he helped to transform landscape painting from an overlooked background setting to an autonomous, emotive subject.

The integration of spiritual significance within the landscape attracted wide acclaim. In *Wanderer Above the Sea of Fog*, a man wearing a frock coat and holding a cane stands on a crag, surveying the rocks and mist before him. He is a Rückenfigur, or a person seen from behind. Through the Rückenfigur's contemplation of the scene, the viewer is forced to share the experience. The unknown world before him is vast and immeasurable. The outline of the mountains is barely visible through the fog. Worryingly, it seems that with one false step, the figure could plunge to his death. Or if he lingers longer, will he be enveloped by the fog?

Although this painting is atmospheric and lifelike, Friedrich never painted directly from nature. He made detailed sketches of the land, but back in his studio, he used elements of these from different settings, building up an entirely imagined view. For instance, the Zirkelstein, a rock that appears in the background mist of the painting, is real but in a changed location. This small table mountain offers spectacular views across the countryside, especially at sunrise and sunset. Located near the River Elbe, only 2 kilometres (1 mile) from Schöna train station in Saxony, hikers can reach the summit and admire the scenery that inspired Friedrich's mysterious works.

During his early career, Friedrich achieved great success; a fellow artist described him as a man who had discovered 'the tragedy of landscape' but later, his art became perceived as fanciful, melancholy and old-fashioned, and he died in obscurity. In the 1920s and 1930s, however, the Expressionists and Surrealists admired his work and he once again came to the fore, only for his equivocal art – and especially his *Wanderer Above the Sea of Fog* – to be adopted by the Nazi regime to symbolise German nationalism during the Second World War. It was not until the 1970s that his dramatic renditions of places such as the Elbe Sandstone Mountains were reassessed and admired once more.

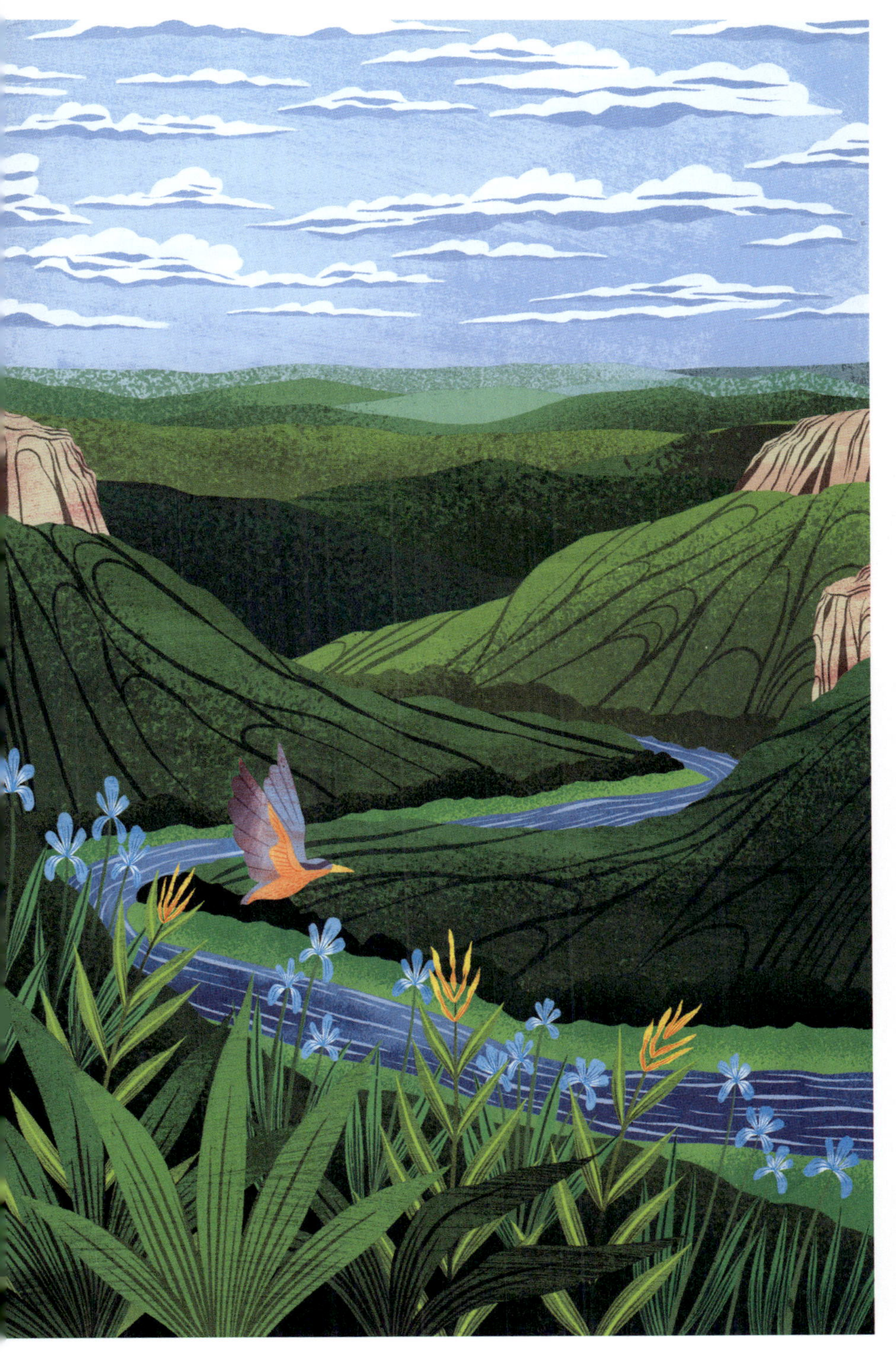

Where?	Lake Attersee, Austria
Which?	*Lake Attersee* (1900) by Gustav Klimt
What?	Ethereal, glass-like tranquil lake

LAKE ATTERSEE

COOL AND still, the air hangs over the waters of Lake Attersee at the edge of the Austrian Alps. The glass-like surface is surrounded by soft green hills and blue-grey mountains, and depending on the sky and where you are standing, the crystal water changes colour throughout the day, from turquoise to sapphire, to cobalt and indigo. In the beautiful Salzkammergut region, Attersee is the largest lake in Austria, and popular for boating, bathing, walking, hiking and picnicking. Although the shores of the lake have been populated since Neolithic times by various settlers, including Romans and the bourgeoisie of the early 19th century, today it remains peaceful and uncrowded. Since the 19th century, paddle steamers, boats and ships have propelled across the shimmering water, ferrying people and goods to the many villages located around the shores – or simply for pleasure. Boats are often helped by the easterly *Rosenwind* (breeze of roses), a soft wind that carries the scent of roses from a castle garden across the lake. It was here in the summer of 1900 that the artist Gustav Klimt (1862–1918) first visited, escaping the heat of the city, after writing to a friend, 'It's terrible, awful here in Vienna. Everything parched, hot, dreadful.'

After his first visit, Klimt stayed in Lake Attersee for 15 more summers, creating more than 45 of his 50 landscape paintings there, in the tiny lakefront towns of Seewalchen, Litzlberg and Weissenbach. He always stayed with his close companion, Emilie Flöge, and her family, initially in the Flöge family villa not far from the village of Weissenbach, and later in Villa Oleander. Klimt and Emilie first met in 1892, when she was 18 and he was 30. Emilie's sister Helene was

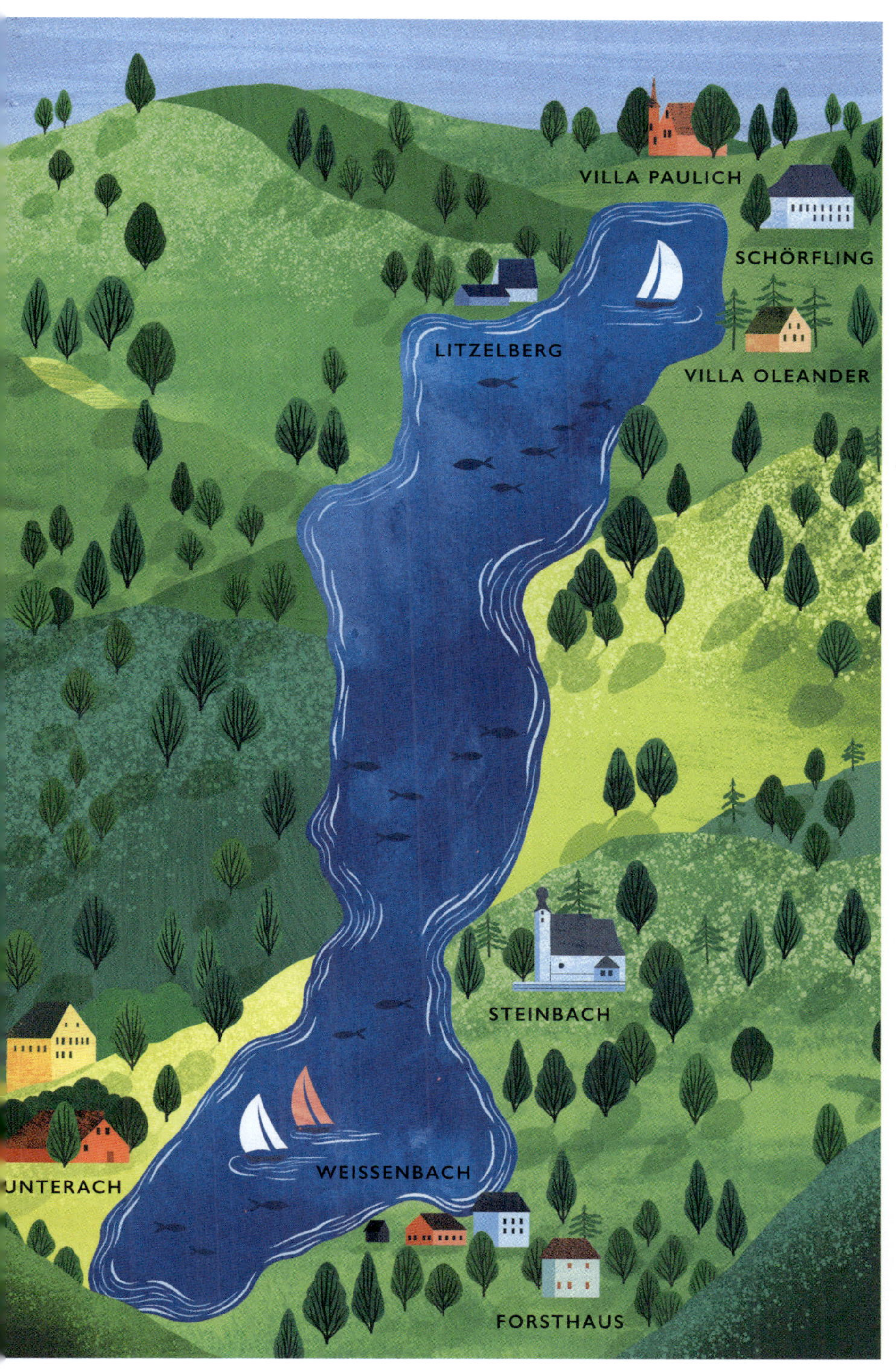
VILLA PAULICH
SCHÖRFLING
LITZELBERG
VILLA OLEANDER
STEINBACH
WEISSENBACH
UNTERACH
FORSTHAUS

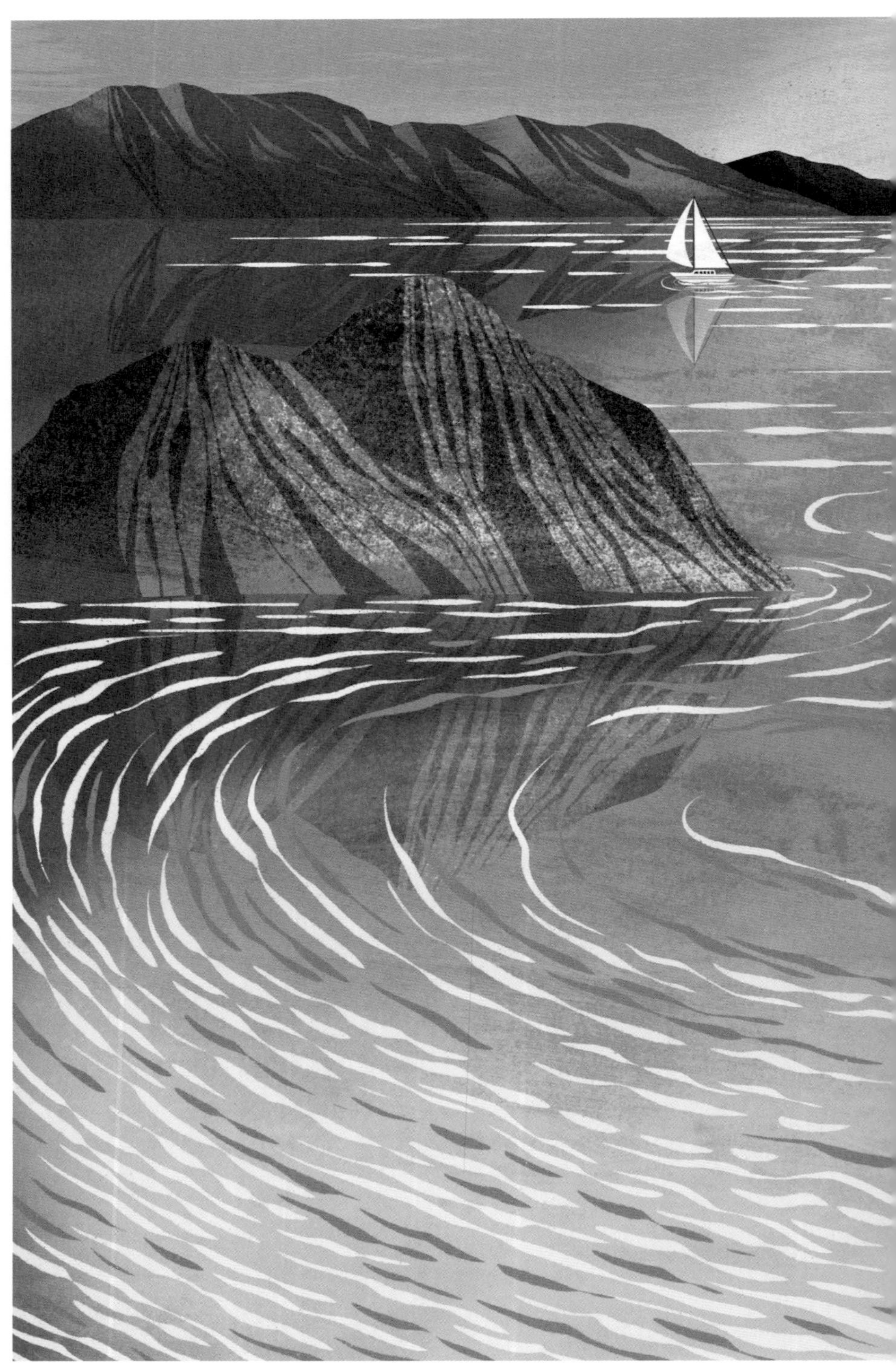

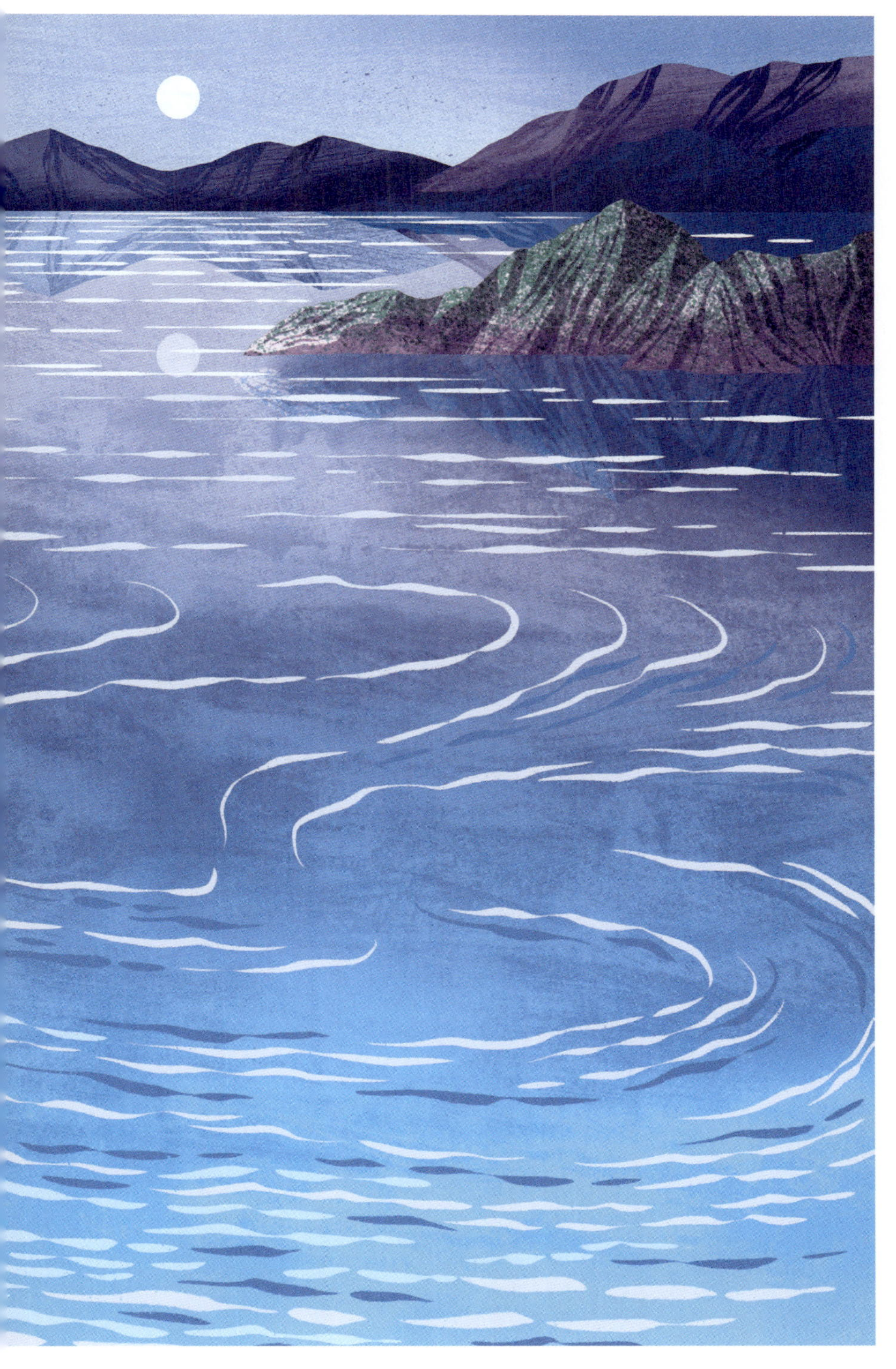

married to Klimt's brother Ernst, who died aged just 28 in 1892, and from then on, Klimt supported Helene and her daughter and became exceptionally close to Emilie. It is not known whether they were lovers, but she became his muse and they often wrote to each other several times a day – disjointed, secret messages between two people who knew each other extremely well. Their friendship lasted 20 years and when Klimt suffered a stroke in 1918, his first words were: '*Emilie soll kommen*' ('Emilie, come').

One of the most important founders of the Vienna Secession – an art and design movement, similar to and concurrent with Art Nouveau – in 1897, Klimt was 38 when he first visited Attersee. There he relaxed, replacing his city clothing with floor-length robes, and abandoning his society portraits for often square landscapes of his summer paradise. He believed this square shape created a sense of tranquillity. Inspired by the presence of Emilie and the breathtaking scenery, Klimt's landscapes were unlike any other painted at the time. They did not explore skies or light or atmospheric views, but they resembled richly embellished or embroidered textiles, combining vivid colour, interesting shapes and flowing rhythms.

In his earliest visits to Attersee, Klimt rowed on the lake to paint, but after a few years he bought a stylish motorboat, which he used as a floating studio, often painting directly onto his canvases from the water. For his painting *Lake Attersee* (1900), which he executed during his first summer there, he worked from the jetty of a small boathouse by the Flöge residence. With most of the square composition filled with the lake, he focused on the surface of the water, applying short, broken, modulated brushstrokes in harmonious, luminous colours – with the palette he used only at Attersee. He reduced the scene to almost an abstraction, eliminating all detail and evoking the sheer expanse of still, calm, blue-green lake. Fascinated by the water, Klimt could spend hours just staring at the lake, watching the changing patterns of light and colour.

The Attersee became his favourite lake, and on what would have been his 150th birthday in July 2012, the Gustav Klimt Centre opened in Kammer-Schörfling along Schloss Kammer avenue that he once also painted. Today, with the Klimt Centre and the stunning lake and surroundings that have barely changed since Klimt was there, you can follow in the artist's footsteps. In particular, you can walk along the Klimt Artist Trail, where you can retrace his and Emilie's steps and witness the breathtaking scenery for yourself.

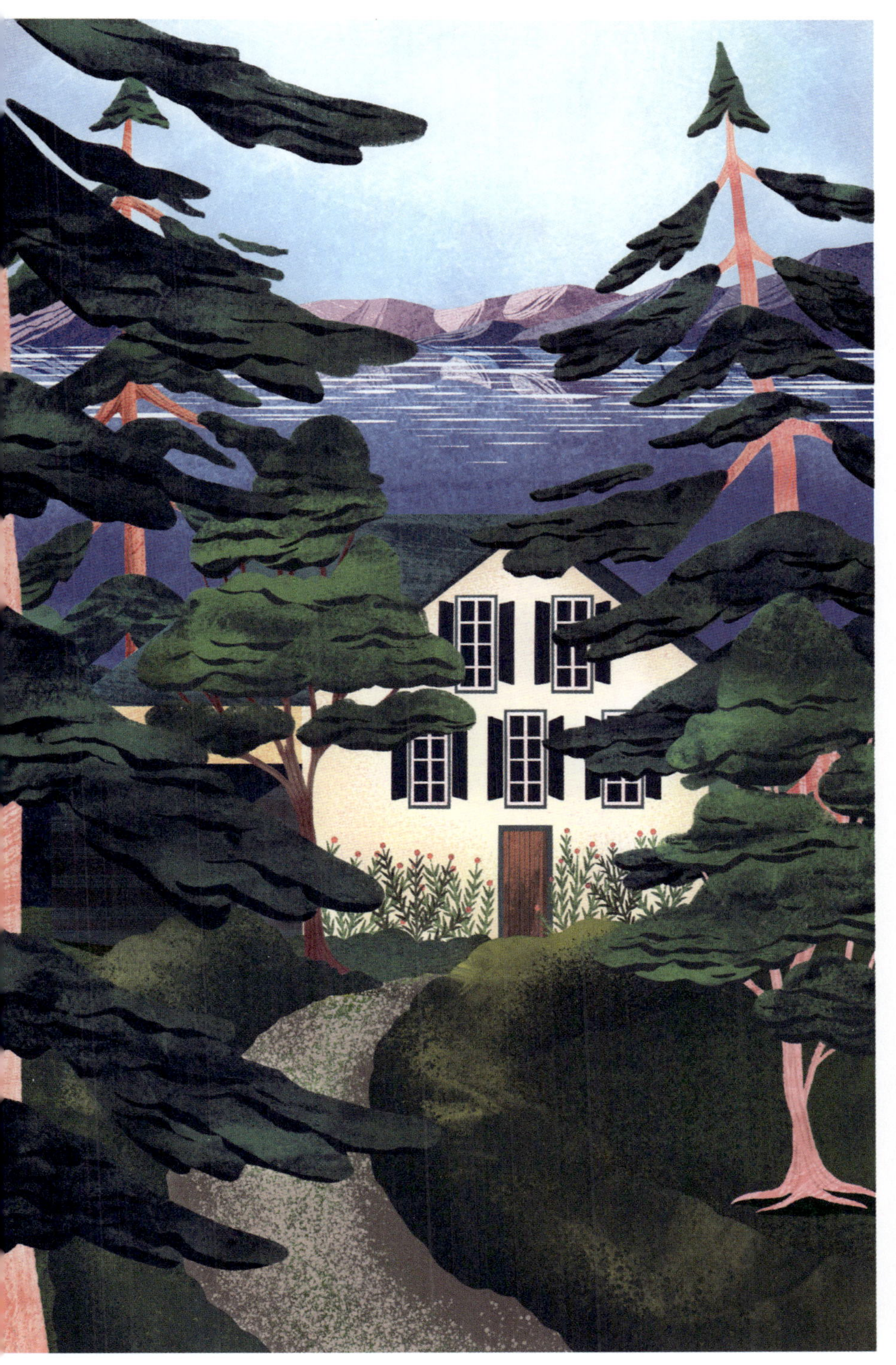

Where?	Oslo, Norway
Which?	*The Scream* (1893) by Edvard Munch
What?	Emotive, inspiring Norwegian fjordland

OSLO

SITTING BETWEEN dense forests and a glittering fjord, Oslo is unique among capital cities, with one of the lowest carbon footprints in the world, created by efficient public transport, a commitment to sustainable food production, refreshing water that sparkles from the tap and an abundance of open spaces. The air in this energised metropolis feels fresh and clear, and there are beautiful views over the Oslo Fjord and the surrounding mountains, forests, parks, waterways and ski slopes. Bars, cafés and restaurants are bustling but chilled, and it is easy to relax in the unhurried atmosphere beneath the clear sunlight that shines for much of the year, whether in the height of summer or during the crisp, cold winter.

Although Oslo is modern and progressive, aspects of the city date back nearly a thousand years, when it was founded by King Harald Hardrada in around 1050. In approximately 1300, the Akershus Fortress was built by Haakon V. After the town was destroyed by fire in 1624, Christian IV of Denmark–Norway built a new city slightly to the west of the original, under the walls of the Akershus Fortress, and called it Christiania, or Kristiania, after himself. It was not until 1925 that its name changed from Kristiania to Oslo. These days, as with most cities, examples of old and new nestle alongside each other; in the architecture of the museums, galleries, university, theatres, concert halls and opera houses.

There is a great diversity of culture to admire, from the Historical Museum and the National Museum of Art, Architecture and Design, to the botanical gardens, the Norwegian Folk Museum and the Viking Ship Museum. More contrasts include the large, airy Frogner

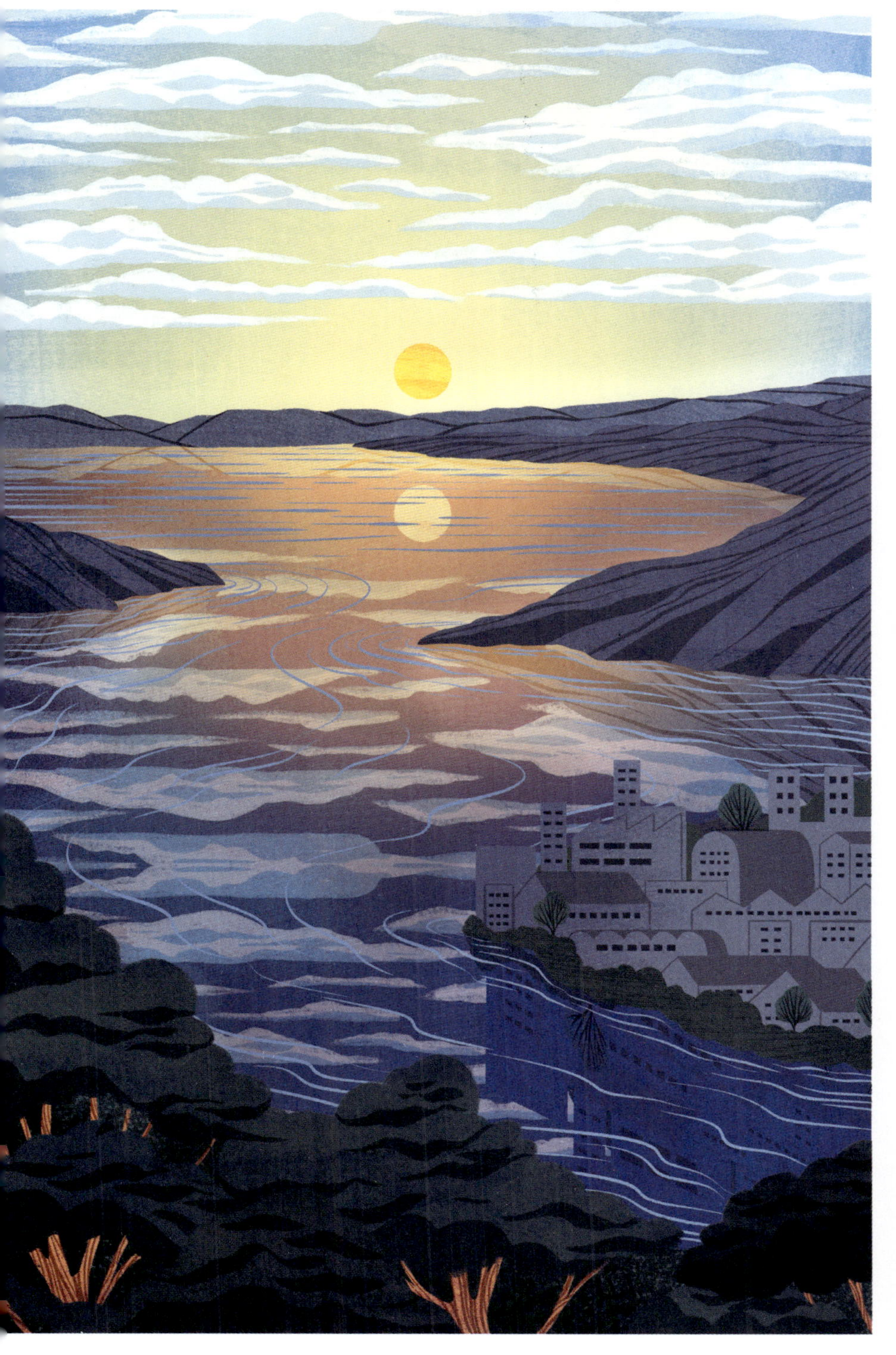

Park with its lake and sculptures, the modernist Ekeberg restaurant set on a hill, the Neoclassical Royal Palace and twin towers of City Hall in the city centre, the Holmenkollen ski slope that rises above the sea to the fjord, the award-winning opera house where waves lap around its glass façade, and the Munch Museum, named after acclaimed artist, Edvard Munch (1863–1944), whose 1893 painting *The Scream* turned the city, and especially the fjord, into an icon.

Munch grew up in Oslo, and although he moved away for several years, he began his career there and returned for the last decades of his life. When he was one year old, his family moved to Nedre Slottsgate, a street in the Kvadraturen area of Kristiania. They later moved to Pilestredet and various addresses in the Grünerløkka neighbourhood, east of the River Akerselva. A stroll around this borough gives a good idea of the Oslo that Munch would have known – a former industrial and working class area; while some gentrification has since taken place, the architecture remains, perhaps surprisingly, much as it was when Munch lived there.

Munch rented his first studio opposite the Parliament building on Karl Johans Gate, Oslo's main street. This lively thoroughfare remains a focal point of the city today, and a leisurely stroll down this street takes you past bustling cafés, restaurants and shops, as well as local street performers, artists and musicians. Munch painted a number of works featuring Karl Johans Gate, such as *Spring Day on Karl Johan Street* in 1890 and *Evening on Karl Johan Street* in 1892. In 1893, he produced four versions of a painting that he initially called *The Scream of Nature*. It has become one of the most recognised paintings in the world. An agitated figure stands in a distorted Oslo landscape against a fiery red sky. Two figures are walking on, unaware of the crisis their friend is experiencing.

Although the image is deliberately exaggerated and misshapen, Munch said he was inspired by the Oslo (Kristiania) Fjord seen from Ekeberg, a neighbourhood within the city. The Ekeberg Park, close to Ekebergparken Sculpture Park, is the spot and is a must-see when you are there to admire the view as Munch once did. Munch was also inspired by the bay of Bjørvika and the Akershus Fortress – seen in the background of the painting and another essential stopping-off point for visitors. More than a landscape, however, the painting represents both personal and universal feelings of anxiety and alienation. It was one of the first works of art to explore inner emotions rather than outer appearances.

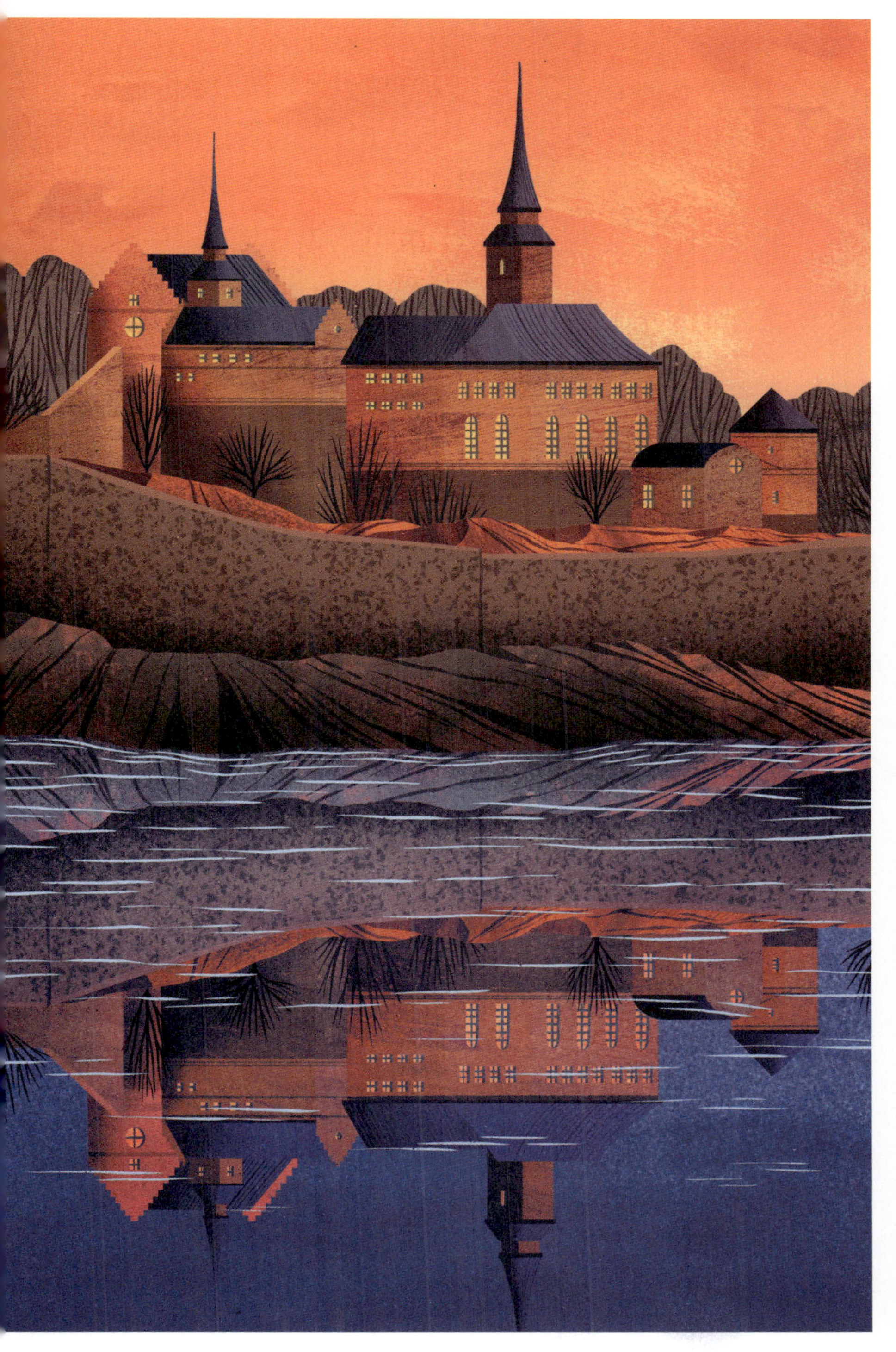

Where?	Lake Mälaren, Sweden
Which?	*The Ten Largest, No 7 Adulthood* (1907) by Hilma af Klint
What?	A fusion of nature and spirituality on a Swedish lake

LAKE MÄLAREN

AT ONE time Lake Mälaren was a bay of the Baltic Sea, inviting boats and ships to sail deep into Sweden. Eventually, as the Earth's crust moved, the bay became a lake that now spills across the countryside west of Stockholm. All around the lake's shores, the soft lapping of water, the hum of insects, gentle calls of birds and erratic scurrying of small wild animals can be heard, while the ripe soil nurtures colourful, delicate wildflowers, including cornflower, honeysuckle and blackthorn. The third-largest freshwater lake in Sweden (after Vänern and Vättern), Lake Mälaren is dotted with thousands of islands, including Selaön, Lovön, Munsö, Björkö and Adelsö.

Around the shoreline are wooded areas, deep forests, sandy beaches, pretty little towns with red wooden cottages and often historical remains, particularly Viking evidence, such as at the archaeological site on Björkö island at Birka of a Viking city from the 9th and 10th centuries. In summer, the lake is busy with boats and ships, and each year, these islands witness mystical natural occurrences including spectacular northern lights and midnight sun. It was in this land of the midnight sun, on the island of Adelsö, west of Stockholm, that Hilma af Klint (1862–1944) spent summers with her family at their manor, Hanmora. In these idyllic surroundings, af Klint came into contact with nature, and her close association with natural forms became an inspiration in her work. Later in life, she lived at Villa Furuheim on Munsö, an island next to Adelsö.

Probably the first artist in the West to produce an abstract painting, af Klint was among the earliest females to receive a higher education at the Royal Academy of Fine Arts in Stockholm.

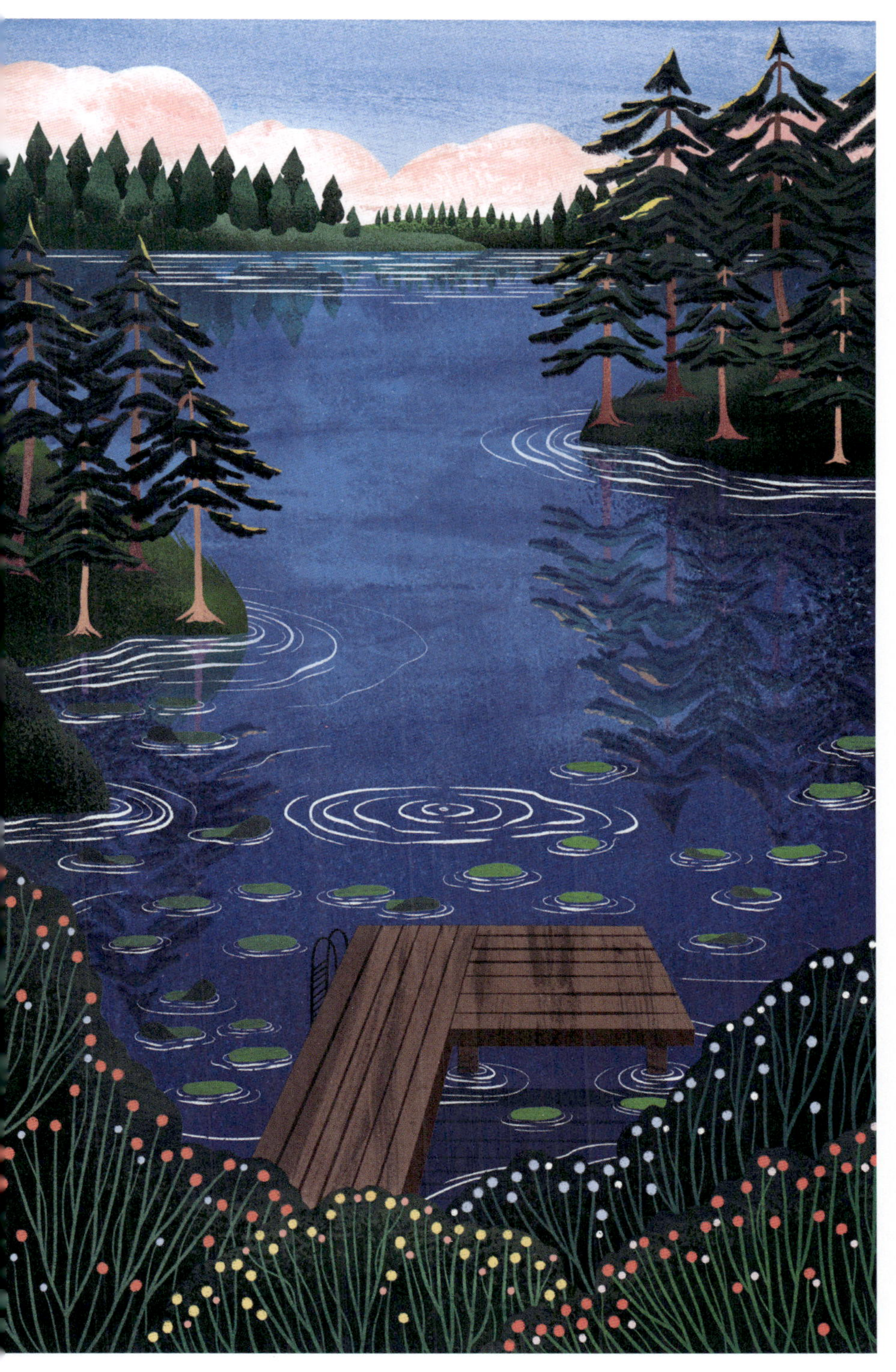

She graduated with honours, and was awarded a scholarship in the form of a studio owned by the Academy in central Stockholm. At the end of the 19th century, spiritualist movements were fashionable in the United States and Europe, especially in literary and artistic circles. Scientific developments were radically altering prevailing ideas about the world. Darwin's evolutionary theories, while not yet entirely accepted in academic circles, affected many, and the discovery of such things as radioactivity and X-rays confirmed for spiritualists that there is an invisible realm of existence.

Inspired by the mystical teachings of theosophy and anthroposophy, af Klint tried to understand both the visible world we are all aware of and the spiritual world that we cannot see. In 1896, with four female artist friends, she began a group called *De Fem* (The Five). They held regular séances and experimented with unconscious writing and drawing, and were apparently successful in making contact with six spirit guides. The women documented their experiences in notebooks, collaborating on automatic drawings filled with biomorphic forms inspired by their visions. In 1904, two of the spirits asked the women to convey the spiritual world through painting, and to design a temple to house the resulting works. The other members of the group refused, believing that such a prolonged, intense engagement with the spirit realm could lead to madness. But in January 1906, af Klint promised to undertake this 'great commission'. From 1906, she produced *Paintings for the Temple*, resulting in 193 works on canvas and paper by 1915. Sometimes resembling diagrams, her paintings were a visual representation of complex spiritual ideas, especially ten that each illustrates a different phase of human life, including childhood, youth, maturity and old age. These huge paintings are called collectively *The Ten Largest*, and there are two themed 'Childhood', two themed 'Youth', four themed 'Adulthood' and two themed 'Old Age'. Af Klint wrote, 'The pictures were painted directly . . . without any preliminary drawings . . . I had no idea what the paintings were supposed to depict; nevertheless, I worked swiftly and surely, without changing a single brushstroke.'

With their free-flowing organic forms of different sizes and bright colours, the *Paintings for the Temple* are at once meditative and calm, dynamic and flowing, neatly echoing the artist's botanical studies of the wild flowers around Lake Mälaren.

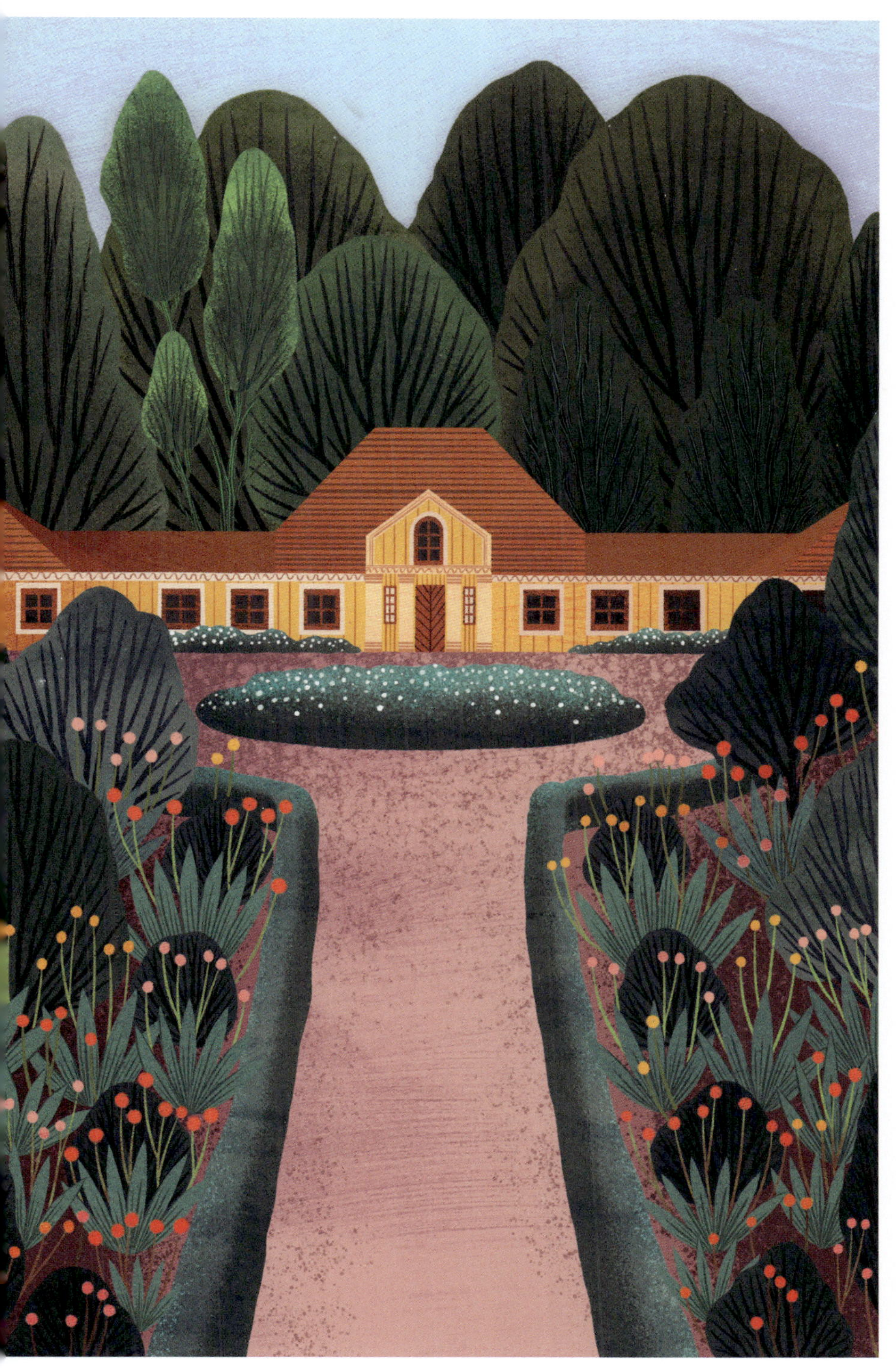

Where?	Tangier, Morocco
Which?	*Paysage Vu d'une Fenêtre (Landscape Viewed from a Window)* (1913) by Henri Matisse
What?	City filled with evocative North African light

TANGIER

THE LIGHT is distinctive in Tangier. At dawn, it pierces through the early morning mist; at midday, it splinters into shafts of light; the golden sunset transforms everything into glowing embers; and at night, silver studs punctuate the deep velvet sky. Just before sunrise, the call to morning prayer echoes from numerous towers across the city, rising in volume before darkness melts into day.

Tangier sits on the northernmost tip of Africa, overlooking both the inky Mediterranean Sea and the azure Atlantic Ocean. Not far away is the Strait of Gibraltar, and these geographical cross-currents result in a synergy of nationalities and languages, mainly French, Arabic and English. Blending these influences and its unique location, Tangier is Europe's gateway to Africa. For a time, it was semi-independent from Africa as an international zone, which attracted diplomats, artists, writers and holiday-makers. After the 1950s, its popularity dipped, but its charm is once again rising. Now you can appreciate anew the same sights that attracted French artists Eugène Delacroix in 1832 and Henri Matisse in 1912 and 1913.

Many different civilisations have occupied Tangier, starting from before the 10th century BC when it was a Phoenician trading post and later became a Carthaginian settlement. It has been a Berber town and was occupied by the Romans, captured by the Byzantine Empire, and it has also been under Spanish and British rule. This eclectic mix of cultures has resulted in a rich diversity of inhabitants and influences. Tangier combines old and new, with its *kasbah* (citadel), *medina* (old walled city), colonial-era neighbourhoods, high-speed train line and regal, elaborate palaces. The medina is a

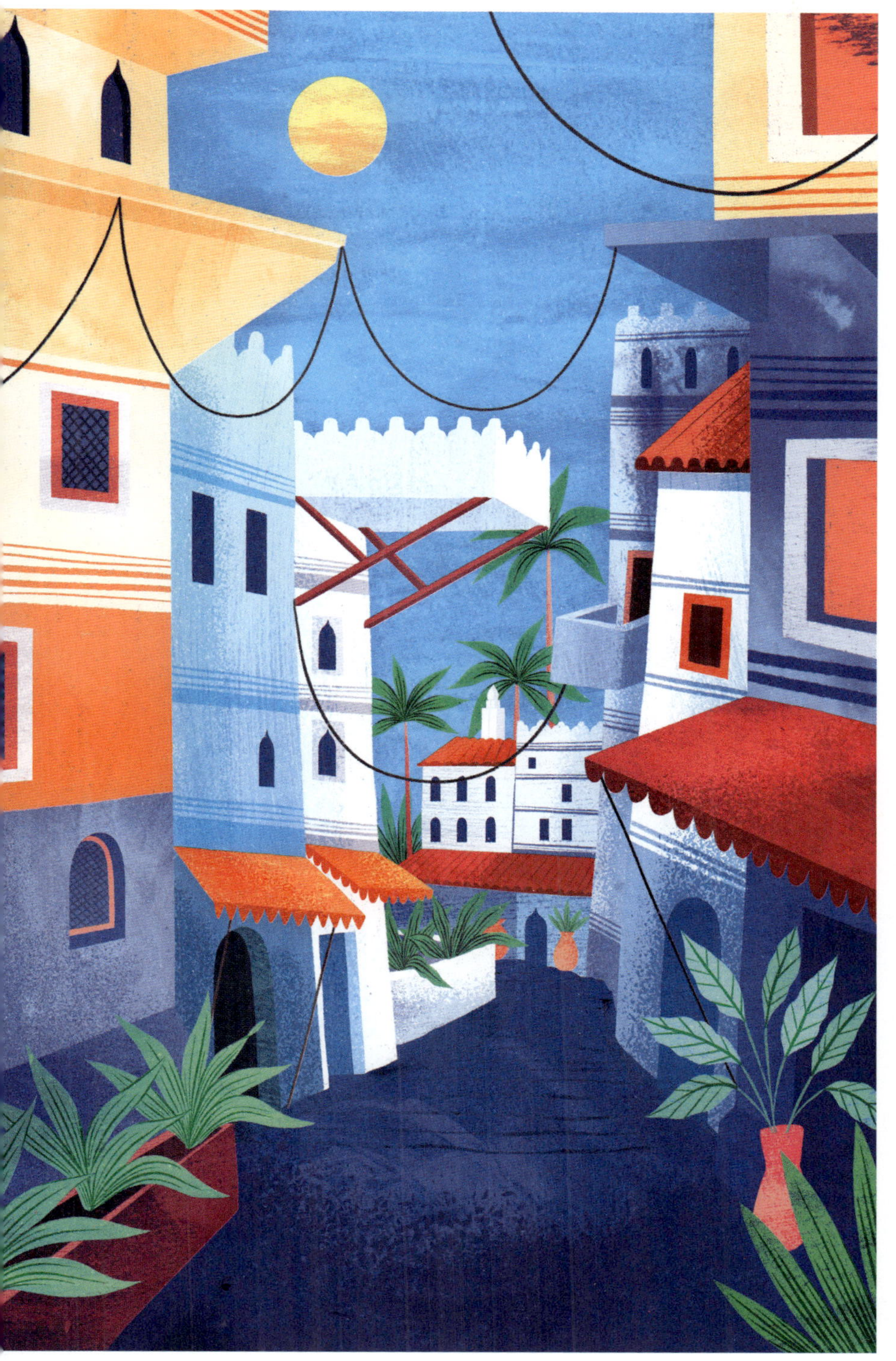

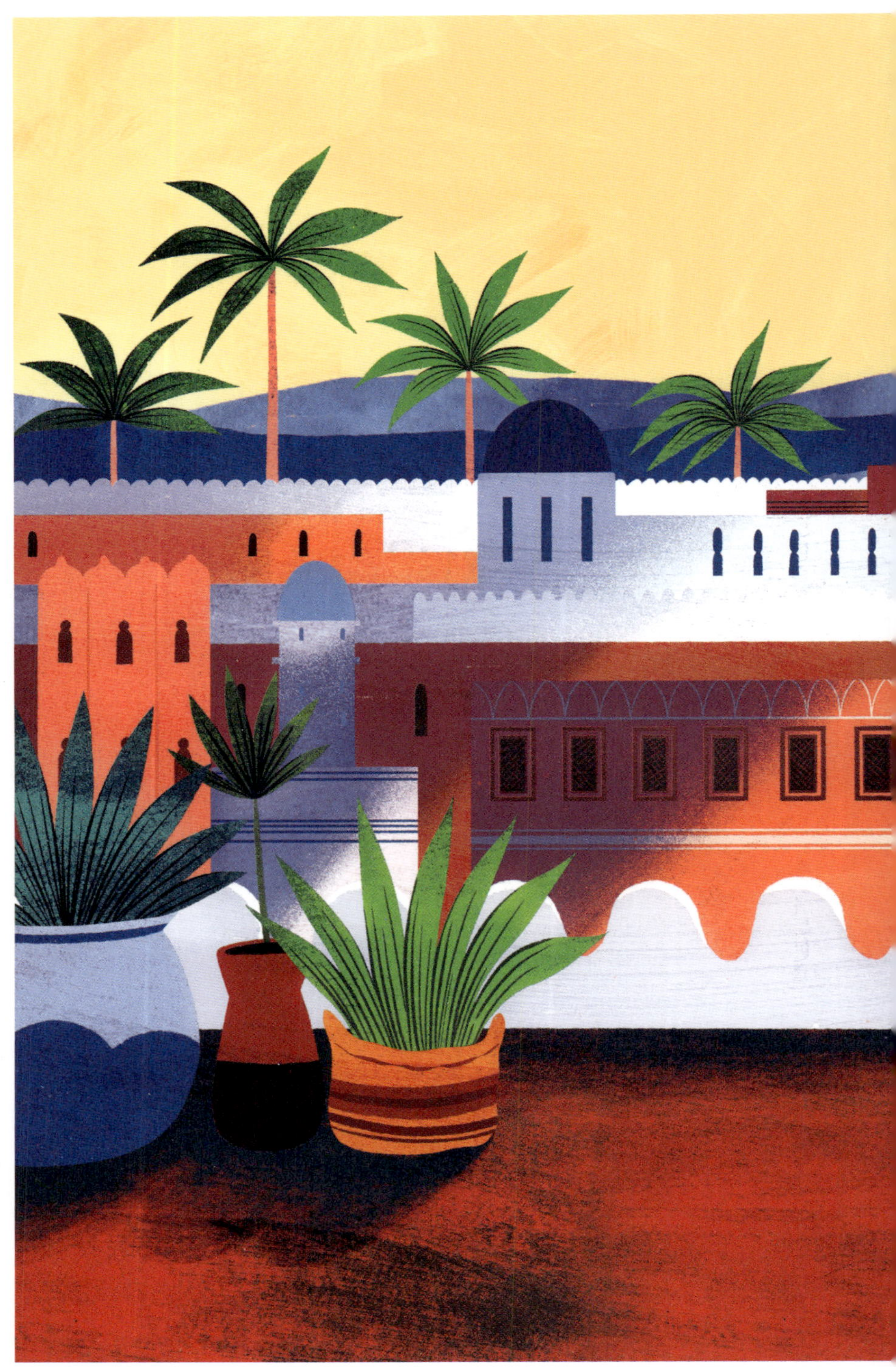

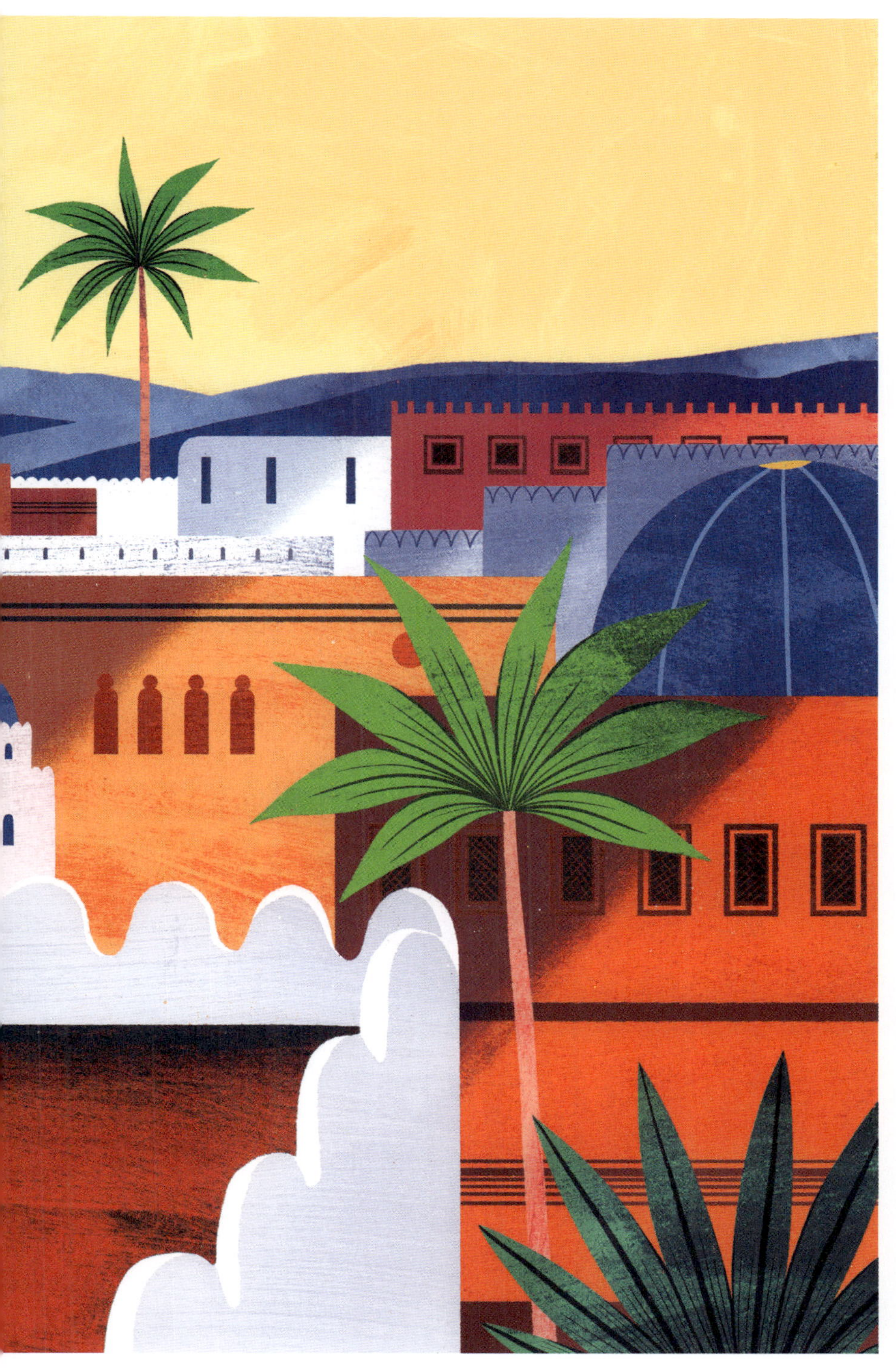

network of alleyways, brimming with lively shops filled with trinkets, artisanal goods, carpets and local food, as well as teahouses serving tea from delicate filigree glasses. Close to the long palm-fringed beaches is a thriving, youthful café culture.

In the early 20th century, Tangier attracted the avant-garde Fauve painter Henri Matisse (1869–1954), seeking a new direction for his art. He was charmed by the cosmopolitan city, its bright and luminous light, vivid colours, variegated sunshine and striking, exotic architecture. With his ardent appreciation of Persian art, and his admiration of Delacroix's North African paintings, as well as advice on colour that he was given by Paul Gauguin, Matisse was delighted with his visits to the city and they had a profound effect on his work and career. He described the light of Tangier as 'mellow' and the city as 'a painter's paradise', and he interpreted it all with rich pigments, animated brushwork and contrasting patterns. The landscapes of Tangier were far more luxuriant than any he had seen before. On his arrival, he went almost immediately into the gardens of the Villa Brooks, a private estate not far from his hotel, and spent weeks painting the acanthuses, palms and periwinkles that grew there.

While in Tangier, Matisse produced approximately 20 oil paintings and even more sketches, using bold shapes and vibrant, expressive colours. On his arrival in the city, it was raining, and he painted a vase of irises in his hotel room, emphasising the pattern created by the flowers against the dressing table and mirror, but among his most evocative paintings of Tangier are his 1912 landscapes *Vue sur la Baie de Tangier (View of the Bay of Tangier)* and *La Porte de la Casbah (Entrance to the Kasbah),* and *Paysage Vu d'une Fenêtre (Landscape Viewed from a Window)* of 1913. Mainly captured in brilliant blue, evoking the reflection of the sky on the stark white buildings, this last image was painted directly from his window in Room 35 of the Grand Hôtel Villa de France, looking out over St Andrew's Church to the kasbah beyond. Most of Matisse's Tangier paintings feature vivid pinks, yellows, blues and greens, circles, stripes and other shapes, all created with thin washes of pigment. Although he spent only a few months there, the experiences and inspiration remained with Matisse for the rest of his life and completely shaped his subsequent art. Later in the 1920s, his paintings of odalisques that he produced in Nice, of reclining females set against patterned cushions, wallpaper and carpets, are clearly the direct result of the way in which the magical light of Tangier affected him.

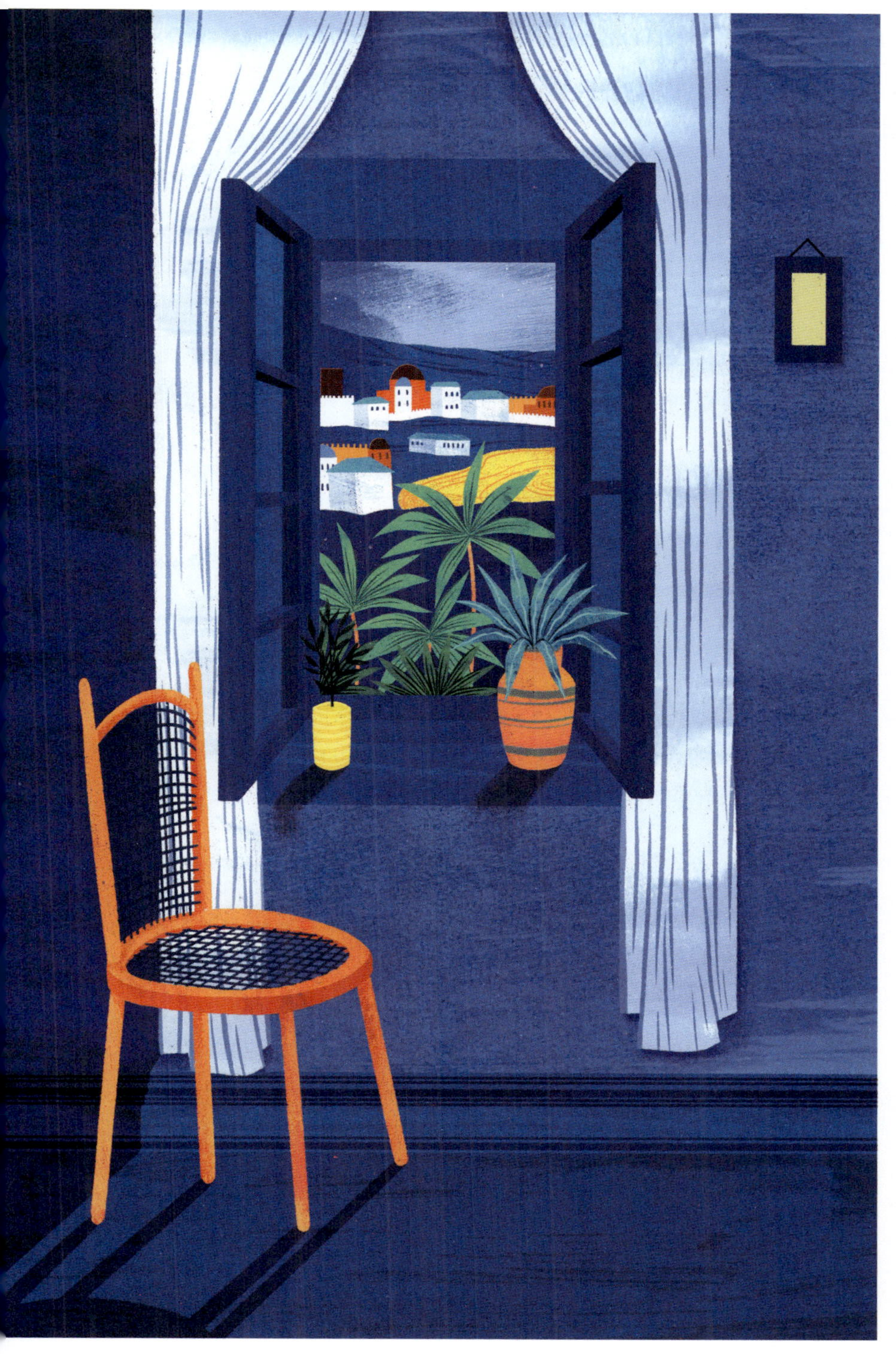

Where?	Mount Fuji, Japan
Which?	*The Great Wave off Kanagawa* (c.1829) by Katsushika Hokusai
What?	Nature's power before a sacred mountain

MOUNT FUJI

EVEN ON the clearest of days, Mount Fuji, Japan's highest mountain and an active volcano, is usually enshrouded in mist and clouds. With its perfect conical shape, it has long been considered the sacred symbol of Japan and an essential part of national identity. In Buddhist and Daoist tradition, it was thought to hold the secret of immortality.

From a distance, Fuji can sometimes be seen in its full splendour during the colder months and in the early mornings or late evenings, when the air is clearest. Rising between Yamanashi and Shizuoka prefectures, it can be viewed from the window of the Shinkansen bullet train that runs from Tokyo to Osaka, and particularly from the Shin-Fuji station. It is actually a composite of three successive volcanoes: at the bottom is Komitake; in the middle is Ko Fuji (Old Fuji); and at the top is Shin Fuji (New Fuji). On its northern slopes are the Fuji Goko (Five Lakes), all formed by lava flows, and to the south-east are wooded areas and hot springs. As it is such a sacred place, it is surrounded by temples and shrines, and climbing to the shrine at the peak has long been a religious practice for Buddhists, Daoists and especially those who follow the Shinto religion. Every summer, mostly during July and August, thousands flock there, often setting out at night in order to reach the summit by dawn.

Famously, Mount Fuji has been captured as a majestic, remote spectacle in a series of woodblock prints created by the Ukiyo-e (Pictures of the Floating World) painter and printmaker, Katsushika Hokusai (1760–1849). Originally published between 1830 and 1833, his *Thirty-Six Views of Mount Fuji* depict Fuji in different seasons, weather conditions, times of day and from different locations.

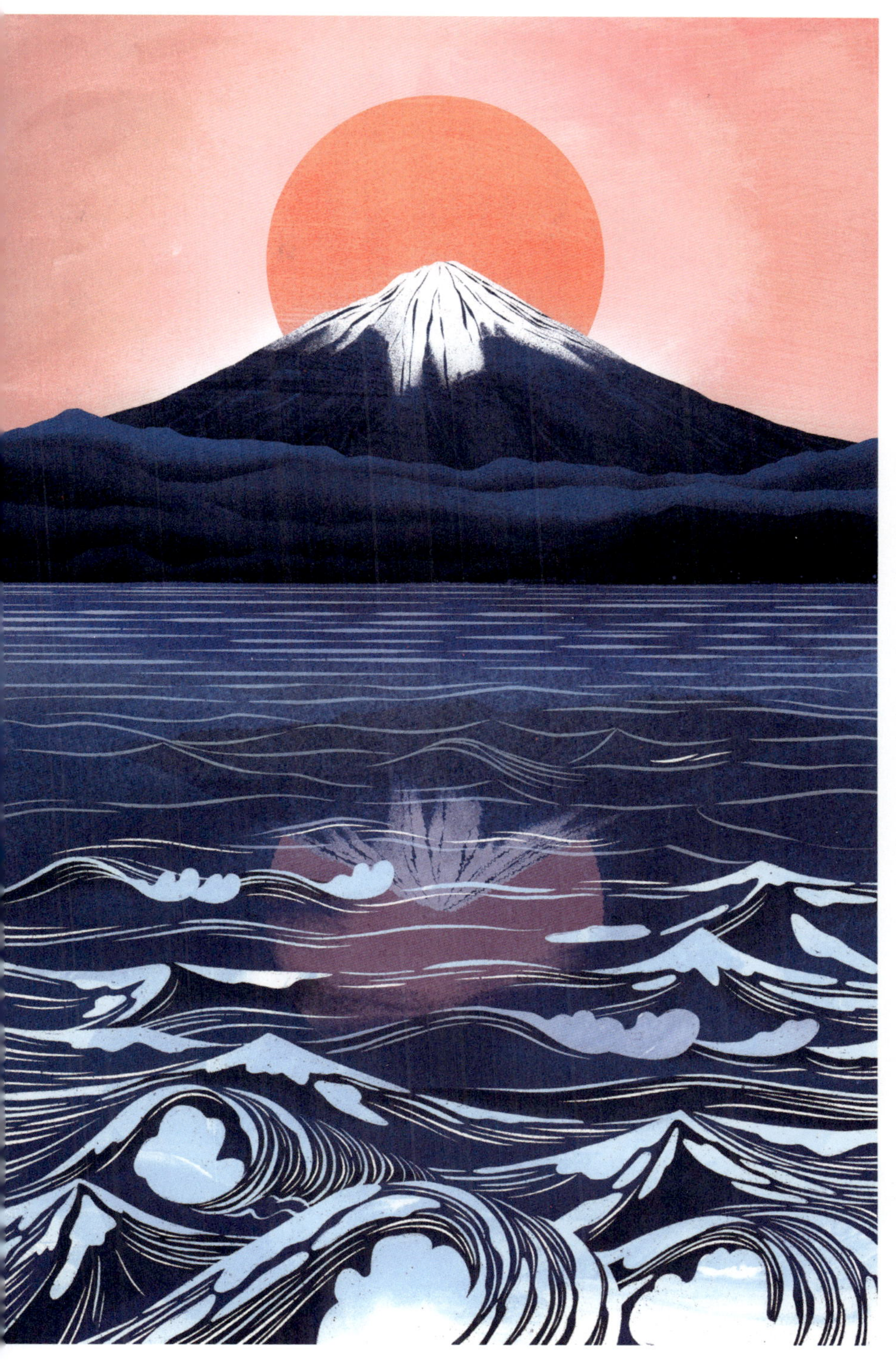

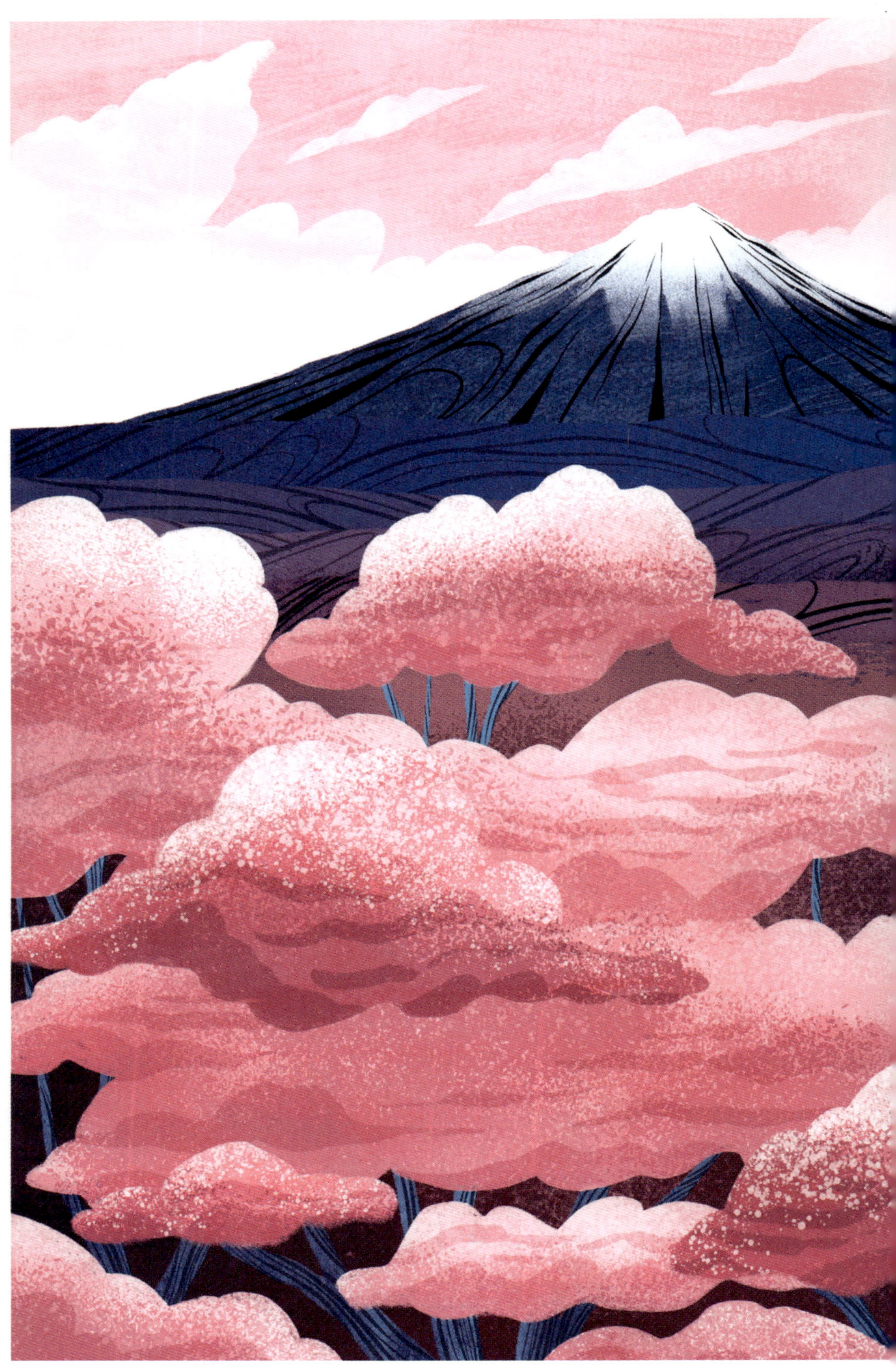

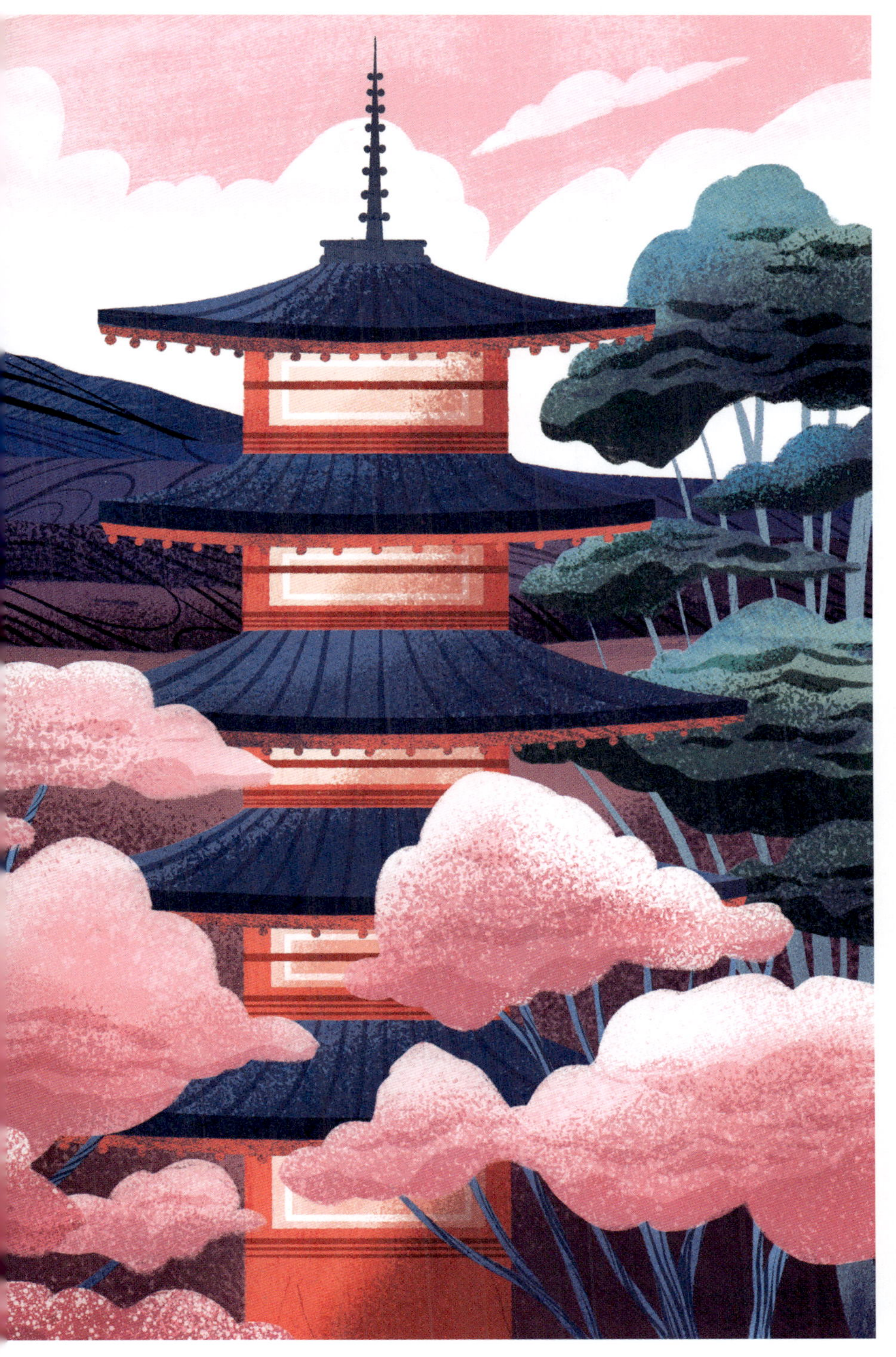

Hokusai was 70 when he began the series, and he added 10 more after the first 36 had been printed and were being sold, making it actually Forty-Six Views, only he kept the original title. Born in Edo (now Tokyo), Hokusai started painting when he was six years old and was nationally renowned before he created this series. He produced it both as a response to a domestic travel boom at the time and because he was obsessed with the sacred powers of Mount Fuji. The mountain appears in each view in different ways. Sometimes prominently in the centre, sometimes as background detail. The first five in the series were printed entirely in shades of blue (a combination of traditional indigo and Prussian blue, which was a recently invented chemical pigment), suggesting the mountain at dawn. Then more colours were added, including delicate and rosy pinks, warm greys and gold, to show the illumination of the world as the sun rises. His process of woodblock printing was complex and precise, requiring the use of a separate block for each individual colour.

Of all the 46 images, the most famous is *The Great Wave off Kanagawa*, which made Hokusai internationally recognised. The scene depicts three boats being threatened by a large wave in front of Mount Fuji. The huge wave about to break dominates the composition and creates a sense of tension. Amid the waves are three *oshiokuri-bune* (fast boats) that carry fish from the Izu and Bōsō peninsulas to the markets in the bay of Edo. Eight rowers are in each boat, each clinging to their oars, with two passengers in the front. The boats and figures convey the enormity of the wave and so the might and power of nature. In the foreground, a small wave forms the shape of a miniature Fuji and, through perspective, is larger than the distant mountain. Storm clouds hang in the sky between the viewer and Mount Fuji, while the sun rises from behind, illuminating the mountain's snowy peak. A dark outline around Mount Fuji suggests that it is early morning. Hokusai's colours are restricted: three shades of blue for the water; yellow for the boats; dark grey for the sky behind Fuji and on the boat below; pale grey for the sky above Fuji and on the foreground boat; and pink clouds in the sky, glowing over the venerated distant mountain. Climbers can take any of the four challenging trails that lead to the summit of Mount Fuji. Once reaching the peak, the magnificent landscape stretches out before you; a view that inspired so many faithful followers and such an epic series of images.

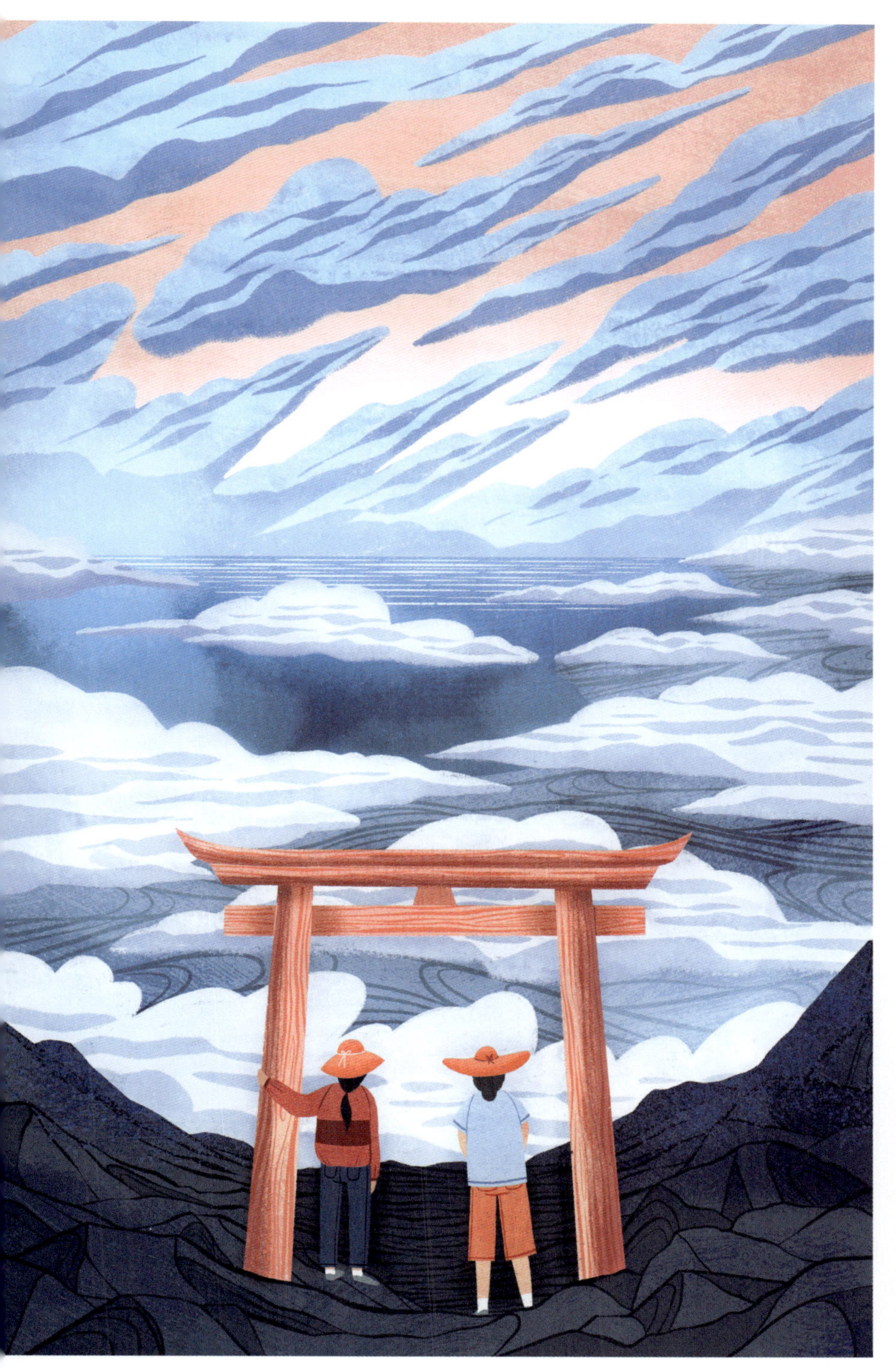

Where?	Tahiti, French Polynesia
Which?	*Where Do We Come From What Are We? Where Are We Going?* (1897) by Paul Gauguin
What?	Exotic, allegorical meanings in dense, tropical surroundings

TAHITI

TREES TOP-HEAVY with bananas and giant flowers greet you. Glorious colours and perfumes pervade; a blend of coconut, hibiscus, jasmine, ginger, frangipani, vanilla and the lemony scent of the national tiare flower. Even in the early morning, the warmth is palpable. A gentle breeze hovers expectantly, sometimes warm and humid, sometimes mild and light, and always heavy with fragrant floral notes.

With high mountains, coral reefs, turquoise lagoons, palm-fringed beaches, tropical vegetation and sparkling waterfalls, the islands of Tahiti in the South Pacific Ocean, epitomise the luxuriance of the tropics. Papeete, the capital, is a lively, bustling port with markets selling local produce and a mix of languages. Leaving his wife and children, this is where Paul Gauguin (1848–1903) arrived in June 1891 from Paris, in search of artistic regeneration. An inherent traveller, Gauguin lived in Peru, Martinique, Paris, Arles and Copenhagen. After joining the merchant navy, he sailed the seas from Le Havre to Rio de Janeiro, and on returning to Paris, worked as a stockbroker for 11 years. But his early travels left him with a loathing of modern cities, and he yearned for mystical, distant lands where he could immerse himself in ancient cultures, abundant nature and simple living. However, his romantic image of Tahiti as an untouched paradise was dashed when he saw the extent to which French colonisation had taken over. He had moved to Tahiti in search of new, exciting motifs and to escape European civilisation, and was disappointed that it was not what he had dreamed of.

Gauguin spent the first few months in Papeete, then moved approximately 45 kilometres (28 miles) down the coast to the

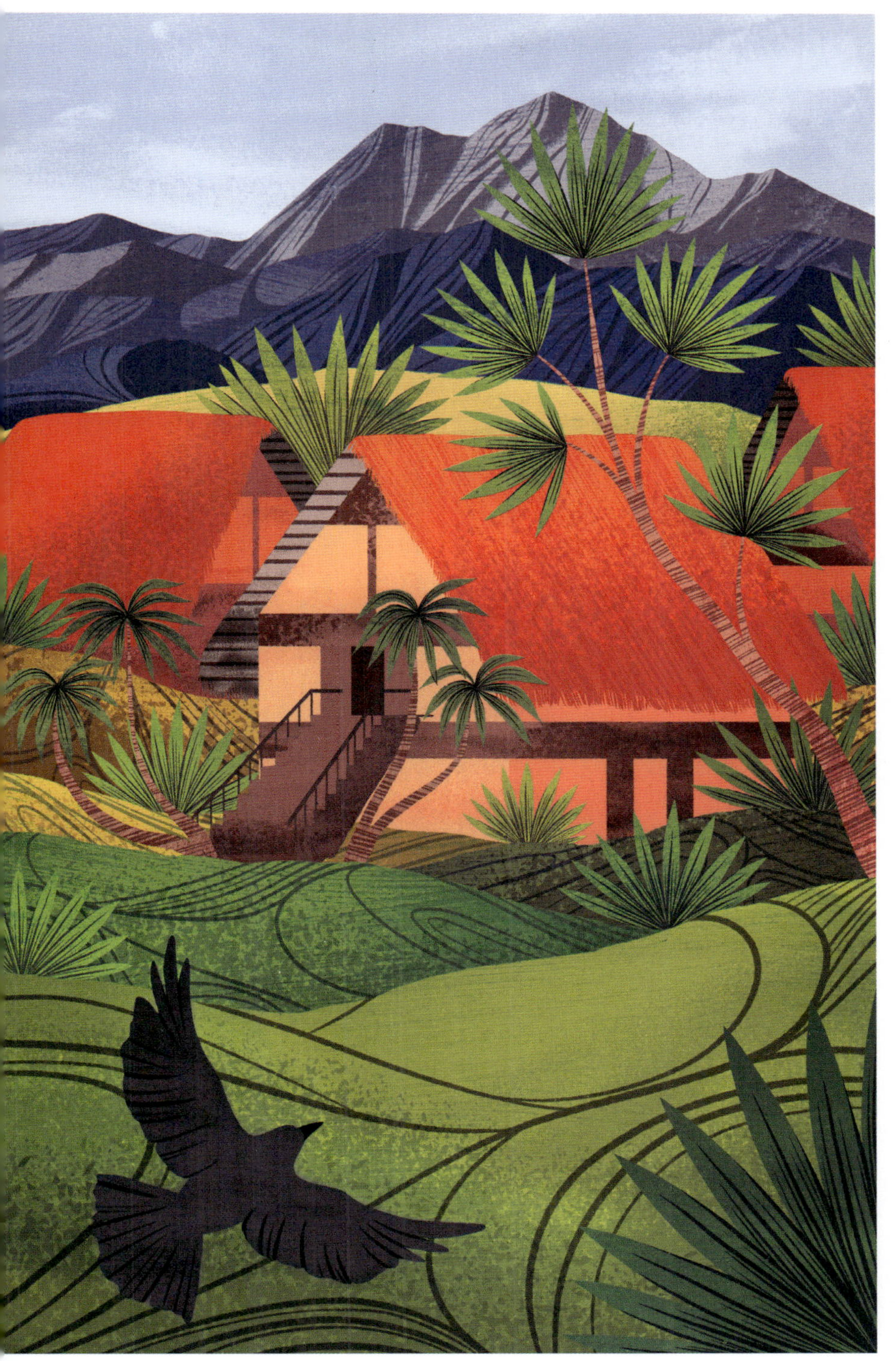

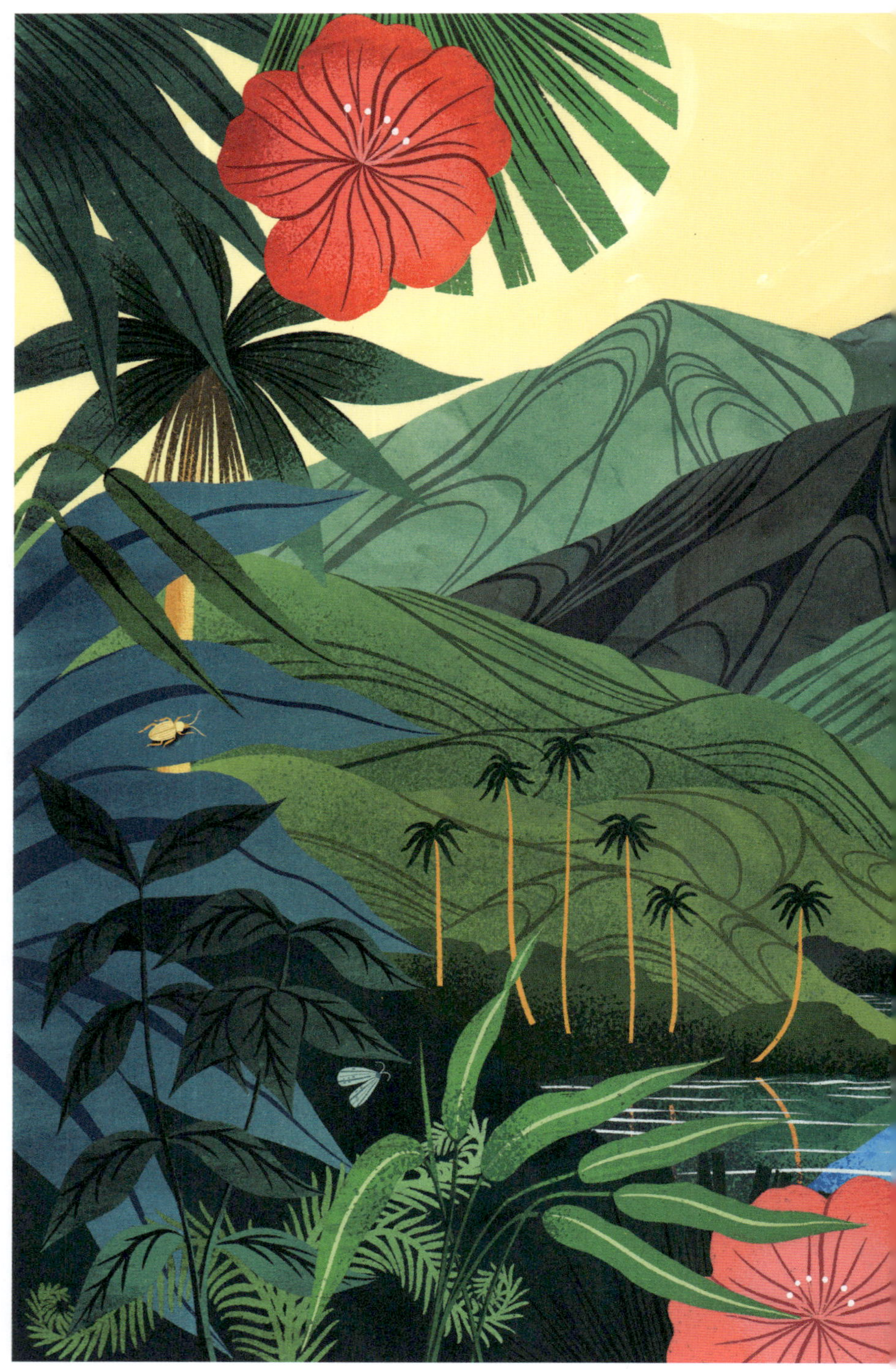

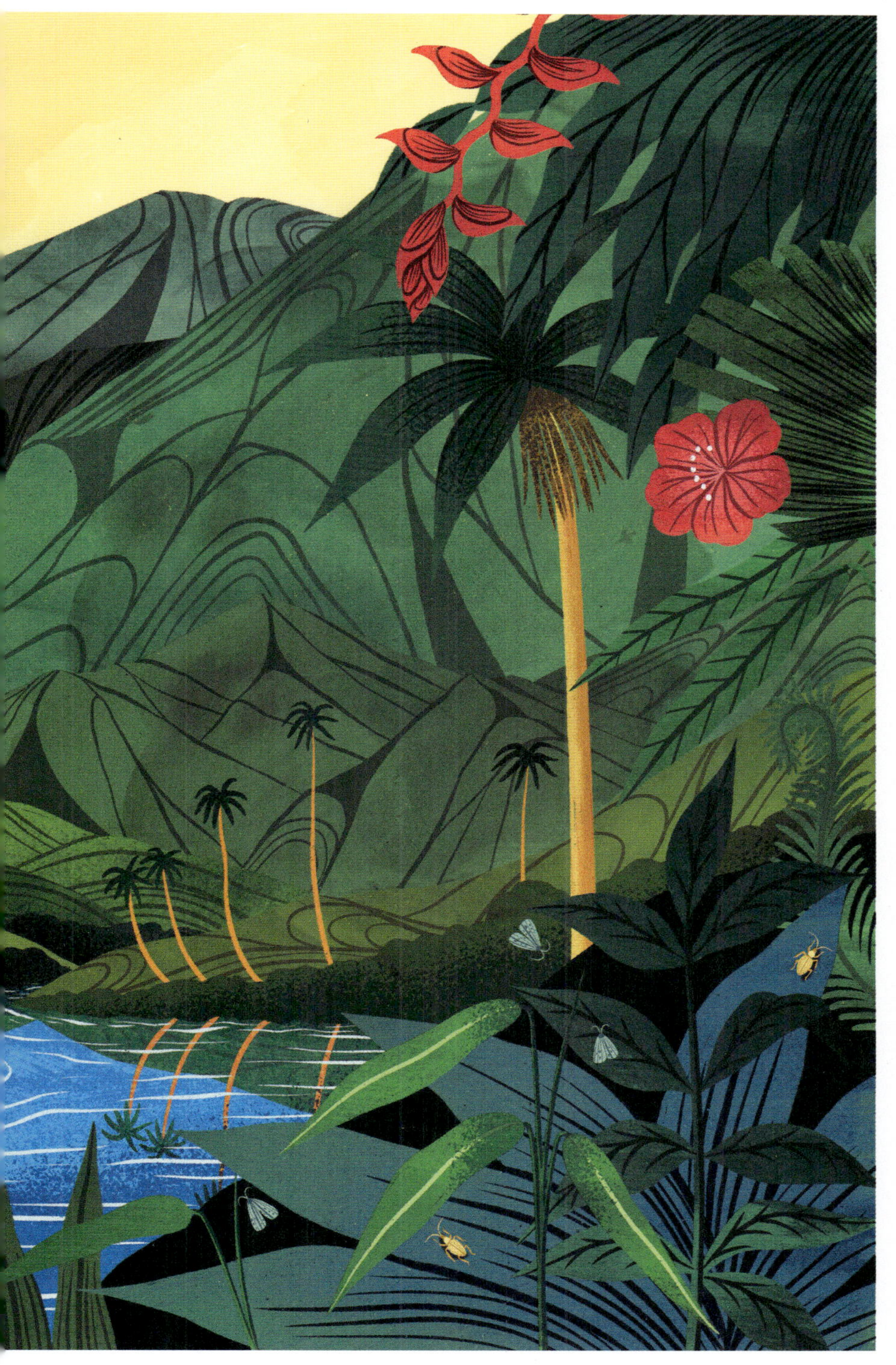

remote village of Mataiea. There, he lived in a native-style bamboo hut with no windows and a roof made of pandanus leaves, close to the beach, surrounded by tropical vegetation, shaded from the sultry heat. From the door of his hut, Gauguin could see the distant mountains at the centre of the island, and from the beach, he could see the peninsula of Taiarapu. Mataiea was quiet, inhabited only by natives to the island, and so was closer to the island life he had hoped for. Almost as soon as he arrived, using a palette of tropical colours, he began painting images of Tahitian life.

Although Tahiti became Gauguin's home for most of the last 12 years of his life, he stayed there for just two years on his first visit, producing paintings that broke with traditionally accepted art. They included richly coloured, flat-looking idyllic landscapes and evocative figures, suggesting mystical notions through his own personal symbolism. Due to increasing poverty, he used coarse canvases and thinly applied paint, and his imagery emulated local Oceanic styles, with a deliberately crude, naïve appearance. With darkly outlined, sinuous contours, his palette of jewel-bright colours convey joy, serenity, mystery and hope. In order to communicate an extra sense of exoticism to European viewers, he gave his works Tahitian titles, such as *Fatata te Miti* (*By the Sea*) and *Manao Tupapau* (*The Spirit of the Dead Watching*), both of 1892.

In 1897, Gauguin painted his largest work. With *Where Do We Come From? What Are We? Where Are We Going?* he aspired to compare with great fresco painters of the past, including Giotto. Calling the vast painting his 'testament', he explored the human condition and his personal struggle with the meaning of existence. In three main sections, the painting presents Tahiti as an earthly Garden of Eden. The first part represents Eve as an old woman holding her head, conveying the guilt of humanity. Towards the centre, a figure picks fruit, referencing the Tree of Knowledge and the forbidden fruit of the Old Testament. On the right, a baby suggests new beginnings. In the background is the vibrant, luxurious vegetation of Tahiti, including flowers, plants and banana trees.

In 1901, Gauguin moved to Atuona on the island of Hiva Oa, in the Marquesas Islands, where today you can visit a reconstruction of his two-storey thatched home in the Paul Gauguin Cultural Centre. He died there in 1903 and was buried in the local Calvary Cemetery, situated at the top of a steep hill, but the climb is worth it as once there, you can enjoy spectacular views of the bay below.

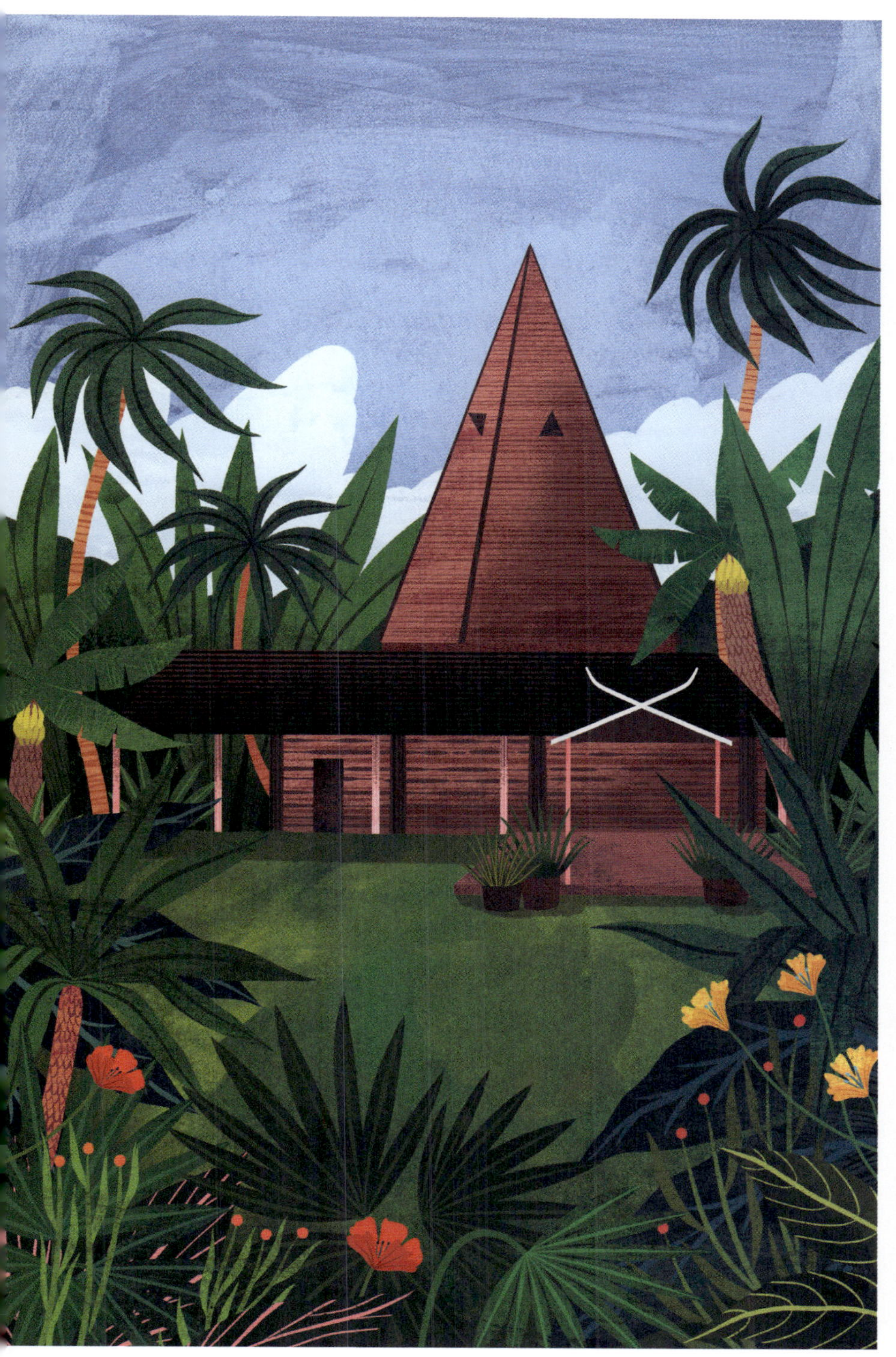

Where?	New York, USA
Which?	*Per Capita* (1981) by Jean-Michel Basquiat
What?	Multicultural, diverse city of opportunity

NEW YORK

TEEMING WITH cabs, buses, shoppers, workers and visitors, New York famously never sleeps. Art Deco skyscrapers, glass-fronted hotels, concrete and steel offices, loft apartments, vast stores, museums, restaurants, bars, booksellers, delis and diners all crowd into the networks of streets and avenues. You can mingle among steaming noodle shops in Chinatown, marvel at the buzz and spectacle of Times Square or lose yourself in Central Park. Every neighbourhood offers a different version of the city. The most densely populated city in the United States, New York is situated on one of the world's largest natural harbours, divided into five boroughs: Brooklyn, Queens, Manhattan, The Bronx and Staten Island. These were consolidated into a single city in 1898, and today, as many as 800 languages are spoken there, making it the most linguistically diverse city in the world. With its ideals of liberty and peace, New York continues to attract people from disparate backgrounds and cultures. And that just about sums up Jean-Michel Basquiat (1960–88): culturally diverse and daring.

Drawing inspiration from his mixed Haitian and Puerto Rican heritage, Basquiat played a crucial role in bringing graffiti into the established art world. His artistic interests were encouraged by his parents, especially his mother who regularly took him to some of New York's greatest art museums, including The Met, MoMA, the Guggenheim and Brooklyn Museum – where he became a member at six years of age. With no formal art training, in the 1970s, he and his friend Al Diaz began creating graffiti in and around Lower Manhattan, adding the tag SAMO© – an abbreviation of Same Old

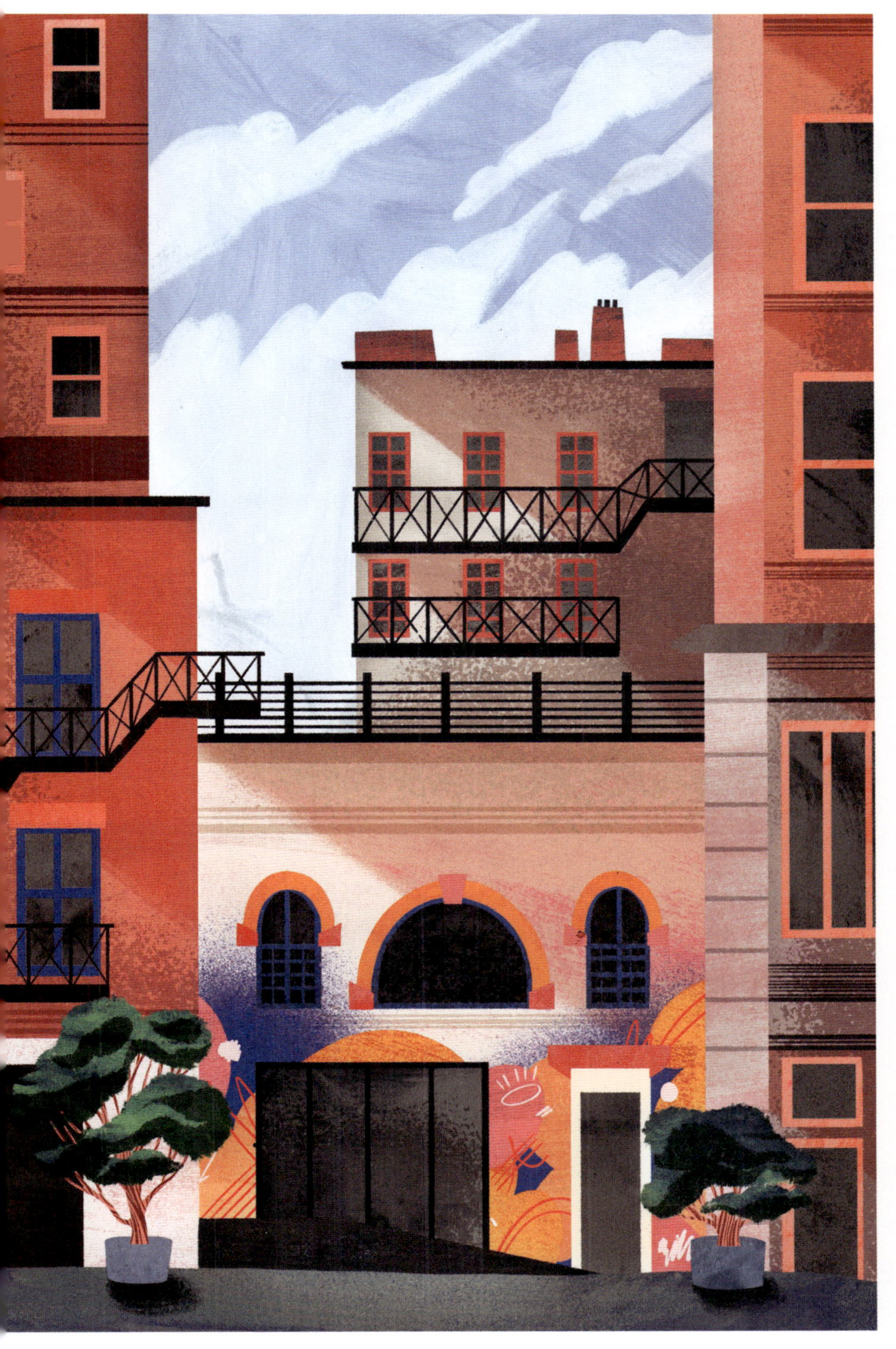

Shit. Their spray-painted graffiti included politically-oriented poems, rhymes and phrases, and it was soon noticed by contemporary artists and journalists. Spray-painting on walls and in subways, the art soon became part of the fabric of the city. Art critic Jeffrey Deitch remembered that, 'Back in the late 70s, you couldn't go anywhere interesting in Lower Manhattan without noticing that someone named SAMO had been there first.' Nowadays, however, no confirmed SAMO© works survive.

After Basquiat and Diaz fell out in 1979, Basquiat wrote 'SAMO© IS DEAD' on buildings around Lower Manhattan. Then in 1980, he exhibited paintings in The Times Square show, held in an abandoned building on the corner of 41st Street and 7th Avenue. Along with Basquiat, exhibitors included established artists such as Keith Haring, Nan Goldin and Jenny Holzer, and it was hailed as 'the first radical art show of the 1980s' by the respected magazine *The Village Voice*. From that time, Basquiat was 'discovered' as a fine artist, and in less than 10 years, he produced over 1,000 paintings and more than 2,000 drawings. Borrowing imagery from African, Caribbean, Aztec and Hispanic cultures, his childlike style conveyed complex ideas and he worked with all kinds of media, including pastels, pencils, charcoal, watercolours, oil sticks, spray paint and the end of his paintbrush, as well as with more traditional brushstrokes.

Basquiat first met Pop artist Andy Warhol in a chance encounter when selling postcards of his work. Two years later, Warhol and Basquiat met properly at Warhol's studio, the Factory. The two became great friends; Warhol mentored Basquiat and Basquiat helped to revitalise Warhol's career. Suddenly famous at 20 years old, Basquiat was soon frequenting the unique nightclub Studio 54, socialising with Warhol's outrageous friends. From 1983, Basquiat lived and worked in NoHo at 57 Great Jones Street, an East Village loft owned by Warhol. By then, he had become one of the world's most sought-after artists; but his drug addiction was severe. In 1988, at just 27, Basquiat died of an overdose.

Despite his short life, Basquiat made a massive impact on hip-hop post-punk and street art with work that appropriated poetry, drawing and painting to draw attention to the gulf between poverty and wealth, segregation and integration, and his artistic legacy is huge. Basquiat was buried at Green-Wood Cemetery in Brooklyn, close to where he was born; his life and legacy forever linked with the city that influenced and inspired him.

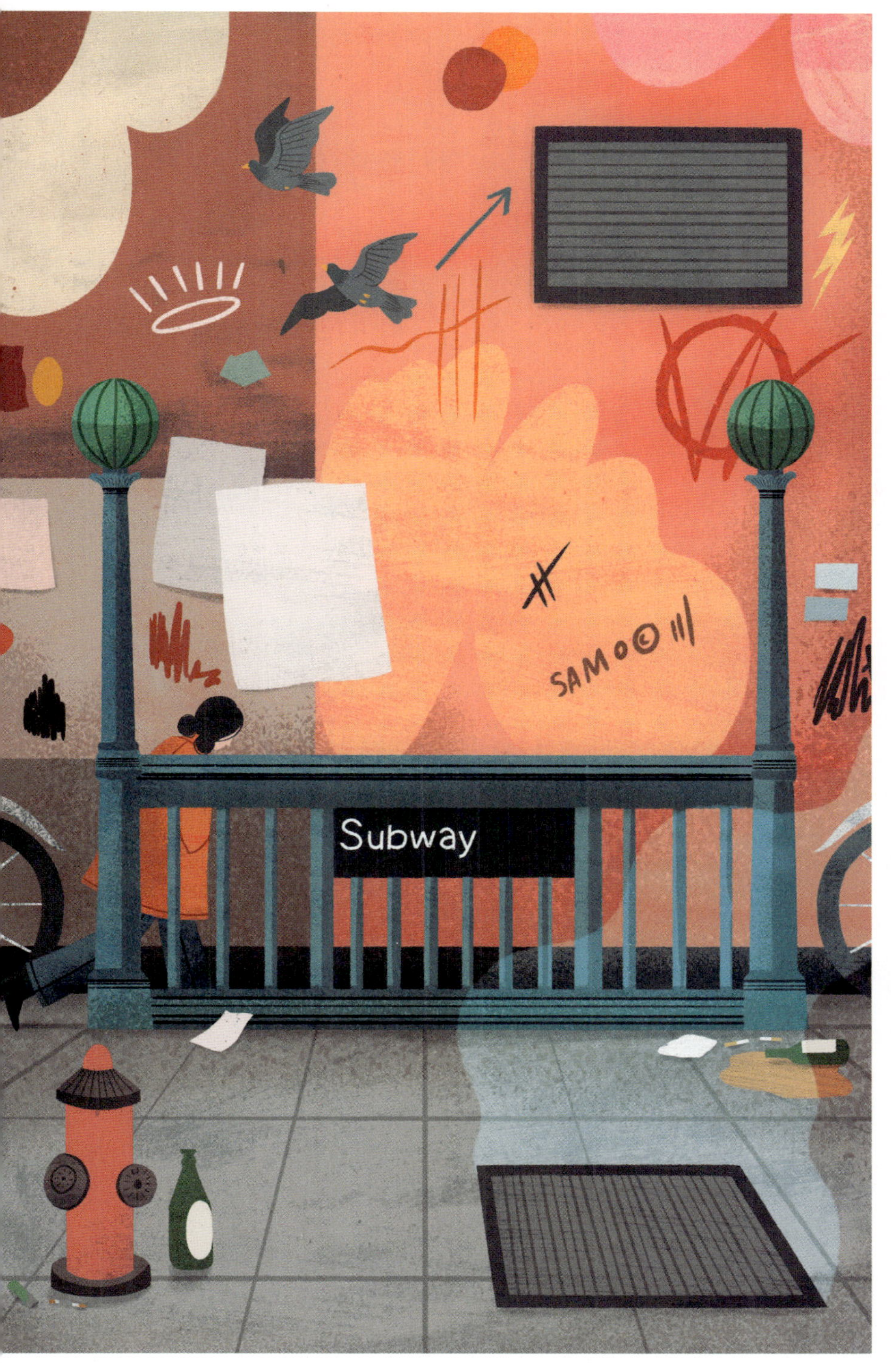
SAMO© III
Subway

Where?	Iowa, USA
Which?	*American Gothic* (1930) by Grant Wood
What?	Quiet state conveying rural American values

IOWA

BORDERED BY the Mississippi River to the east and the Missouri and Big Sioux Rivers to the west, Iowa sits in America's Midwest, in the heart of the Corn Belt. It's a peaceful, welcoming state – predominantly agricultural, featuring prairies, savannas, forests and wetlands. In the early morning, songbirds whirl and soar above the Great River Road that hugs the Mississippi and meanders through rolling farmland, country byways and remote, picturesque towns.

Also on the banks of a river, Cedar Rapids is the second-largest city in Iowa, and it was here that the artist Grant Wood (1891–1942) lived from the age of ten, after his father died. Famous for his Regionalist style, Wood painted with a detailed, realistic approach that, like other Regionalists, reflected the traditional old-fashioned values of small-town America. In 1930, after the stock market crash of 1929 and the onset of the Great Depression, Wood passed through Eldon, in the southern part of Iowa, and saw a white wooden house. It appealed to his idea of Americans embodying the values of hard work, community and austerity. Eldon was a small, sleepy country town with fewer than 1,000 inhabitants, and the house, built in 1881, was in a modest style known as Carpenter Gothic. Also known as the Dibble House, because it was built and first owned by Eldon resident Charles Dibble, it was a small house with a gable and pointed arched window on the upper level. Wood photographed it and made a sketch of it on the back of an envelope. After obtaining permission from the owners, he returned the next day and made another sketch, this time in oil on paperboard, exaggerating the angle of the roof and lengthening the window.

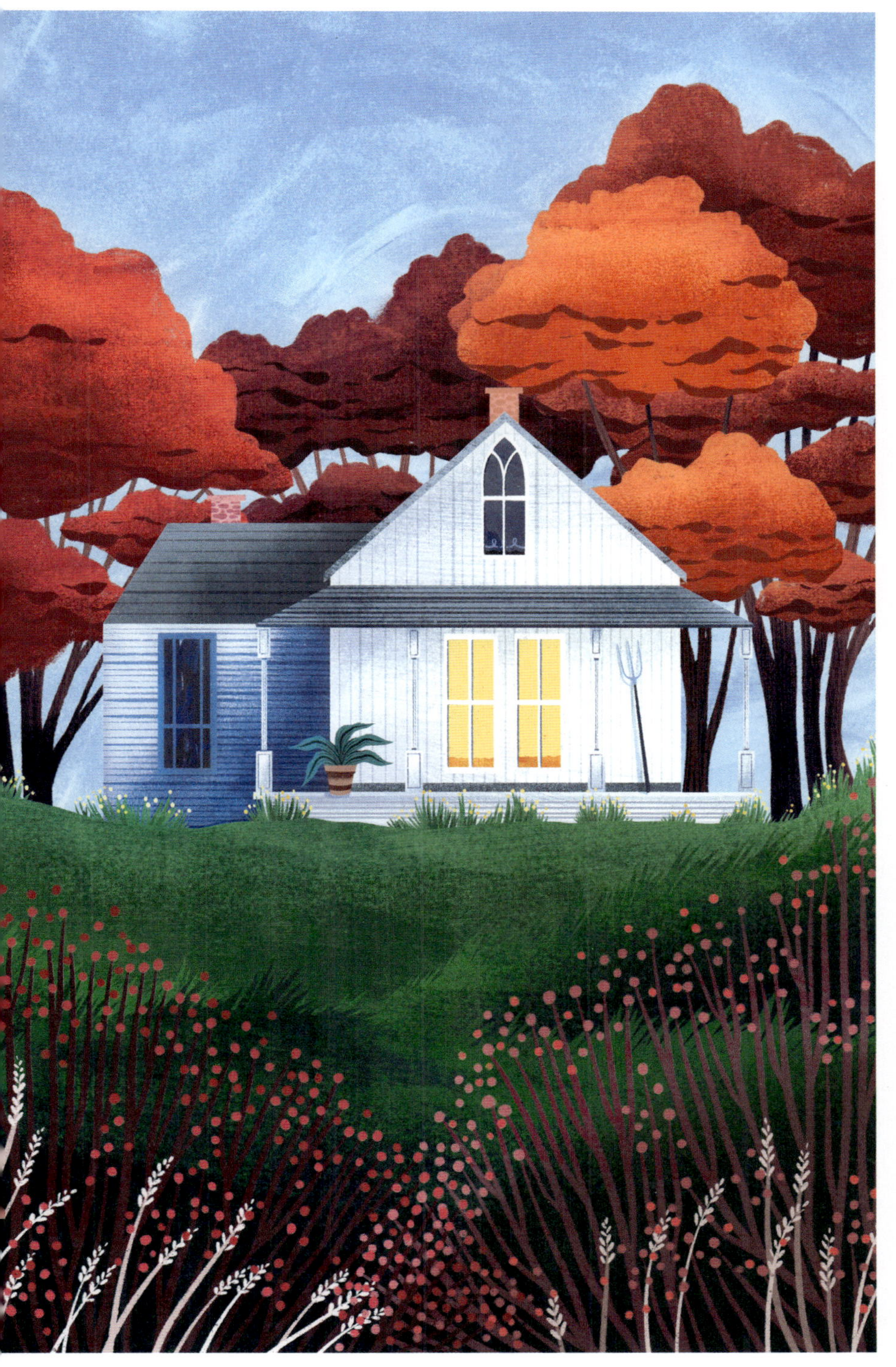

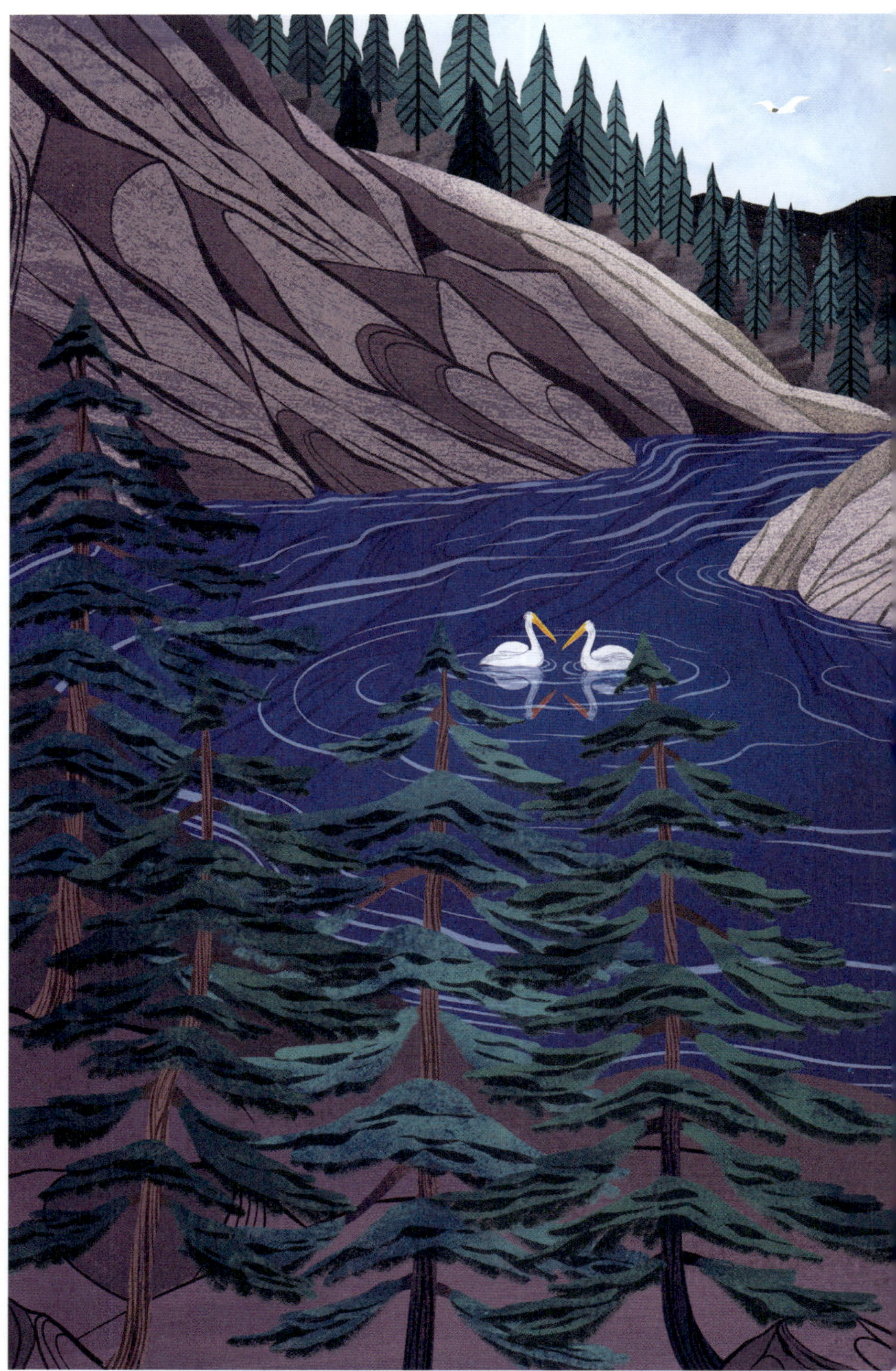

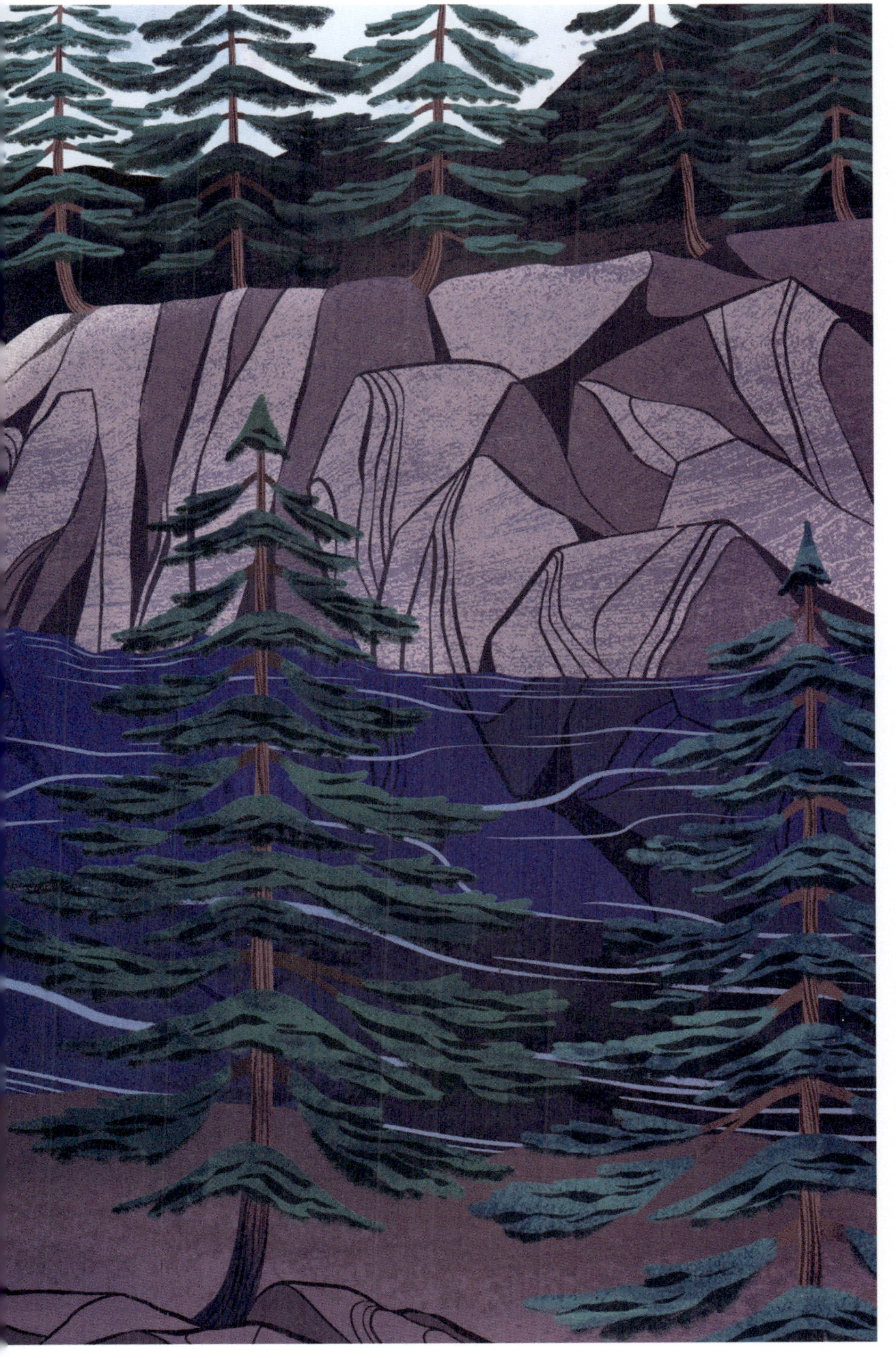

At the time, the country was sinking deeper into the Great Depression, and there was a sense of desperation. Wood concentrated on the general longing for a return to traditional American values and lifestyles, and said he decided to paint the house with 'the kind of people I fancied should live in that house'.

Back at 5 Turner Alley in Cedar Rapids, Wood's home and studio, which you can visit today, he painted the house in what became one of America's most famous artworks, *American Gothic* (1930). He added two models in front of the house: his sister Nan and his dentist, Dr Byron McKeeby, representing a farmer and his spinster daughter. He painted all three elements, the house and the two figures, separately, they were never in the studio together. Nan wears an old-fashioned pinafore and a cameo brooch with her hair pulled back; McKeeby wears a collarless shirt, jacket and overalls and holds a pitchfork pointing to the sky that echoes both the Gothic window behind him and the stitching on the pocket of his overalls. Bald-headed, dark-eyed and stern-looking, he looks directly at viewers, while Nan looks with a concerned expression into the distance. Within the painting, Wood used several repeating and rhythmic forms and lines to unify the composition: the curtains in the Gothic window echo the pattern of Nan's dress, and the cameo and potted plants on the porch echo the shape of her head. Those plants, plus the green trees, church spire and red barn in the background, are all neat and precise, and the overall meticulous, highly detailed, polished style was inspired by Flemish Renaissance art, which Wood studied during his travels to Europe between 1920 and 1928.

Although interpretations and reception varied, as soon as Wood completed the painting, it was accepted to the Art Institute of Chicago's annual exhibition of American paintings (one of the major shows of the year in the United States), where it won an award of $300. Wood intended the painting to be a positive statement about rural American values, an image of reassurance at a time of great hardship. The man and woman represent survivors, and the strength and dependability of the American Midwest.

Listed on the National Register of Historic Places, the now iconic Gothic House is open to the public and can be rented for special events. Combined with a visit to his studio in Cedar Rapids, you can completely immerse yourself in Grant Wood's world.

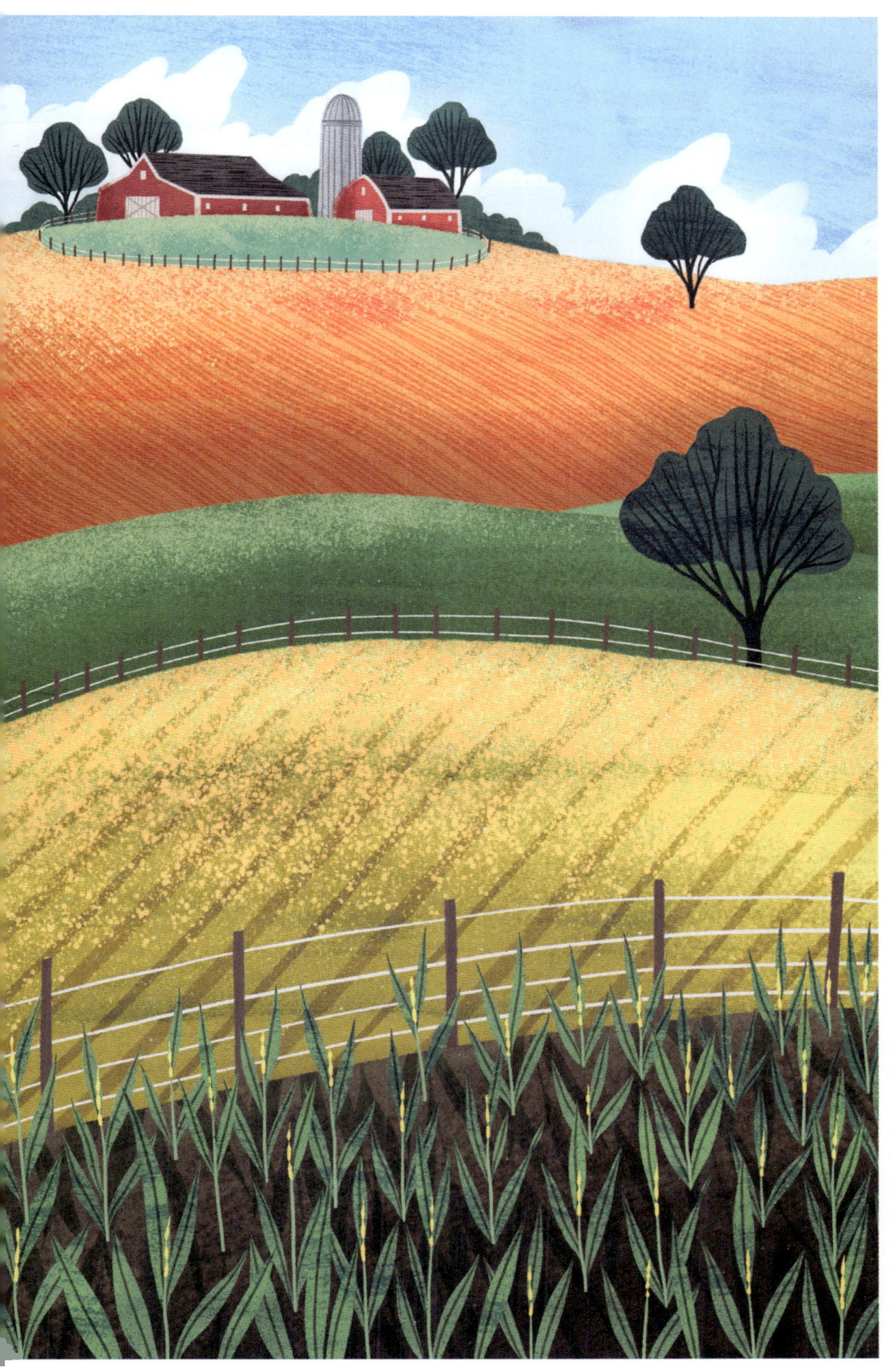

Where?	New Mexico, USA
Which?	*My Front Yard, Summer* (1941) by Georgia O'Keeffe
What?	Faraway otherworldliness in the New Mexican desert

NEW MEXICO

AS THE amber sun turns to vivid orange and lowers behind the mountains, the rocks turn an even more spectacular red and the distant mesas glow purple. With its sharp light, expansive skies and ethereal rock formations, the tiny village of Abiquiú was the starting point of the pioneering trade route of the Old Spanish Trail that connected the northern settlements of New Mexico with California. In the Tewa language, Abiquiú means 'wild chokecherry place', and in 1742, 24 Tewa Pueblo families were the first settlers there, led by a Roman Catholic priest as part of the strategy by the Spanish to defend New Mexico's borders against Native American tribes.

Almost 200 years later, New Mexico captivated the artist Georgia O'Keeffe (1887–1986) when she first stayed at Taos in 1929. Instantly enchanted by the rugged, open scenery and the spiritual atmosphere, she began painting the undulating, multi-coloured landscape in her smooth, semi-abstract style. Over the following years, she travelled back and forth to New Mexico several times from her home in New York and gradually stayed for longer periods on a 21,000-acre dude – or guest – ranch, among the colourful bluffs of Abiquiú, called Ghost Ranch. 'As soon as I saw it, I knew I must have it,' she later wrote about the place.

O'Keeffe also described her feelings about the entire location: 'When I got to New Mexico, that was mine. As soon as I saw it, that was my country. I'd never seen anything like it before, but it fitted to me exactly. It's something that's in the air, it's just different.' Eventually, she moved into the house at Ghost Ranch and lived there for the last 40 years of her life, first of all for part of the year and then from

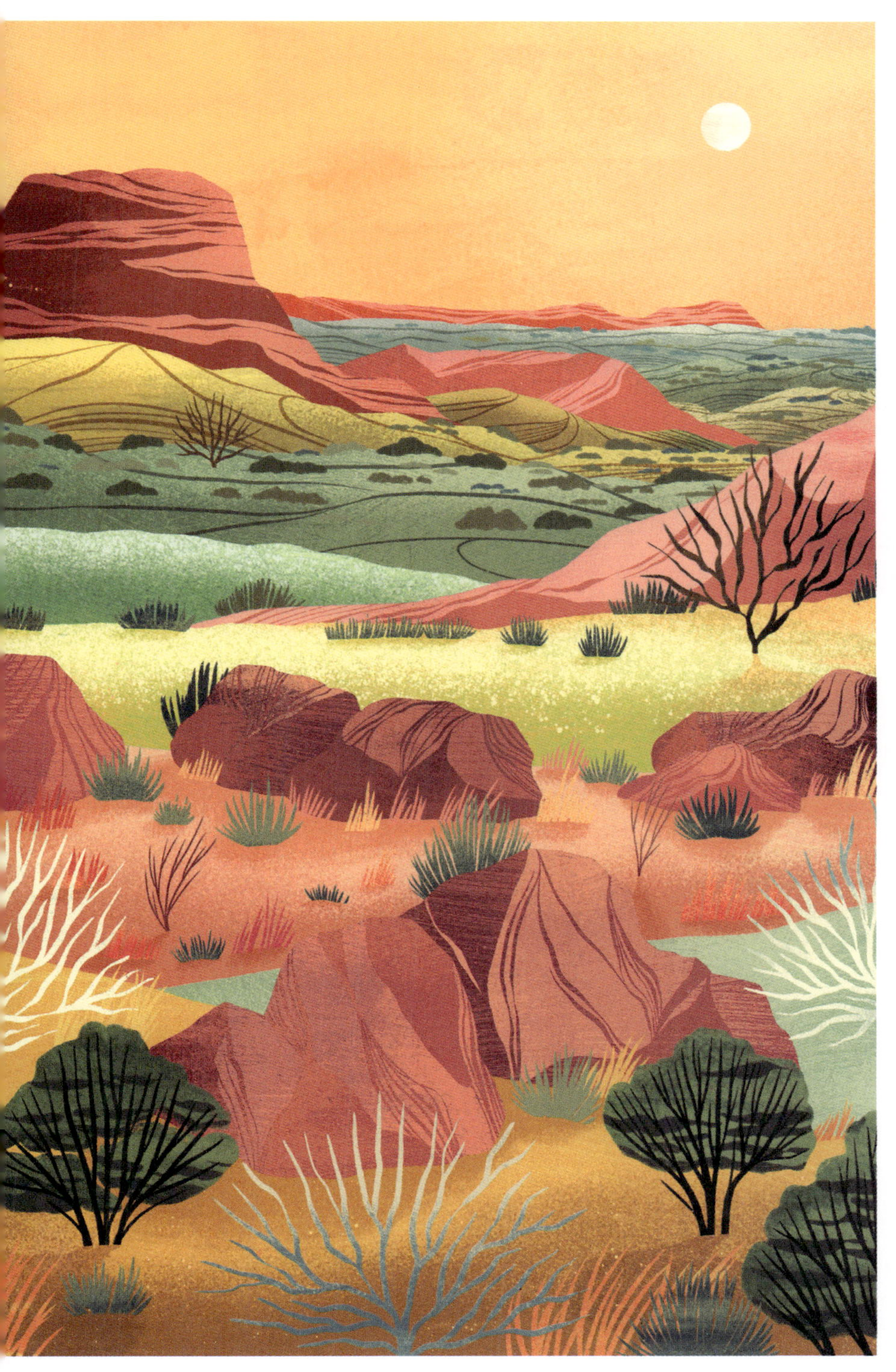

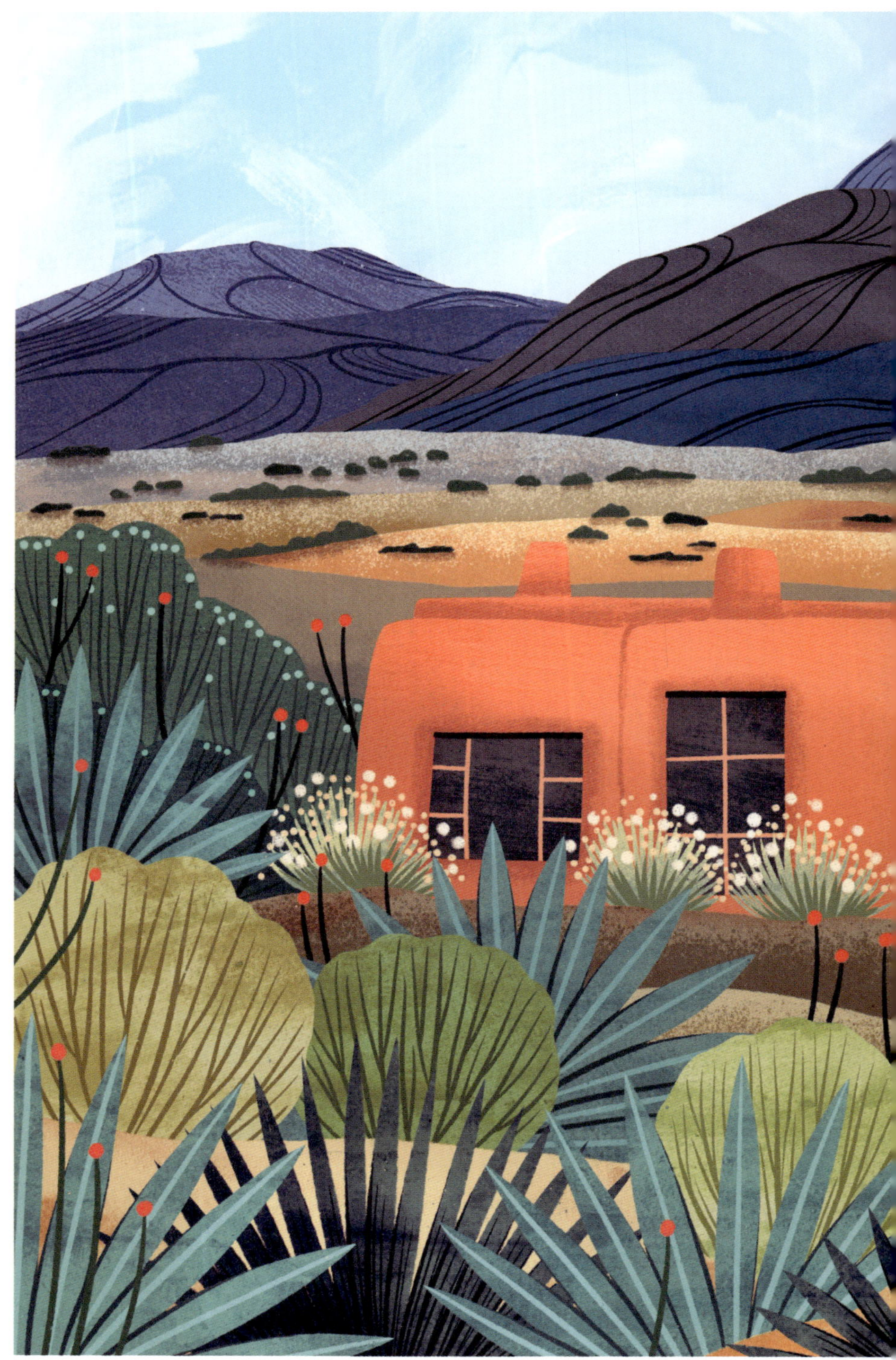

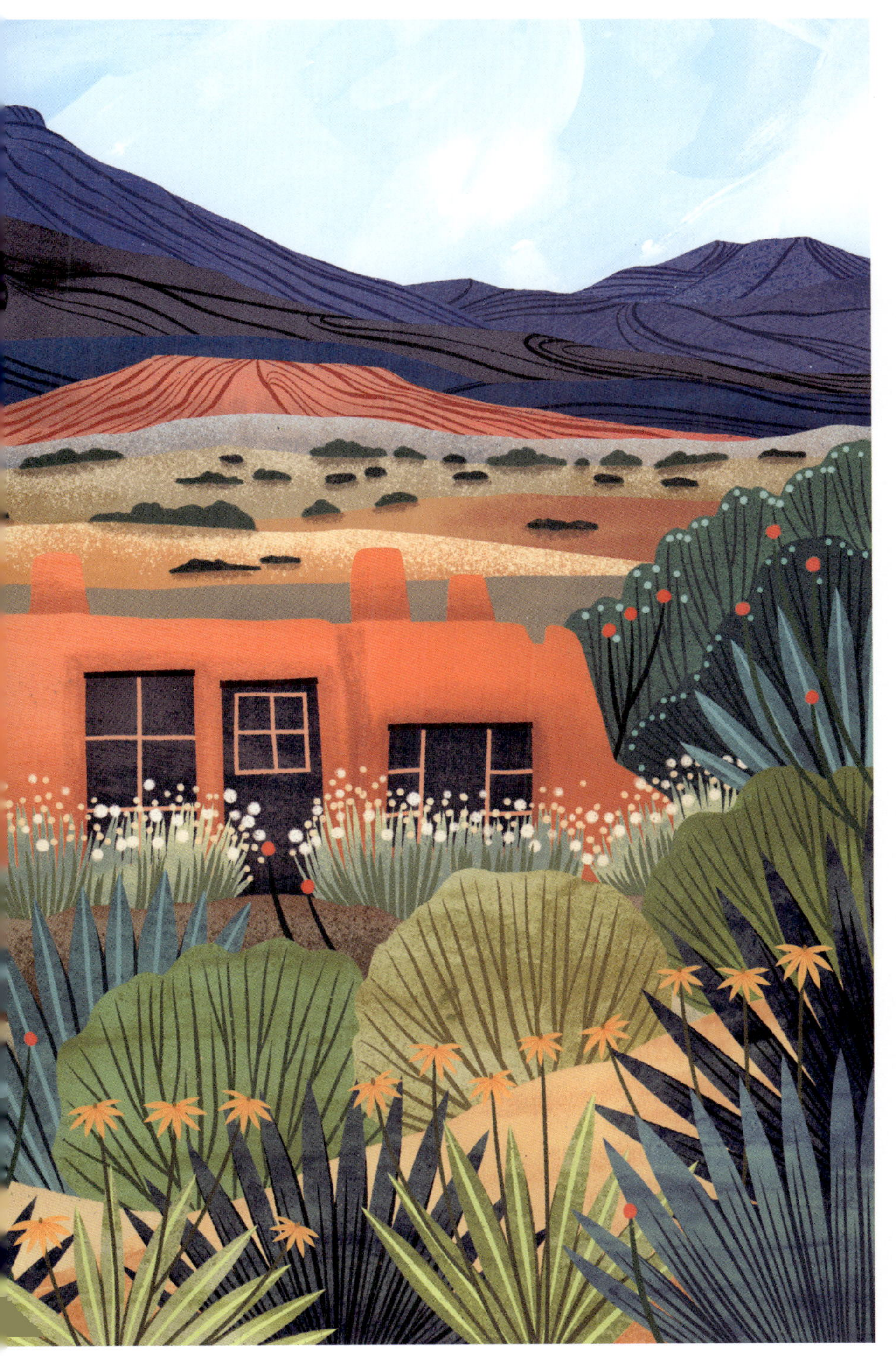

1949, permanently. Blending in with the surroundings, the walls of Ghost Ranch house are punctuated by wide picture windows that open on to majestic vistas. A hand-carved wooden ladder leads to the roof where O'Keeffe often slept under the stars. She lived modestly, collecting rocks, bones and gnarled branches from the desert, and she painted them and the landscape constantly, emphasising the curving forms and bright sunlight. In 1942, she wrote to her friend, fellow artist Arthur Dove: 'I wish you could see what I see out the window; the earth pink and yellow cliffs to the north, the full pale moon about to go down in an early morning lavender sky … pink and purple hills in front and the scrubby fine dull cedars and a feeling of much space – it is a very beautiful world.'

A year before writing that letter, O'Keeffe painted *My Front Yard, Summer* (1941), capturing the panoramic view from her front window. The predominant motif is what she called her 'private mountain', and she captured its shifting colours, sensuous contours and harmonious shape, conveying her deep connection with nature. It is an abbreviated, semi-abstract image, in which she distils what she saw in front of her to its essence, conveying the image and her own emotional reaction to it. By minimising details, she reduces the view to areas of light, shadow and pattern. One aspect she particularly admired about New Mexico was that she could see clearly and expansively over vast distances.

Eleven years after her death, in 1997, the Georgia O'Keeffe Museum opened in Santa Fe. With over 3,000 works, including 140 of her oil paintings, nearly 700 drawings and hundreds of other works, the museum offers insights into her creative processes, as well as the light and land that inspired her. The O'Keeffe Museum also maintains her home and studio in the village of Abiquiú, 95 kilometres (60 miles) north-west of Santa Fe, along the Chama River. Ghost Ranch, O'Keeffe's first home in New Mexico, is now run by the Presbyterian Church and is around 48 kilometres (30 miles) north-west of Abiquiú. You can book a tour through the O'Keeffe Museum. Limited to 12 people, it lasts an hour and takes you on a scenic ride on a shuttle bus to many of O'Keeffe's most inspirational sites, including the dramatic 21,000-acre landscape around Ghost Ranch. According to the Pueblo people, the unique landscape here is suffused with spirits of the past, including, presumably, one of the world's greatest artists who so loved the ancient, sacred place, and made it her home for nearly half a century.

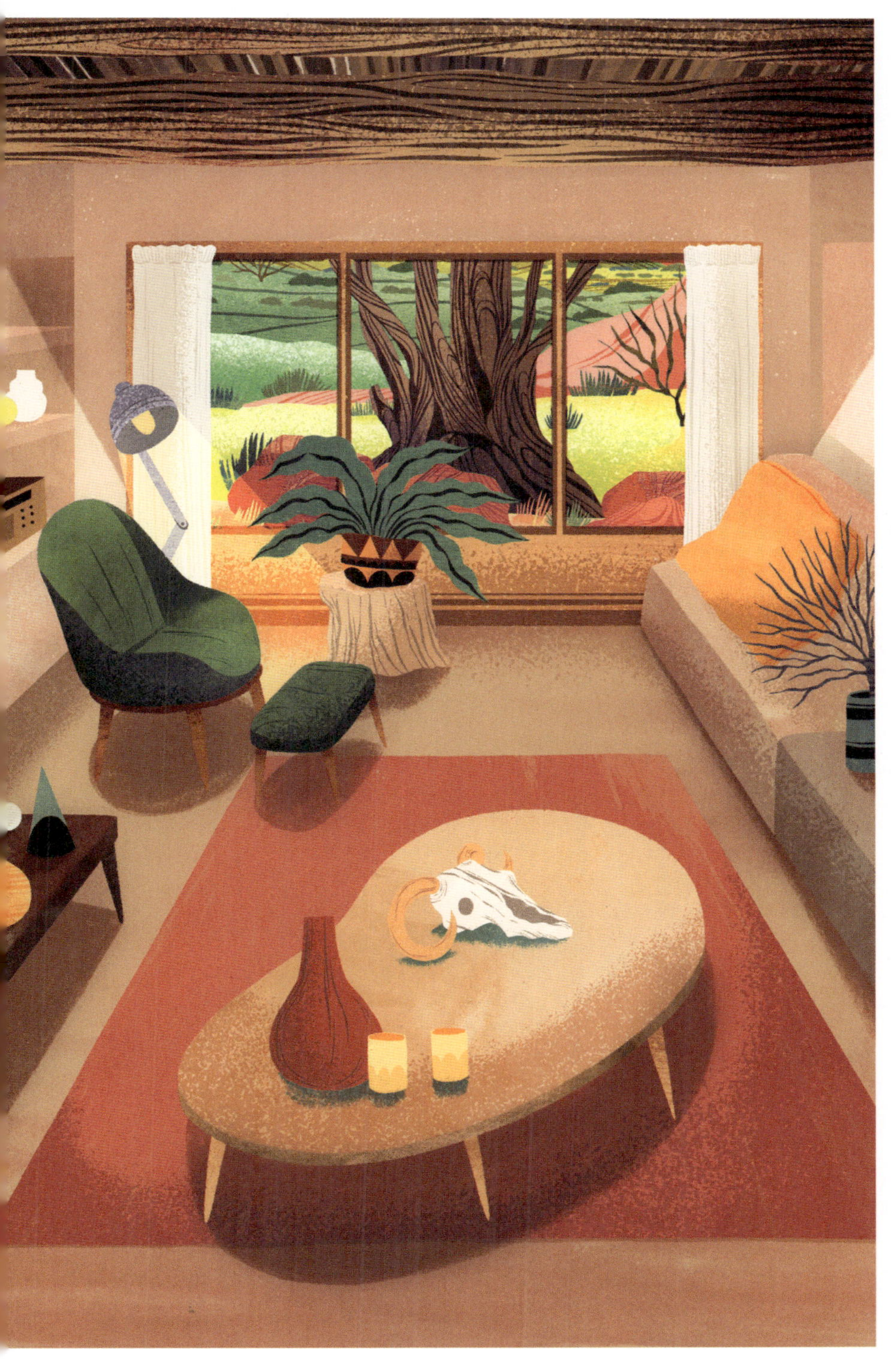

Where?	Coyoacán, Mexico
Which?	*The Two Fridas* (1939) by Frida Kahlo
What?	Sultry, magical neighbourhood steeped in history

COYOACÁN

IN THE lazy afternoon heat, the scent of orchids, dahlias and honeysuckle hangs in the air, fruit ripens on trees and cicadas chirrup. Hugged by a sapphire sky, the borough of Coyoacán – meaning 'place of coyotes' – in Mexico City retains much of its original 16th-century layout, with narrow streets, cobblestoned plazas and vibrant markets, selling fruit, flowers and handcrafted goods. Its epicentre is a pair of plazas, the larger, cobblestoned Plaza Hidalgo and the Jardín del Centenario, with rustling trees and exotic plants, a central fountain where coyotes frolic, and the 16th-century Baroque parish church of San Juan Bautista – one of the oldest churches in Mexico, dating to the mid-16th century, which blends the influences of indigenous Indian craftsmen with Spanish Baroque building styles. Leading on from the Plaza Hidalgo, is Coyoacán's main plaza, Plaza de la Conchita – a leafy colonial town square. All around are street vendors, bars, cafés, and people enjoying the colourful atmosphere.

It was here in Coyoacán, at La Casa Azul (The Blue House), named after its cobalt-blue walls, that Frida Kahlo (1907–54) grew up. Built in 1904, La Casa Azul is, like most of the other buildings in the area, formed around a central courtyard and garden. Over two floors, it incorporates bedrooms, studio space, a large kitchen and a dining room. Everywhere is painted with rich, vivid colours, and the entrance hall is decorated with mosaics. Now preserved as the Museo Frida Kahlo, it was made into a museum in 1958, four years after Kahlo's death. On entering, Kahlo's spirit can be felt everywhere – her paints are still in her studio by her easel, and the house is filled with paintings, period furnishings and pre-Columbian

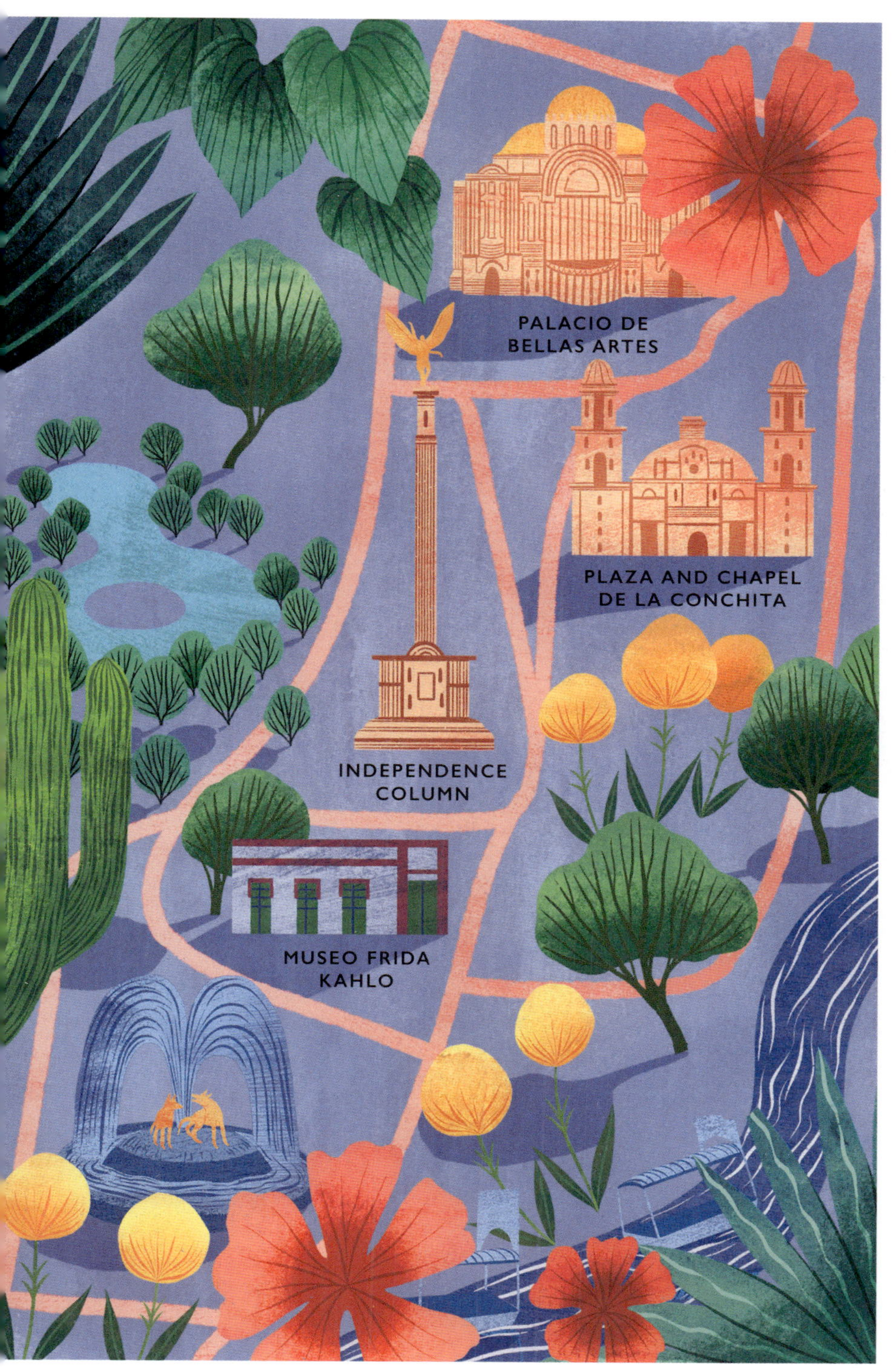
PALACIO DE
BELLAS ARTES
PLAZA AND CHAPEL
DE LA CONCHITA
INDEPENDENCE
COLUMN
MUSEO FRIDA
KAHLO

artefacts. Today, it is one of the most popular museums in Mexico City, with queues of Frida fans flocking to explore her home, work and fascinating life, immersing themselves in the creative living space she inhabited.

Kahlo spent much time in Casa Azul convalescing, first in 1918 after contracting polio, then when she suffered a terrible accident aged 18 while on her school bus that left her permanently physically damaged. She spent almost 2 years confined to her bed and endured 32 operations over the rest of her life. During her convalescence, she began to paint, and after she met Diego, she invited him to the Casa Azul to see her work. Rivera began visiting regularly, and soon other artists started meeting at the house. After her marriage to Rivera in 1934, Kahlo began wearing traditional Tehuana costume and drew greater artistic inspiration from Mexican folk art. Yet the marriage was not happy. Diego's infidelities took a toll on Kahlo's fragile health. She plunged into affairs with men and women, miscarried twice, had two abortions, suffered an appendectomy and had two gangrenous toes amputated.

Influenced by her health and personal problems, Kahlo produced soul-searching, introspective paintings such as the double self-portrait *The Two Fridas* (1939) that expressed her feelings of being broken by physical and psychological pain. At La Casa Azul, you can see where Kahlo lived, painted and also, sadly, where she died. An urn in the form of her face lies on her bed, holding her ashes. Beside this is the mirror in which she observed herself to paint her famous self-portraits. Her clothes, jewellery and personal objects remain where she left them. Book your tickets in advance and give yourself a few hours to explore. Then stroll into the cobbled streets or take the red tram that passes through Coyoacán. The charming Cantina La Guadalupana was a favourite local bar often frequented by Kahlo and Rivera, and while it's now closed, you can still see the original signage marking the spot. To the north is Coyoacán's colourful market, brimming with the scent of flowers, exotic fruits and delicious Mexican street food, including crispy tostadas and spicy quesadillas. Nearby is the Coyoacán Mexican Artisans Bazaar and the Museo de las Culturas Populares, where the diverse artistic heritage of Mexico can be seen. In the Frida Kahlo Park are life-sized bronze statues of Kahlo and Rivera. Wherever you go in this vibrant place, you will take in the same sights, sounds and scents that were experienced by Kahlo herself.

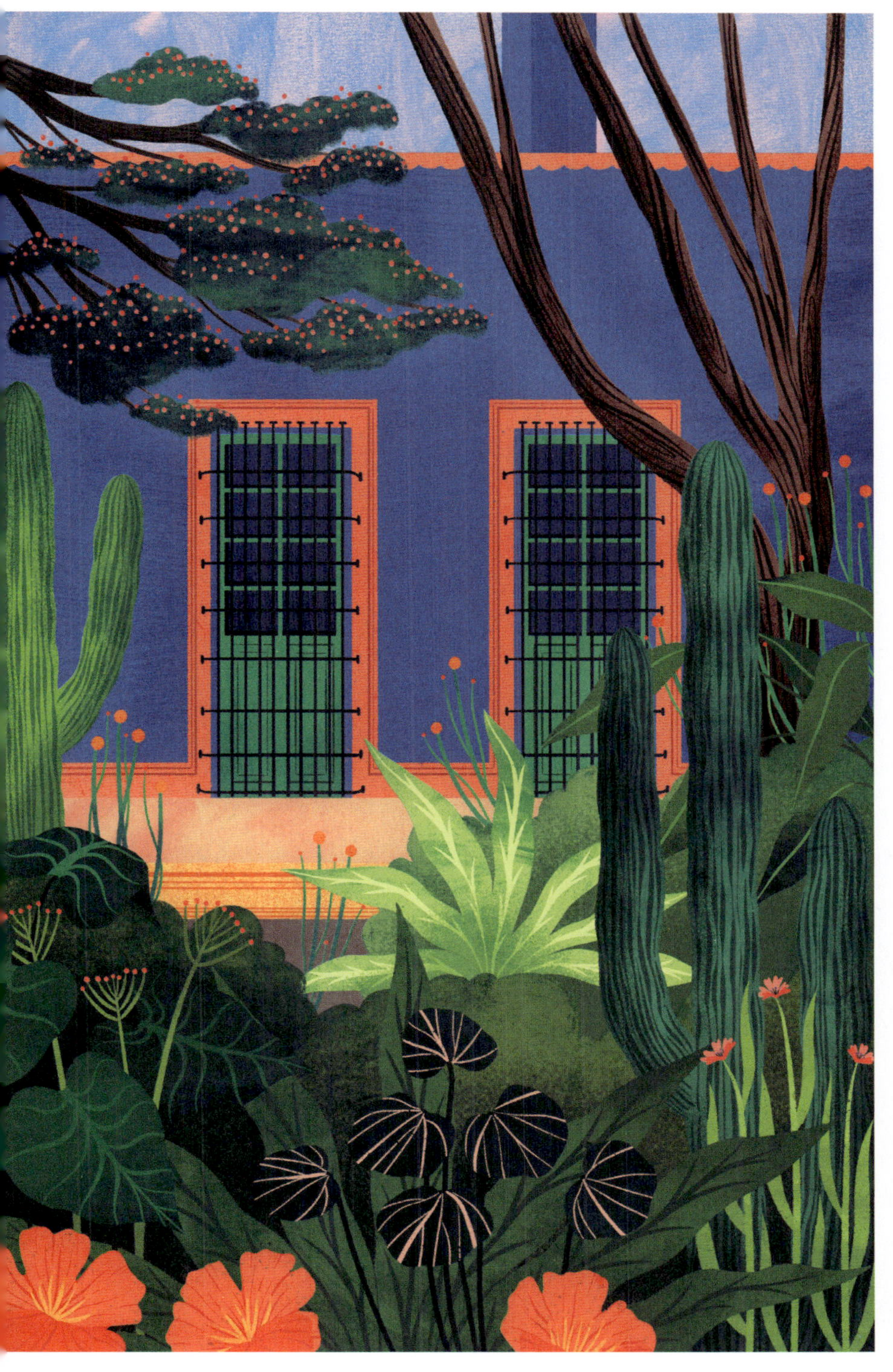

SUSIE HODGE, MA FRSA, is an art historian, author and artist with over 150 books published, mainly on art and design history, practical art and history. She also writes magazine articles, web resources for museums and galleries, and provides workshops and lectures for schools, universities, museums, galleries, businesses, groups and societies around the world. A regular contributor to radio and TV news programmes and documentaries, Susie's previous books include *Why Your Five Year Old Could Not Have Done That: Modern Art Explained*, *I Know An Artist: The Inspiring Connections Between the World's Greatest Artists* and *Painting Masterclass: Creative Techniques of 100 Great Artists*.

AMY GRIMES is an illustrator based in London. Particularly inspired by nature and the natural patterns found there, Amy's work often features bright and bold illustrated motifs, floral icons and leafy landscapes. As well as working on design and publishing commissions, Amy has an illustrated brand selling prints, textiles and stationery under the name of Hello Grimes.

ALSO AVAILABLE:

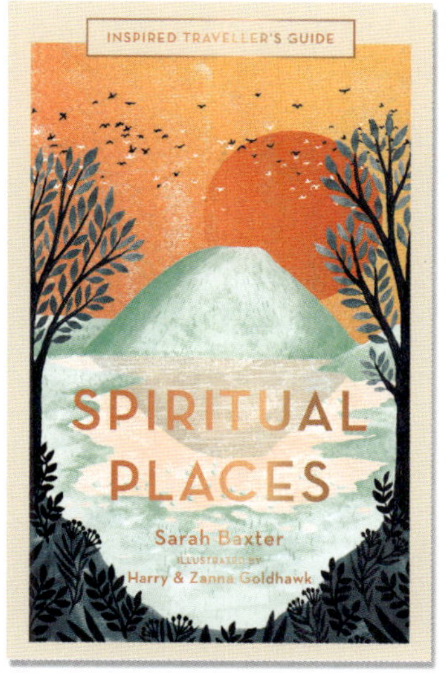

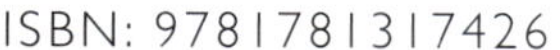
ISBN: 9781781317426

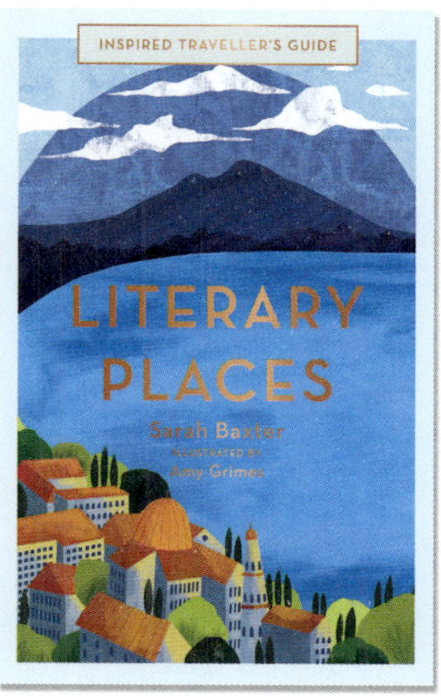

ISBN: 9781781318102

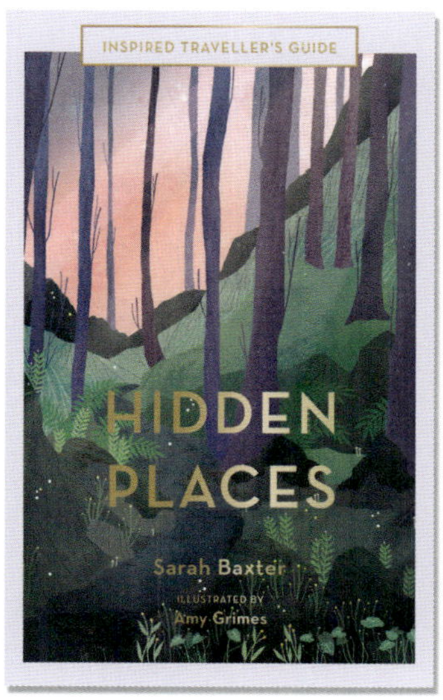

ISBN: 9781781319208

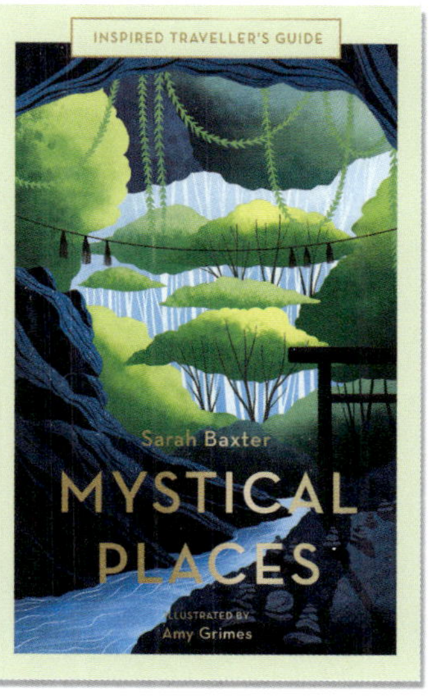

ISBN: 9781781319581